HOPE AGAIN

Publications by Charles R. Swindoll

BOOKS

Active Spirituality
The Bride
Come Before Winter
Compassion: Showing We Care in a Careless
    World
Dear Graduate
Dropping Your Guard
Encourage Me
The Finishing Touch
Flying Closer to the Flame
For Those Who Hurt
The Grace Awakening
Growing Deep in the Christian Life
Growing Strong in the Seasons of Life
Growing Wise in Family Life
Hand Me Another Brick
Improving Your Serve
Intimacy with the Almighty
Killing Giants, Pulling Thorns
Laugh Again

Leadership: Influence That Inspires
Living Above the Level of Mediocrity
Living Beyond the Daily Grind, Books I and II
Living on the Ragged Edge
Make Up Your Mind
Man to Man
Paw Paw Chuck's Big Ideas in the Bible
The Quest for Character
Recovery: When Healing Takes Time
Sanctity of Life
Simple Faith
Standing Out
Starting Over
Strengthening Your Grip
Stress Fractures
Strike the Original Match
The Strong Family
Three Steps Forward, Two Steps Back
Victory: A Winning Game Plan for Life
You and Your Child

MINIBOOKS

Abraham: A Model of Pioneer Faith
David: A Model of Pioneer Courage
Esther: A Model of Pioneer Independence

Moses: A Model of Pioneer Vision
Nehemiah: A Model of Pioneer
    Determination

BOOKLETS

Anger
Attitudes
Commitment
Dealing with Defiance
Demonism
Destiny
Divorce
Eternal Security
Fun Is Contagious
God's Will
Hope
Impossibilities

Integrity
Leisure
The Lonely Whine of the Top Dog
Moral Purity
Our Mediator
Peace . . . in Spite of Panic
Prayer
Sensuality
Stress
Tongues
When Your Comfort Zone Gets the Squeeze
Woman

Hope Again

Charles R. Swindoll

WORD PUBLISHING

DALLAS LONDON VANCOUVER MELBOURNE

WORD PUBLISHING

1996

Unless otherwise indicated, Scripture quotations used in this book are
from the New American Standard Bible NASB © 1960, 1962, 1963, 1968, 1971, 1972,
1973, 1975, 1977 by The Lockman Foundation. Used by permission.
The King James Version of the Bible (KJV). *The Living Bible* (TLB),
copyright 1971 by Tyndale House Publishers, Wheaton, Ill. Used by permission.
The Message (MSG). Copyright © 1993. Used by permission of NavPress
Publishing Group. The Holy Bible, New International Version (NIV).
Copyright © 1973, 1978, 1984 International Bible Society. Used by
permission of Zondervan Bible Publishers. J. B. Phillips: The New Testament
in Modern English, Revised Edition (PHILLIPS). Copyright © J. B. Phillips
1958, 1960, 1972. Used by permission of Macmillan Publishing Co., Inc.

Book design by Mark McGarry
Set in Monotype Dante

Library of Congress Cataloging-in-Publication Data
Swindoll, Charles R.
Hope Again / Charles R. Swindoll
p. cm.
ISBN 0–8499–1132–x (hardcover)
ISBN 0–8499–3994–1 (foreign edition)
1. Suffering — Religious aspects — Christianity. 2. Hope — Religious
aspects — Christianity. 3. Consolation. 4. Bible. N.T. Peter,
1st — devotional literature. I. Title.
BV4909.S95 1996 248.8'6 — dc20
96–8962
CIP

Printed in the United States of America.

6 7 8 0 1 2 3 4 9 BVG 9 8 7 6 5 4 3 2 1

I dedicate this book to two of my closest colleagues and
faithful friends on the leadership team at
Dallas Theological Seminary:

Dr. Wendell Johnston
and
Dr. Charlie Dyer

Without their invaluable assistance, there is no way these
recent years could have been so satisfying and
rewarding. These men have given me
fresh encouragement to press on . . . to finish strong
. . . to hope again.

Contents

Acknowledgments   ix

The Old Fisherman's Letter   xi

1 Hope Beyond Failure
   The Broken Man Behind the Book   1

2 Hope Beyond Suffering
   How We Can Smile Through Suffering   9

3 Hope Beyond Temptation
   Staying Clean in a Corrupt Society   25

4 Hope Beyond Division
   Reasons for Pulling Together   43

5 Hope Beyond Guilt
   Becoming Living Stones   59

6 Hope Beyond Unfairness
   Pressing On Even Though Ripped Off   79

7 Hope Beyond "I Do"
   The Give-and-Take of Domestic Harmony   97

8   Hope Beyond Immaturity
Maturity Checkpoints   113

9   Hope Beyond Bitterness
When Life "Just Ain't Fair"   131

10 Hope Beyond the Creeds
Focusing Fully on Jesus Christ   149

11 Hope Beyond the Culture
How to Shock the Pagan Crowd   163

12 Hope Beyond Extremism
Marching Orders for Soldiers of the Cross   179

13 Hope Beyond Our Trials
"When Through Fiery Trials . . ."   197

14 Hope Beyond Religion
A Job Description for Shepherds   215

15 Hope Beyond Dissatisfaction
A Formula That Brings Relief   233

16 Hope Beyond the Battle
Standing Nose-to-Nose with the Adversary   249

17 Hope Beyond Misery
Lasting Lessons   265

Notes   281

Acknowledgments

I WANT TO ACKNOWLEDGE, with great gratitude, my longstanding friendship with several important people.

First, my friends on the leadership team at Word Publishing: Byron Williamson, Kip Jordon, Joey Paul, and David Moberg. There are others I could name, but these four have been especially encouraging and helpful on this particular project. Thank you, men, for continuing to believe in me and for knowing how to turn dreams into books.

I also want to express my gratitude to writer Ken Gire for his excellent work many years ago on our Insight for Living study guide on 1 Peter. I found several of his insights and illustrations helpful as I worked my way through this volume.

Judith Markham has again proven herself invaluable to me as my editor. Her ability to transform my primitive lines and disjointed phrases into understandable sentences and meaningful paragraphs is something to behold! I am especially grateful for her wise and seasoned counsel throughout this process. Without her help this book would have been twice as long and half as interesting.

Although I've already mentioned them in my dedication, I want to repeat my thanks to Wendell Johnston and Charlie Dyer for giving me hope again and again on numerous occasions since I began my work as president of Dallas Theological Seminary back in the summer of 1994. The Dallas heat during that July was enough to wilt the most stouthearted, but there they were right from the start, smiling, serving, and sweating alongside me, giving constant affirmation and providing plenty of wind beneath my wings. Without their wholehearted commitment and assistance, rather than soaring like an eagle, I would have wandered around those halls like a turkey wondering where to roost. So thank you, men, for your faithful and supportive presence.

Finally, I want to acknowledge the encouragement of my wife, Cynthia, and express my thanks for her unswerving loyalty and compassionate understanding. We have been through a whale of a transition (we're still in it!), but because I haven't had to travel alone, the journey hasn't been nearly as difficult as it could have been. Having her by my side and knowing she is always in my corner and excited about my work has freed me up to finish what I started, regardless of the time and effort required. Thanks to her, I never felt the challenging task of finishing another project this extensive was hopeless.

CHUCK SWINDOLL
DALLAS, TEXAS

The Old Fisherman's Letter

HOPE IS A wonderful gift from God, a source of strength and courage in the face of life's harshest trials.

- When we are trapped in a tunnel of misery, hope points to the light at the end.
- When we are overworked and exhausted, hope gives us fresh energy.
- When we are discouraged, hope lifts our spirits.
- When we are tempted to quit, hope keeps us going.
- When we lose our way and confusion blurs the destination, hope dulls the edge of panic.
- When we struggle with a crippling disease or a lingering illness, hope helps us persevere beyond the pain.
- When we fear the worst, hope brings reminders that God is still in control.
- When we must endure the consequences of bad decisions, hope fuels our recovery.

- When we find ourselves unemployed, hope tells us we still have a future.
- When we are forced to sit back and wait, hope gives us the patience to trust.
- When we feel rejected and abandoned, hope reminds us we're not alone . . . we'll make it.
- When we say our final farewell to someone we love, hope in the life beyond gets us through our grief.

Put simply, when life hurts and dreams fade, nothing helps like hope.

Webster defines hope: "Desire accompanied by expectation of or belief in fulfillment . . . to desire with expectation of obtainment . . . to expect with confidence." How vital is that expectation! Without it, prisoners of war languish and die. Without it, students get discouraged and drop out of school. Without it, athletic teams fall into a slump and continue to lose . . . fledgling writers, longing to be published, run out of determination . . . addicts return to their habits . . . marriage partners decide to divorce . . . inventors, artists, entertainers, entrepreneurs, even preachers, lose their creativity.

Hope isn't merely a nice option that helps us temporarily clear a hurdle. It's essential to our survival.

Realizing the vital role hope plays in life, I decided several years ago to do a serious, in-depth study on the subject. To my surprise, one of the best sources of information was a letter located toward the end of the New Testament that was written by the old fisherman himself, Peter. He should know the subject well, having found himself in great need of hope at a critical moment in his own life—when he failed miserably.

And so . . . here it is, a book for all who sincerely search for ways to hope again . . . when your life hurts and when your dreams fade.

Hope Beyond Failure

The Broken
Man Behind
the Book

THIS IS A BOOK ON HOPE. *Hope*. It is something as important to us as water is to a fish, as vital as electricity is to a light bulb, as essential as air is to a jumbo jet. Hope is that basic to life.

We cannot stay on the road to anticipated dreams without it, at least not very far. Many have tried—none successfully. Without that needed spark of hope, we are doomed to a dark, grim existence.

How often the word "hopeless" appears in suicide notes. And even if it isn't actually written, we can read it between the lines. Take away our hope, and our world is reduced to something between depression and despair.

There once lived a man who loved the sea. Rugged, strong-willed, passionate, and expressive, he did nothing halfheartedly. When it came to fishing, he was determined—and sometimes obnoxious. But he was loyal when it came to friendships . . . loyal to the core, blindly coura-geous, and overconfident, which occasionally caused him to overstate his commitment. But there he stood, alone if necessary, making prom-ises with his mouth that his body would later be unable to keep.

3

As you probably realize by now, the man's name was Peter, not just one of the Twelve, but the spokesman for the Twelve (whether they liked it or not). Once he decided to follow Christ, there was no turning back. As time passed, he became all the more committed to the Master, a devoted and stubborn-minded disciple whose loyalty knew no bounds.

Ultimately, however, his commitment was put to the test. Jesus had warned him that Satan was hot on his heels, working overtime to trip him up. But Peter was unmoved. His response? "Lord, with You I am ready to go both to prison and to death!" (Luke 22:33). Jesus didn't buy it. He answered, "Peter, the cock will not crow today until you have denied three times that you know Me" (Luke 22:34). Though that prediction must have stung, Peter pushed it aside . . . self-assured and overly confident that it would never happen.

Wrong. That very night, Jesus' words turned to reality. The loyal, strong-hearted, courageous Peter failed his Lord. Deliberately and openly he denied that he was one of the Twelve. Not once or twice but three times, back to back, he turned on the One who had loved him enough to warn him.

The result? Read these words slowly as you imagine the scene.

And the Lord turned and looked at Peter. And Peter remembered the word of the Lord, how He had told him, "Before a cock crows today, you will deny Me three times." And he went out and wept bitterly. (Luke 22:61–62)

No longer loyal and strong, far from courageous and committed, the man was suddenly reduced to heaving sobs. What guilt he bore! How ashamed he felt! Words cannot adequately portray his brokenness. Emotionally, he plunged to rock bottom, caught in the grip of hopelessness; the effect on Peter was shattering. Every time he closed his eyes he could see the face of Jesus staring at him, as if asking, "How could you, Peter? Why would you?" That look. Those words. The man was haunted for days. The Savior's subsequent death by crucifixion must have been like a nail driven into Peter's heart.

The one thing he needed to carry him on was gone . . . gone forever, he thought. *Hope.* Until that glorious resurrection day, the first Easter morn, when we read not only of Jesus' miraculous, bodily resurrection from the dead but also those great words of grace, "Go, tell His disciples and Peter . . ." (Mark 16:7). *And Peter!* The significance of those two words cannot be overstated.

They introduced hope into the old fisherman's life . . . the one essential ingredient without which he could otherwise not recover. Upon hearing of his Savior's resurrection and also his Savior's concern that *he* especially be given the message, Peter had hope beyond his failure. Because of that, he could go on.

And, not surprisingly, he would later be the one who would write the classic letter of hope to those who needed to hear it the most . . . those who were residing "as aliens, scattered" across the vast landscape of the Roman Empire (1 Pet. 1:1).

Between his earlier failure and his writing this letter, Peter had been used of God as the catalyst in the formation of the early church. But having been broken and humiliated, his leadership was altogether different than it would have been without his failure. Now that he had been rescued by grace and restored by hope, he had no interest in playing "king of the mountain" by pushing people around. Rather, he became a servant-hearted shepherd of God's flock.

I like the way Eugene Peterson describes Peter in his introduction to 1 and 2 Peter:

> The way Peter handled himself in that position of power is even more impressive than the power itself. He kept out of the center of attention, he didn't parade his power, because he kept himself under the power of Jesus. He could have easily thrown around his popularity, power, and position to try to take over, using his close association with Jesus to promote himself. But he didn't. Most people with Peter's gifts couldn't have handled it then *or* now, but he did. Peter is a breath of fresh air.[1]

I cannot speak for you, but I certainly can for myself—this is a time when I could use some of Peter's "fresh air" in the form of a big dose of hope! These past two and a half years of my life and ministry have been anything but relaxed and settled. Having left a thriving, flourishing church where I had ministered for almost twenty-three years with a staff many would consider among the best in the country, and having stepped into a whole new arena of challenges—including endless commuting, facing the unknown, and accepting responsibilities outside the realm of my training, background, and expertise—I have found myself more than ever in need of hope. Solid, stable, sure hope. Hope to press on. Hope to endure. Hope to stay focused. Hope to see new dreams fulfilled.

And so it follows naturally that a book with this title has begun to flow from my pen. I trust that you who once smiled with me as we learned to laugh again by working our way through Paul's words to the Philippians are ready to travel with me through Peter's words as we now learn to hope again.

The journey will be worth the effort, I can assure you. We'll find hope around the corner of many of life's contingencies: hope beyond suffering and temptation . . . hope beyond immaturity and bitterness and the realities of our culture . . . hope beyond our trials and beyond times of dissatisfaction, guilt, and shame, to name only a few.

Best of all, we'll be guided on this journey by one who knew hopelessness firsthand, thanks to his own failures . . . and who experienced, firsthand, what it was like to hope again and again and again.

If that sounds like the kind of journey you need to take, read on. It will be a pleasure to travel with you, to be your companion on a road that leads to the healing of hurts and dreams fulfilled.

A Prayer for Hope Beyond Failure

Dear Father, every person reading these words, including the one writing them, has experienced failure. It has left us broken and disappointed in ourselves. And there are times when a flashback of those failures returns to haunt us. How sad it makes us when we recall those moments! Thank You for the remarkable transformation made possible by forgiveness. Thank You for understanding that "we are but dust," often incapable of fulfilling our own promises or living up to our own expectations.

Renew our hope—hope beyond failure—as we read and reflect on the words of Peter, with whom we can so easily identify. Remind us that, just as You used him after he had failed repeatedly, You will also use us, by Your grace.

May we find fresh encouragement from his words and new strength from his counsel as we journey together with Peter as our guide. We look to You for the ability to hope again, for You, alone, have the power to make something beautiful and good out of lives littered with the debris of words we should never have said and deeds we should never have done.

Our only source of relief comes through Your grace. Bring it to our attention again and again as we discover the truths You led the old fisherman to write so many years ago. In the gracious name of Jesus, I ask this.

AMEN

2

Hope Beyond Suffering

How We Can Smile Through Suffering

WE DON'T LOOK ALIKE. We don't act alike. We don't dress alike. We have different tastes in the food we eat, the books we read, the cars we drive, and the music we enjoy. You like opera; I like country. We have dissimilar backgrounds, goals, and motivations. We work at different jobs, and we enjoy different hobbies. You like rock climbing; I like Harleys. We ascribe to a variety of philosophies and differ over politics. We have our own unique convictions on child-rearing and education. Our weights vary. Our heights vary. So does the color of our skin.

But there is one thing we all have in common: We all know what it means to hurt.

Suffering is a universal language. Tears are the same for Jews or Muslims or Christians, for white or black or brown, for children or adults or the elderly. When life hurts and our dreams fade, we may express our anguish in different ways, but each one of us knows the sting of pain and heartache, disease and disaster, trials and sufferings.

Joseph Parker, a great preacher of yesteryear, once said to a group of aspiring young ministers, "Preach to the suffering and you will never lack a congregation. There is a broken heart in every pew."

Truly, suffering is the common thread in all our garments.

This has been true since the beginning, when sin entered the world and Adam and Eve were driven from the Garden. It shouldn't surprise us, therefore, that when the apostle Peter wrote his first letter to fellow believers scattered throughout much of Asia Minor he focused on the one subject that drew all of them together. Suffering. These people were being singed by the same flames of persecution that would take the apostle's life in just a few years. Their circumstances were the bleakest imaginable. Yet Peter didn't try to pump them up with positive thinking. Instead, he gently reached his hand to their chins and lifted their faces skyward—so they could see beyond their circumstances to their celestial calling.

> Peter, an apostle of Jesus Christ, to those who reside as aliens, scattered throughout Pontius, Galatia, Cappadocia, Asia, and Bithynia, who are chosen according to the foreknowledge of God the Father, by the sanctifying work of the Spirit, that you may obey Jesus Christ and be sprinkled with His blood: May grace and peace be yours in fullest measure. (1 Pet. 1:1–2)

The men and women Peter wrote to knew what it was like to be away from home, not by choice but by force. Persecuted for their faith, they had been pushed out into a world that was not only unfamiliar but hostile.

Warren Wiersbe, in a fine little book entitled *Be Hopeful*, says this about the recipients of the letter:

> The important thing for us to know about these "scattered strangers" is that they were going through a time of suffering and persecution. At least fifteen times in this letter, Peter referred to suffering; and he used eight different Greek words to do so. Some of these Christians were suffering because they were living godly lives and doing what was good and right. . . . Others were suffering reproach for the name of Christ . . . and being railed at by unsaved people. . . . Peter wrote to

encourage them to be good witnesses to their persecutors, and to remember that their suffering would lead to glory.[1]

Take another look at the beginning of that last sentence: "Peter
wrote to encourage them to be good witnesses to their persecutors."
It is so easy to read that. It is even easier to preach it. But it is extremely difficult to do it. If you have ever been mistreated, you know
what a great temptation it is to retaliate, to defend yourself, to fight
back, to treat the other person as he or she has treated you. Peter
wants to encourage his fellow believers to put pain in perspective
and find hope beyond their suffering.

While most of us are not afflicted by horrible persecution for
our faith, we do know what it means to face various forms of
suffering, pain, disappointment, and grief. Fortunately, in the letter
of 1 Peter we can find comfort and consolation for our own brand of
suffering. Just as this treasured document spoke to the believers scattered in Pontius or Galatia or Cappadocia or Asia, so it speaks to us
in Texas and California, Arizona and Oklahoma, Minnesota and
Maine.

The first good news Peter gives us is the knowledge that we are
"chosen by God." What a helpful reminder! We aren't just thrown
on this earth like dice tossed across a table. We are sovereignly and
lovingly placed here for a purpose, having been chosen by God. His
choosing us was *according to His foreknowledge, by the sanctifying work
of the Spirit, that we may obey Jesus Christ, having been sprinkled with His
blood.* Powerful words!

God has given us a purpose for our existence, a reason to go on,
even though that existence includes tough times. Living through
suffering, we become sanctified—in other words, set apart for the
glory of God. We gain perspective. We grow deeper. We grow up!

Can you imagine going through such times without Jesus Christ?
I can't. But frankly, that's what most people do. They face those
frightening fears and sleepless nights in the hospital without Christ.
They struggle with a wayward teenager without Christ. Alone, they
endure the awful words from a mate, "I don't want to live with you

any longer. I want my freedom. I don't love you any more. I'm gone." And they go through it all without Christ.

For souls like these, life is one painful sting after another. Just imagining what life must be like without Christ, I am surprised that more people who live without hope don't take their own lives. As appalled as I am by Jack Kevorkian and his death-on-demand philosophy, I am not surprised. What surprises me is that more people don't simply put an end to it all.

Yet if we will only believe and ask, a full measure of God's grace and peace is available to any of us. By the wonderful, prevailing mercy of God, we can find purpose in the scattering and sadness of our lives. We can not only deal with suffering but rejoice through it. Though our pain and our disappointment and the details of our suffering may differ, there is an abundance of God's grace and peace available to each one of us.

These truths form the skeleton of strong doctrine. But unless the truths are fleshed out they remain hard and bony and difficult to embrace. Knowing this, Peter reminds his readers of all they have to cling to so that they can actually rejoice in times of suffering, drawing on God's grace and peace in fullest measure.

Rejoicing Through Hard Times

As I read and ponder Peter's first letter, I find six reasons why we as believers can rejoice through hard times and experience hope beyond suffering.

We Have a Living Hope

Blessed be the God and Father of our Lord Jesus Christ, who according to His great mercy has caused us to be born again to a living hope through the resurrection of Jesus Christ from the dead. (1 Pet. 1:3)

As difficult as some pages of our life may be, nothing that occurs to us on this earth falls into the category of "the final chapter." That chapter will not be completed until we arrive in heaven and step into the presence of the living God. Our final meeting is not with the antagonist in our life's story but with the author Himself.

"Who can mind the journey," asks the late, great Bible teacher James M. Gray, "when the road leads home?"

How can we concern ourselves that much over what happens on this temporary planet when we know that it is all leading us to our eternal destination? Peter calls that our "living hope," and he reminds us that it is based on the resurrection of Jesus Christ. If God brought His Son through the most painful trials and back from the pit of death itself, certainly He can bring us through whatever we face in this world, no matter how deep that pit might seem at the time.

Do you realize how scarce hope is to those without Christ? One cynical writer, H. L. Mencken, an American newspaperman during the early half of this century, referred to hope as "a pathological belief in the occurrence of the impossible."

To the unsaved, hope is nothing more than mental fantasy, like wishing upon a star. It's the kind of Disneyland hope that says, "I sure hope I win the lottery." . . . "I hope my boy comes home someday." . . . "I hope everything works out OK." That's not a living hope. That's wishful thinking.

But those who are "born again" in the Lord Jesus Christ have been promised a living hope through His resurrection from the dead.

So if you want to smile through your tears, if you want to rejoice through times of suffering, just keep reminding yourself that, as a Christian, what you're going through isn't the end of the story . . . it's simply the rough journey that leads to the right destination.

"Hope is like an anchor," someone has said. "Our hope in Christ stabilizes us in the storms of life, but unlike an anchor, it does not hold us back."

We Have a Permanent Inheritance

Blessed be the God and Father of our Lord Jesus Christ, who according to His great mercy has caused us . . . to obtain an inheritance which is imperishable and undefiled and will not fade away, reserved in heaven for you. (1 Pet. 1:3–4)

We also can rejoice through suffering because we have a permanent inheritance—a secure home in heaven. And our place there is reserved under the safekeeping, under the constant, omnipotent surveillance of Almighty God. Nothing can destroy it, defile it, diminish it, or displace it. Isn't that a great relief?

Have you ever had the disconcerting experience of finding someone else in the theater or airplane seat you had reserved? You hold the proper ticket, but someone else is in your seat. At best it's awkward; at worst it can lead to an embarrassing confrontation.

Have you ever made guaranteed reservations at your favorite hotel for a "nonsmoking" room and arrived late at night to find they have given it to someone else? What a disappointment! You give them your guaranteed reservation number and they punch endless information into the computer, then they look at you as though you've just landed from Mars. Your heart sinks. You force a smile and ask to speak to the manager. He comes out, stares at the same computer screen, then gives you the same look with a slightly deeper frown. "Sorry," he says. "There must be some kind of mistake."

Well, that's not going to happen in glory! God will not look at you like, "Now, what did you say your name was again?" The living God will ultimately welcome you home to your permanent, reserved inheritance. Your name is on the door.

I don't know what that does to you, but it sure gives me a reason to rejoice. The more difficult life gets on this earth, the better heaven seems.

We Have a Divine Protection

[We] . . . are protected by the power of God, through faith for a salvation ready to be revealed in the last time. (1 Pet. 1:5)

Under heaven's lock and key, we are protected by the most efficient security system available—the power of God. There is no way we will be lost in the process of suffering. No disorder, no disease, not even death itself can weaken or threaten God's ultimate protection over our lives. No matter what the calamity, no matter what the disappointment or depth of pain, no matter what kind of destruction occurs in our bodies at the time of death, our souls are divinely protected.

Our world is filled with warfare, with atrocities, with terrorism. Think of those men and women, especially those precious, innocent children, whose lives were shattered in an instant on that April 1995 morning in Oklahoma City when the world blew up around them. What happens in such times of tragic calamities? Is our eternal inheritance blown away with our bodies? Absolutely not. Even through the most horrible of deaths, He who made us from the dust of the earth protects us by His power and promises to deliver us to our eternal destination.

"God stands between you and all that menaces your hope or threatens your eternal welfare," James Moffatt wrote. "The protection here is entirely and directly the work of God."

Two words will help you cope when you run low on hope: *accept* and *trust*.

Accept the mystery of hardship, suffering, misfortune, or mistreatment. Don't try to understand it or explain it. Accept it. Then, deliberately *trust* God to protect you by His power from this very moment to the dawning of eternity.

We Have a Developing Faith

In this you greatly rejoice, even though now for a little while, if necessary, you have been distressed by various trials, that the proof of your faith, being more precious than gold which is perishable, even though tested by fire, may be found to result in praise and glory and honor at the revelation of Jesus Christ. (1 Pet. 1:6–7)

Here is the first of several references in Peter's letter to rejoicing. The words "even though" indicate that the joy is unconditional. It does not depend on the circumstances surrounding us. And don't overlook the fact that this joy comes *in spite of* our suffering, not because of it, as some who glorify suffering would have us believe. We don't rejoice because times are hard; we rejoice in spite of the fact that they are hard.

These verses also reveal three significant things about trials.

First, trials are often necessary, proving the genuineness of our faith and at the same time teaching us humility. Trials reveal our own helplessness. They put us on our face before God. They make us realistic. Or, as someone has said, "Pain plants the flag of reality in the fortress of a rebel heart." When rebels are smacked by reality, it's amazing how quickly humility replaces rigidity.

Second, trials are distressing, teaching us compassion so that we never make light of another's test or cruelly force others to smile while enduring it.

How unfair to trivialize another person's trial by comparing what he or she is going through with what someone else has endured. Even if you have gone through something you think is twice as difficult, comparison doesn't comfort. It doesn't help the person who has lost a child to hear that you endured the loss of two.

Express your sympathy and weep with them. Put your arm around them. Don't reel off a lot of verses. Don't try to make the hurting person pray with you or sing with you if he or she is not ready to do that. Feel what that person is feeling. Walk quietly and compassionately in his or her shoes.

Third, trials come in various forms. The word *various* comes from an interesting Greek term, *poikolos,* which means "variegated" or "many colored." We also get the term "polka dot" from it. Trials come in a variety of forms and colors. They are different, just as we are different. Something that would hardly affect you might knock the slats out from under me—and vice versa. But God offers special grace to match every shade of sorrow.

Paul had a thorn in the flesh, and he prayed three times for God to remove it. "No," said God, "I'm not taking it away." Finally Paul said, "I've learned to trust in You, Lord. I've learned to live with it." It was then God said, "My grace is sufficient for that thorn." He matched the color of the test with the color of grace.

This variety of trials is like different temperature settings on God's furnace. The settings are adjusted to burn off our dross, to temper us or soften us according to what meets our highest need. It is in God's refining fire that the authenticity of our faith is revealed. And the purpose of these fiery ordeals is that we may come forth as purified gold, a shining likeness of the Lord Jesus Christ Himself. That glinting likeness is what ultimately gives glory and praise and honor to our Savior.

We Have an Unseen Savior

And though you have not seen Him, you love Him, and though you do not see Him now, but believe in Him, you greatly rejoice with joy inexpressible and full of glory. (1 Pet. 1:8)

Keep in mind that the context of this verse is suffering. So we know that Peter is not serving up an inconsequential, theological hors d'oeuvre. He's giving us solid meat we can sink our teeth into. He's telling us that our Savior is standing alongside us in that furnace. He is there even though we can't see Him.

You don't have to see someone to love that person. The blind mother has never seen her children, but she loves them. You don't have to see someone to believe in him or her. Believers today have never seen a physical manifestation of the Savior—we have not visibly seen Him walking among us—but we love Him nevertheless. In times of trial we sense He is there, and that causes us to "greatly rejoice" with inexpressible joy.

Some, like the struggling, reflective disciple Thomas, need to see and touch Jesus in order to believe. But Jesus said, "Blessed are they who did not see, and yet believed" (John 20:29). Even though we can't see Jesus beside us in our trials, He is there—just as He was when Shadrach, Meshach, and Abednego were thrown into the fiery furnace.

We Have a Guaranteed Deliverance

> . . . obtaining as the outcome of your faith the salvation of your souls. (1 Pet. 1:9)

How can we rejoice through our pain? How can we have hope beyond our suffering? Because we have a living hope, we have a permanent inheritance, we have divine protection, we have a developing faith, we have an unseen Savior, and we have a guaranteed deliverance.

This isn't the kind of delivery the airlines promise you when you check your bags. ("Guaranteed arrival. No problem.") I'll never forget a trip I took a few years ago. I went to Canada for a conference with plans to be there for eight days. Thanks to the airline, I only had my clothes for the last two! When I finally got my luggage, I noticed the tags on them were all marked "Berlin." ("Guaranteed arrival. No problem." They just don't guarantee when or where the bags will arrive!) That's why we now see so many people boarding airplanes with huge bags hanging from their shoulders and draped over both arms. Don't check your bags, these folks are saying, because they probably won't get there when you do.

But when it comes to spiritual delivery, we never have to worry. God guarantees deliverance of our souls, which includes not only a deliverance from our present sin but the glorification of our physical bodies as well. Rejoice! You're going to get there—guaranteed.

Rejoicing, Not Resentment

When we are suffering, only Christ's perspective can replace our resentment with rejoicing. I've seen it happen in hospital rooms. I've seen it happen in families. I've seen it happen in my own life.

Our whole perspective changes when we catch a glimpse of the purpose of Christ in it all. Take that away, and it's nothing more than a bitter, terrible experience.

Nancy and Ed Huizinga in Grand Rapids, Michigan, know all about this. In December 1995, while they were at church rehearsing for the annual Christmas Festival of Lights program, their home burned to the ground. But that wasn't their only tragedy that year. Just three months earlier, Nancy's long-time friend, Barb Post, a widow with two children, had died of cancer. Nancy and Ed had taken her two children, Jeff and Katie, into their home as part of their family, something they had promised Barb they would do. So when Ed and Nancy's house burned to the ground just before Christmas, it wasn't just their home that was lost; it was the home of two teenagers who had already lost their mother and father.

As circumstances unfolded, irony went to work. The tragedy that forced the Huizingas from their home allowed Jeff and Katie to move back to theirs. Since their home had not yet been sold following their mother's death, they and the Huizinga family moved in there the night after the fire.

On the following Saturday, neighbors organized a party to sift through the ashes and search for anything of value that might have survived. One of the first indications they received of God's involvement in their struggle came as a result of that search. Somehow a piece of paper survived. On it were these words: "Contentment: Realizing that God has already provided everything we need for our present happiness."

To Nancy and Ed, this was like hearing God speak from a burning bush. It was the assurance they needed that He was there . . . and He was not silent.

Nancy's biggest frustration now is dealing with insurance companies and trying to assess their material losses. Many possessions, of course, were irreplaceable personal items such as photographs and things handed down from parents and grandparents. But her highest priority is Jeff and Katie, along with her own two children, Joel and Holly. The loss has been hardest on them, she says.

"They don't have the history of God's faithfulness that Ed and I have. We've had years to make deposits in our 'faith account,' but they haven't. We've learned that if you fail to stock up on faith when you don't need it, you won't have any when you do need it. This has been our opportunity to use what we've been learning."

While the world might view this as a senseless tragedy, deserving of resentment, Nancy and Ed have seen God reveal Himself to them and refine them through this fire as He pours out a full measure of grace and peace.[2]

Suffering comes in many forms and degrees, but His grace is always there to carry us beyond it. I've lived long enough and endured a sufficient number of trials to say without hesitation that only Christ's perspective can replace our resentment with rejoicing. Jesus is the central piece of suffering's puzzle. If we fit Him into place, the rest of the puzzle—no matter how complex and enigmatic—begins to make sense.

Only Christ's salvation can change us from spectators to participants in the unfolding drama of redemption. The scenes will be demanding. Some may be tragic. But only then will we understand the role that suffering plays in our lives. Only then will we be able to tap into hope beyond our suffering.

A Prayer for Hope Beyond Suffering

Lord, mere words about hope and encouragement and purpose can really fall flat if things aren't right in our lives. If we're consumed by rage and resentment, somehow these words seem meaningless. But when our hearts are right, we hear with new ears. Then, rather than resisting these words, we appreciate them, and we love You for them.

Give us grace to match our trials. Give us a sense of hope and purpose beyond our pain. And give us fresh assurance that we're not alone, that Your plan has not been aborted though our suffering intensifies.

Help those of us who are on our feet right now to maintain a compassion for those who aren't. Give us a word of encouragement for others living in a world of hurt.

Let us never forget that every jolt in this rugged journey from earth to heaven is a reminder that we're on the right road.

I ask this in the compassionate name of the Man of Sorrows who was acquainted with grief.

AMEN

3

Hope Beyond Temptation

Staying Clean in a Corrupt Society

WOULDN'T IT BE wonderful if God would save us and then, within a matter of seconds, take us on to glory? Wouldn't that be a great relief? We would never have any temptations. We would never have to battle with the flesh. We would never even have the possibility of messing up our lives. We could just be whisked off to glory—saved, sanctified, galvanized, glorified! Trouble is, I have a sneaking suspicion that many, if not most, would wait until fifteen minutes before takeoff time to give their lives to Christ and then catch the jet for glory.

Since that's not an option and since it's clearly God's preference that we prove ourselves blameless and innocent and above reproach, we obviously have to come up with an alternative route. Some have suggested sanctification by isolation, believing the only way to keep evil and corruption from rubbing off on you is to withdraw from the world. After all, how can you walk through a coal mine without getting dirty? The logic seems irrefutable.

But God, in His infinite wisdom, has deliberately left us on this earth. He has sovereignly chosen to give many of us more years *in* Christ than *out* of Christ—many more years to live for Him "in the midst of a crooked and perverse generation, among whom you appear as lights in the world" (Phil. 2:15). Or, as one of my mentors, the late Ray Stedman, so succinctly put it, "Crooked and perverse simply means we are left in a world of crooks and perverts." That's the kind of world God left us in on purpose.

Don't think for a minute, however, that the Lord has made a mistake leaving us here. We are His lights in a dark world. In fact, just minutes before Jesus' arrest and ultimate death on the cross, He prayed this for His disciples and for us:

> I have given them Thy word; and the world has hated them, because they are not of the world, even as I am not of the world. I do not ask Thee to take them out of the world, but to keep them from the evil one. (John 17:14–15)

Think about that. "I'm not asking You to take them out from among the midst of a crooked and perverse generation," Jesus said. "But I do ask You to guard them, to protect them." Jesus doesn't ask the Father to isolate His disciples from the world but to insulate them, "to keep them from the evil one."

He has left us in the world on purpose and for His purpose. In a world where the majority are going the wrong way, we are left as lights—stoplights, directional lights, illuminating lights—as living examples, as strong testimonies of the right way. We are spiritual salmon swimming upstream.

The Seductive Cosmos Mentality

Few things are more awesome than pictures of earth the astronauts have taken from space. Our big, blue-and-white marble planet stands out so beautifully against the deep darkness of space. However, that's not the "world" Jesus has in mind here. He's not talking about

28

the visible planet named Earth; He's talking about a philosophy that envelopes earthlings. It's not a place but a system—a system that finds its origin in the Enemy himself. It's a figure of speech that encapsulates the mind-set and morality of the unregenerate. It's what John calls the *cosmos*.

> Do not love the world, nor the things in the world. If anyone loves the world, the love of the Father is not in him. For all that is in the world [the *cosmos*], the lust of the flesh and the lust of the eyes and the boastful pride of life, is not from the Father, but is from the world. And the world is passing away, also its lusts; but the one who does the will of God abides forever. (1 John 2:15–17)

The physical world upon which we have our feet planted is visible. It can be measured. It can be felt. It has color and odor and texture. It's tangible . . . obvious. What is not so obvious is the system that permeates and operates within lives on this earth. It is a world-system manipulated by the pervasive hand of Satan and his demons, who pull the strings to achieve the adversary's wicked ends. If we are ever to extricate ourselves from those strings, we must be able to detect them and understand where they lead.

So what is this system? What is its philosophy? What is the frame of reference of the *cosmos*—its thinking, its drives, its goals?

The first thing we need to know is that it is a system that operates apart from and at odds with God. It's designed to appeal to us, to attract us, to seduce us with its sequined garb of fame, fortune, power, and pleasure. God's ways are often uncomfortable, but the world-system is designed to make us comfortable, to give us pleasure, to gain our favor, and ultimately to win our support. The philosophy of the world-system is totally at odds with the philosophy of God.

Greek grammarian Kenneth Wuest wrote:

> *Kosmos* refers to an ordered system . . . of which Satan is the head, his fallen angels and demons are his emissaries, and the unsaved of the human race are his subjects. . . . Much in this world-system is religious, cultured, refined, and intellectual. But it is anti-God and anti-Christ.

... This world of unsaved humanity is inspired by "the spirit of the age," ... which Trench defines as follows: "All that floating mass of thoughts, opinions, maxims, speculations, hopes, impulses, aims, aspirations, at any time current in the world, which it may be impossible to seize and accurately define, but which constitutes a most real and effective power, being the moral, or immoral atmosphere which at every moment of our lives we inhale, again inevitably to exhale."[1]

You want to know what we are inhaling? Pay close attention to the commercials on television and observe what they're advertising and how virtually every word, picture, and sound is designed to pull you in, to make you dissatisfied with what you have and what you look like and who you are. The great goal is to make you want whatever it is that is being sold.

But it's not just on television. The world-system, the cosmos philosophy, is everywhere. It's going on all the time, even when you can't see it, and especially when you're not thinking about it. It's whistling its appeal, "Come on. Come on. You'll love it. This is so much fun. It'll make you look so good. It'll make you feel so good." It motivates us by appealing to our pride and to that which pleases us, all the while cleverly seducing us away from God.

And over all this realm, don't forget, Satan is prince.

A Challenge to Be Different

The pull of the world is every bit as strong and subtle as gravity. So invisible, yet so irresistible. So relentlessly there. Never absent or passive.

Unless we realize how strong and how subtle the world's influence really is, we won't understand the passion behind Peter's words.

Living in Holiness

Therefore, gird your minds for action, keep sober in spirit, fix your hope completely on the grace to be brought to you at the revelation of Jesus Christ. As obedient children, do not be conformed to the former lusts which were yours in your ignorance, but like the Holy One who called you, be holy yourselves also in all your behavior; because it is written, "You shall be holy, for I am holy." (1 Pet. 1:13–16)

Reading these statements, we can't help but catch something of Peter's assertive spirit. He seems to be saying that this is no time to kick back; this isn't a day to be passive. In fact, I think Peter really bears down with his pen at this point. Look at the forcefulness of his phrases: "gird your minds for action" . . . "keep sober" . . . "fix your hope." He spits them out in staccato form. Today we might say, "Straighten up!" . . . "Get serious!" And then the clincher command from God, saying, in essence: "Be holy like I am."

It's easy to let the world intoxicate us and fuzz our minds. But if we're to shake ourselves out of that dizzying spell, we must resist the power it exerts on us.

I think Peter is saying, "You have to realize that even though you're living in the cosmos, your mind, your eyes, *your focus* must be beyond the present." Kenneth Wuest suggests this: "Set your hope perfectly, unchangeably, without doubt and despondency."

That goes back to what we were thinking about in the previous chapter. No matter how bad things get, fix your mind beyond what's happening around you and what's happening to you. Otherwise you'll erode into the cosmos mentality.

I love the way verse 14 begins, "As obedient children. . . ." Isn't that affirming? Rather than coming down on his fellow believers, assuming they're disobedient, Peter assumes just the opposite here. "You're obedient children."

Through the years, my wife, Cynthia, and I found that if we referred to our children as good kids, obedient kids, kids we were proud of, that attitude instilled in them a sense that Mom and Dad had confidence and trust in them. And that's the attitude Peter employs when he tells the believers scattered throughout the ancient world: "As obedient children, do not be conformed." This also reminds me of Paul's words to believers in Romans 12:2: "And do not be conformed to this world, but be transformed. . . ."

How easy it is to allow the world, the cosmos, to suck you into its system. If you do, if you conform, then you are adopting the kind of lifestyle that was yours when you were in ignorance, when you didn't know there was another way to live. That was back when the cosmos was your comfort zone.

Have you been in Christ so long that you have forgotten what it was like to be without Him? Remember, He has called us to follow in His footsteps—to be *holy* "like the Holy One who called you, be holy yourselves also in all your behavior; because it is written, 'YOU SHALL BE HOLY, FOR I AM HOLY.'" We have a Father who is holy, and as His children, we're to be like Him.

But what does it mean to be *holy*? That's always a tough question to answer. Stripped down to its basics, the term *holy* means "set apart" in some special and exclusive way. Perhaps it will help if we think of it in another context. In holy matrimony, for example, a man and a woman are set apart, leaving all others as they bond exclusively to each other.

When I was a young man and a young husband serving in the marines, I was eight thousand miles away from my wife. I knew Cynthia existed. I could read her letters and occasionally hear her voice on the phone, but I couldn't see her or touch her. I had only the memory of our standing together three years earlier before God and a minister who had pronounced us husband and wife, setting us apart exclusively to each other for the rest of our lives. We were wed back in June 1955, but regardless of how long ago it was, we stood together and committed ourselves to a *holy* intermingling of our lives. To be intimate with another woman would break that holy relationship, that exclusive oneness. Remembering that helped keep me faithful to my wife while we were apart those many months . . . and it still helps over forty-one years later!

Church ordinances or sacraments, such as baptism and communion, are often called *holy*. In Holy Communion, for example, the bread and wine are set apart from common use and set aside to God alone. The same meaning lies behind the word *sanctify* in 1 Peter 3:15: "But sanctify Christ as Lord in your hearts." I love that. We are to "set Him apart" as Lord in our hearts.

What a successful way to deal with the cosmos! To begin the morning by saying, "Lord, I set apart my mind for You today. I set apart my passion. I set apart my eyes. I set apart my ears. I set apart my motives. I set apart my discipline. Today I set apart every limb of my body and each area of my life unto You as Lord over my life." When we start our day like that, chances are good that temptation's winks will not be nearly as alluring.

Walking in Fear

> And if you address as Father the One who impartially judges according to each man's work, conduct yourselves in fear during the time of your stay upon earth. (1 Pet. 1:17)

Another secret of living a godly life in the midst of a godless world involves the way we conduct ourselves hour by hour through the day. Peter says we are to do it "in *fear*." We don't hear much about the *fear* of God today, and when we do, some may think only of images of a fire-and-brimstone preacher pounding a pulpit. We need a better perspective. Perhaps the word *reverence* gives us a clearer picture of what Peter means here. In fact, the New International Version translates this phrase "live your lives as strangers here in reverent fear." The point is, if we're going to address God as Father, then we should conduct ourselves on earth in a way that reflects our reverence for Him as our Father.

Also, if you're going to address Him as your Father, if you're going to have a one-on-one relationship with Him in fellowship and in prayer, then conduct yourself as one who knows that you will someday have to account to Him for your life. Why? Well, in case you didn't know, "each one of us shall give account of himself to God" (Rom. 14:12).

When we die, we will be brought before the judgment seat of Christ where we will independently account for our lives before God. He will see us as our lives pass in review, and He will reward us accordingly. It's not a judgment to see if we get into heaven. That's taken care of. As we saw in the previous chapter, we can't lose our salvation. We can, however, lose our reward. At the judgment seat, Christ will judge our works and determine whether they were done in the power of the Spirit or in the energy of the flesh. We will all give an account of the deeds we have done in this life, and God will "test the quality of each man's work" (1 Cor. 3:13). That thought, alone, will instill a big, healthy dose of the fear of God in us!

We don't know how God is going to do this, but it helps me to put it into an everyday image we can understand. So I picture myself in the future standing there all alone before my heavenly Father. Along comes an enormous celestial dump truck, piled high with stuff. The truck backs up, the bed lifts up, and the whole load is dumped out in front me. The Lord and I talk about all the wood, hay, and stubble that's piled there, and then He begins digging through it. "Oh, there's a piece of gold," He says. "Hmm, here's some silver." With that He begins setting aside all the precious and permanent stuff. Then, *whoosh!* The wood, hay, and stubble are gone, instantly consumed by fire. Only the gold, silver, and precious stones that remain are rewarded.

In the 1988 Summer Olympics in Seoul, South Korea, Ben Johnson of Canada won the one-hundred-meter dash, setting a new Olympic record and a new world record. Our American contender, Carl Lewis, came in second, and most were shocked that he hadn't won the gold. After the race, the judges learned that Johnson had had an illegal substance in his body. He ran the race illegally, so the judges took away his medal. Though he ran faster and made an unforgettable impression, he did not deserve the reward.

Though the world and even our fellow Christians may be impressed with and applaud our deeds, let's not forget that God is the final judge! He searches our hearts; He alone knows our motivation. And He will be the One to say, "This deserves a reward. Ah, but that does not."

That's why we conduct ourselves in fear. That's why we walk in reverence. Because we know that He is checking for illegal substances. He knows whether down deep inside we have gotten sucked into the cosmos, whether we have bought into the system. He knows whether our noble acts and deeds are done out of pride and self-aggrandizement or whether they have been carried out in the power of the Spirit. He knows whether our inner, unseen thoughts and motives match our external words and works. He is pleased when our lives honor Him—inside and out. He is grieved when they do not. And it is *His* smile we want. It is *His* reward, not the reward of this world, not the applause of those around us, not the superficial spotlight of fame or fortune or power.

This Christian life is a tough fight. Earlier in this century, Donald Grey Barnhouse, a well-known minister and radio preacher, wrote an entire book on this subject, *The Invisible War*. This conflict is not a war fought with Uzis or tanks or smart bombs or ground-to-air missiles. The land mines, ambushes, and traps set by our enemy are much more subtle than that—and even more deadly, for they aim at the soul. And they are everywhere.

But with the pride and pleasures of the cosmos so alluring, how can weaklings like us run the race without being disqualified and forfeiting our reward? How can we win the battle over an enemy we can't see? The solution to that problem rests within our minds.

Focusing Your Mind

. . . knowing that you were not redeemed with perishable things like silver or gold from your futile way of life inherited from your forefathers, but with precious blood, as of a lamb unblemished and spotless, the blood of Christ. For He was foreknown before the foundation of the world, but has appeared in these last times for the sake of you who through Him are believers in God, who raised Him from the dead and gave Him glory, so that your faith and hope are in God. (1 Pet. 1:18–20)

I'm convinced that the battle with this world is a battle within the mind. Our minds are major targets of the Enemy's appeal. When the world pulls back its bowstring, our minds are the bull's-eyes. Any arrows we allow to become impaled in our minds will ultimately poison our thoughts. And if we tolerate this long enough, we'll end up acting out what we think. So the third technique for counteracting that poison, for dealing with the seduction of the cosmos, the world around us, is to focus our minds on Christ. We can do this by remembering what our Savior has done for us. Or, to paraphrase 1 Peter, "remember what your inheritance cost your Savior."

The first thing Christ did for us was to deliver us from slavery—slavery to a "futile way of life." Whether we knew it or not, we were trapped in a lifestyle that had only empty pleasures and dead-end desires to offer. We were in bondage to our impulses spawned from our sinful nature. In such a condition, we were hopelessly unable to help ourselves. The only way for us to be emancipated from that slavery was to have someone redeem us. That ransom price was paid by Christ, not with gold or silver, but with His precious blood. In doing so, He broke the chains that bound us to this world. He opened the door and said, "Now you're free to live for Me and serve Me." That single emancipation proclamation made possible a life of hope beyond temptation.

The second thing Christ did for us was to come near and make Himself known; He "appeared in these last times for the sake of you who through Him are believers in God . . . so that your faith and hope are in God" (vv. 20–21). That makes the whole thing personal, doesn't it? He realized the enormity of our earth-born emptiness. He knew our inability to free ourselves. And He willingly stepped out of His privileged position in heaven to pay the ransom . . . for us! He gave Himself, not only so we could become free, but so we could be secure, with our faith and hope resting not precariously on our own shoulders but securely on His.

What is life like without Christ? Look at 1 Peter 4:3–4.

> For the time already past is sufficient for you to have carried out the desire of the Gentiles, having pursued a course of sensuality, lusts, drunkenness, carousels, drinking parties and abominable idolatries. And in all this, they are surprised that you do not run with them into the same excess of dissipation, and they malign you.

That's a pretty vivid description of the futile lifestyle of the lost. That's what we see around us every day—a lifestyle promising to satisfy, to bring happiness and pleasure and contentment. Yet it brings just the opposite. This lifestyle leads only to another hangover or another bout with guilt—if there is even enough conscience left for guilt. It's one "happy hour" (strange name!) after another. One high after another. One snort after another. One drug after another. One affair after another. One abortion after another. One partner after another. It's life lived for the highs, which are nothing more than temporary breaks in the lows. It's empty. It's hollow. It's miserable. It's exactly as Peter describes it: a "futile way of life."

And we've been redeemed from that, not with silver or gold, "but with precious blood, as of a lamb unblemished and spotless, the blood of Christ."

Techniques to Remember

When we're in the comfortable conclave of Christian fellowship, it's relatively easy to be holy, to conduct our lives in the fear of God, and to focus our minds on the Savior (at least externally). But when we're out in the world, when we're in the minority, it's different, isn't it?

If you want to stay clean, even when you're walking alone in the dark, low-ceilinged coal mine of the corrupt and secular culture, you need to remember a few practical things—four come to mind.

First, pay close attention to what you look at. This takes us back to verse 13, where we are told to gird our minds for action, keep sober in spirit, and fix our hope completely on the grace that's revealed in Jesus Christ.

Our eyes seem to be the closest connection to our minds. Through our eyes we bring in information and visual images. Through our eyes we feed our imaginations. Through our eyes we focus on things that are alluring and attractive and, don't kid yourself, extremely pleasurable for a while . . . *for a while*. Remember, the Bible says that Moses, by faith, gave up the "passing pleasures of sin" to walk with the people of God (Heb. 11:24–26). The cosmos offers pleasures, no doubt about it, but they are passing. . . .

37

If then you have been raised up with Christ, keep seeking the things above, where Christ is, seated at the right hand of God. Set your mind on things above, not on the things that are on earth. (Col. 3:1–2)

Second, give greater thought to the consequences of sin rather than to its pleasures. One of the characteristics of the cosmos is that nobody ever mentions the ugly underside of pleasurable sins. If you're thinking about having an affair, if you are getting caught in that lustful trap, I strongly suggest that you walk through the consequences in your mind. Stroll slowly . . . ponder details. Think through the effects of that act in your life and in the lives of others whom your life touches.

In a *Leadership* magazine article titled "Consequences of a Moral Tumble," Randy Alcorn says that whenever he is feeling "particularly vulnerable to sexual temptation," he finds it helpful to review the effects such action could have. Some of things he mentions are:

- Grieving the Lord who redeemed me. . . .
- One day having to look Jesus . . . in the face and give an account of my actions. . . .
- Inflicting untold hurt on . . . your best friend and loyal wife. . . . losing [her] respect and trust.
- Hurting my beloved daughters. . . .
- Destroying my example and credibility with my children, and nullifying both present and future efforts to teach them to obey God. . . .
- Causing shame to my family. . . .
- Creating a form of guilt awfully hard to shake. Even though God would forgive me, would I forgive myself?
- Forming memories and flashbacks that could plague future intimacy with my wife.
- Wasting years of ministry training and experience for a long time, maybe permanently. . . .

- Undermining the faithful example and hard work of other Christians in our community.

- Bringing great pleasure to Satan, the enemy of God and all that is good. . . .

- Possibly bearing the physical consequences of such diseases as gonorrhea, syphilis, chlamydia, herpes, and AIDS; perhaps infecting [my wife] or, in the case of AIDS, even causing her death.

- Possibly causing pregnancy, with the personal and financial implications, including a lifelong reminder of my sin. . . .

- Causing shame and hurt to my friends, especially those I've led to Christ and discipled.[2]

And that's just a partial list of the consequences! It doesn't even begin to factor in the consequences for the other person in the affair and the number of people affected by his or her sin.

Take a realistic look at the other side of a moral tumble. For a change, force yourself to give greater thought to the painful consequences than to the passing pleasures of sin.

Third, begin each day by renewing your sense of reverence for God. Start each new day by talking to the Lord, even if that early-morning talk has to be brief.

"Lord, I'm here. I'm Yours. I want You to know that I'm Yours. Also I want to affirm that I reverence You. I give You my day. I will encounter strong seductive forces that will allure me. Since I am frail and fragile, I really need Your help."

If you know of some challenges you'll be facing that day, rehearse the areas of need. If you know a real test is coming, talk to the Lord about it. Then trade off with Him. Hand over your fragility and receive His strength in return. Reverence Him as the source of your power.

Fourth, periodically during each day focus fully on Christ. In his book *Spiritual Stamina,* Stuart Briscoe cites a good example of this:

It's fun watching young men in love. It can be even more fun when the romance is long distance.

You can predict what will happen. There'll be hours of late-night, heart-pounding telephone conversations. The postal service will be overrun with love notes crossing each other in the mail. Pillows will be soaked with tears.

But the most telling symptom is the glazed, faraway look in Romeo's eyes. I'm sure you've seen it. You ask the man a question and you get a blank stare. He's not at home. He's elsewhere. He's in another land. He's with his sweetheart.

You might say his heart is set on things afar, where Juliet is seated right by the telephone.[3]

That's being focused fully on another person. I challenge you to do this with your Lord. Deliberately set aside a few minutes every day when your eyes glaze over, when you don't realize where you are, when a telephone ring means nothing because you are focusing fully on Christ. Imagine Him as he walks with His disciples, touching those who were sick, praying for them in John 17, going to the cross, sitting with His disciples at the seashore and having broiled fish for breakfast. Then imagine Him as He is thinking about you, praying for you, standing with you, living in you.

These four techniques will help you stay clean in a corrupt society—to be in the world but not of it.

A Prayer for Hope Beyond Temptation

Thank You, Father, for Your truth preserved through the centuries. Thank You for the careful concern of a man like Peter who knew both sides of life on planet Earth: what it was to live in this old world and what it was to walk with the Savior, Your Son.

Lord, since You don't save us then suddenly take us home to glory, hear our prayer this day as we ask You to bring to our attention those things that will assist us in staying clean in a corrupt world. Give us an intense distaste for things that displease You and a renewed pleasure in things that bring You honor and magnify Your truth. As You do this, we will have what we need so much, hope beyond temptation.

I ask this for the honor of Him who consistently and victoriously withstood the blast of the Devil's temptations without relief, Jesus our Lord.

AMEN

4

Hope Beyond Division

<u>Reasons for</u>
<u>Pulling Together</u>

BEFORE ANDREW JACKSON became the seventh president of the United States, he served as a major general in the Tennessee militia. During the War of 1812 his troops reached an all-time low in morale. As a result they began arguing, bickering, and fighting among themselves. It is reported that Old Hickory called them all together on one occasion when tensions were at their worst and said, "Gentlemen! Let's remember, the enemy is over *there!*"

His sobering reminder would be an appropriate word for the church today. In fact, I wonder if Christ sometimes looks down at us and says with a sigh, "Christians, your Enemy is over there! Stop your infighting! Pull for one another. Support one another. Believe in one another. Care for one another. Pray for one another. Love one another."

One of the most profound comments made regarding the early church came from the lips of a man named Aristides, sent by the Emperor Hadrian to spy out those strange creatures known as "Christians." Having seen them in action, Aristides returned with a mixed report. But his immortal words to the emperor have echoed down through history: "Behold! How they love one another."

How often do we hear such words today from those who don't know Christ but who have watched those of us who do? I'm inclined to think that it's much more likely that they say, "Behold! How they hurt one another!" . . . "Behold! How they judge one another!" . . . "Behold! How they criticize one another!" . . . "Behold! How they fight with one another!"

This is the generation that has given new meaning to the shameful practice of brother-bashing and sister-smashing. You would think we were enemies rather than members of the same family. Something is wrong with this picture.

The mark of the Christian should be a spirit of unity and genuine love for others, but the church today rarely demonstrates those qualities. We are looked on by the world as self-seeking and factious rather than loving and unified. You question that? Just step into a Christian bookstore and scan the shelves. What impression do you get? Do the books reflect love and unity within the body of Christ? Or do they reflect polarization, criticism, and judgment of one another? Better yet, sit back and observe what's going on in your own church. Are you overwhelmed with the love and unity that exudes from your local body of believers? Or are you saddened and disappointed by the political power plays and petty disagreements that block our ability to get along with one another?

Unity: An Almost Forgotten Virtue

To underscore this important quality, let's consider Jesus' words in John 13, where we find Him with His twelve disciples for the last time. They have met together for a meal in a second-floor room in the city of Jerusalem. Jesus notices that the men have come into the room with dirty feet—not surprising in that rocky, dusty land. What must have been disappointing was that none of the Twelve had voluntarily washed the others' feet. So during supper Jesus arose from the table and poured water into a basin and proceeded to go around the table and wash the disciples' feet.

What a scene it must have been! To this day, I shake my head when I imagine the Savior washing the dirty feet of His disciples.

And so when He had washed their feet, and taken His garments, and reclined at the table again, He said to them, "Do you know what I have done to you?" (John 13:12)

Understand, He wasn't fishing for the obvious answer, "You've washed our feet, Master." He was looking for the answer He has to explain to them a few moments later:

You call Me Teacher and Lord; and you are right, for so I am. If I then, the Lord and the Teacher, washed your feet, you also ought to wash one another's feet. For I gave you an example that you also should do as I did to you. (John 13:13–15)

I think most of Jesus' disciples would have gladly returned the favor and washed *His* feet. Peter out of embarrassment. John out of devotion. That would be easy to do. After all, they loved Him. Why wouldn't they take an opportunity to wash His feet—if only to make a good impression? But that is not what Jesus told them to do. Instead He said, *"Wash one another's feet."*

Then, a bit later, in their final hours together, He changed the subject from washing feet to showing love.

A new commandment I give to you, that you love one another, even as I have loved you, that you also love one another. By this all men will know that you are My disciples, if you have love for one another. (John 13:34–35)

It's easy to love Christ for all He is, for all He's done. It's not so easy, however, to love other Christians. Yet that is the command we have been given. That compelling mark of the Christian will be a powerful witness to non-Christians. It has nothing to do with talking to the lost about their spiritual condition. It has everything to do with how we treat one another. If you want to make an impact on the world around you, this rugged society that is moving in the wrong direction more rapidly every year, He said, "love one another." That's how they'll know that you're different. Your love will speak with stunning eloquence to a lost world.

Then, as the oil lamps flickered away the last hour before His arrest and trial, Jesus prayed to the Father on behalf of His disciples.

> I do not ask in behalf of these alone [the disciples], but for those also who believe in Me through their word [that's you and me]; *that they may all be one*; even as Thou, Father, art in Me, and I in Thee, that they also may be in Us; that the world may believe that Thou didst send Me. And the glory which Thou hast given Me I have given to them; that they may be one, just as We are one; I in them, and Thou in Me, that they may be perfected in unity, that the world may know that Thou didst send Me, and didst love them, even as Thou didst love Me. (John 17:20–23, italics mine)

Look at that! Believe it or not, He was praying for us during those final hours. He was praying that you and I might make an impact on the world because of our unity with Him and with each other.

The margin notes of the New American Standard Bible gives this literal translation: "That they may be perfected *into a unit*." A unit is a team, folks. No more brother-bashing. No more sister-smashing. No more ugly gossip groups. No more sarcastic, judgmental put-downs. Jesus prayed that we would support and encourage and love and forgive each other until we are perfected into a unit.

Unity. That's what He desires for us. Not uniformity, but unity; oneness, not sameness. We don't have to look alike. We don't even have to think alike. The body is made up of many different parts. He doesn't even pray for unanimity. We can disagree. Every vote doesn't have to be 100 percent. But we must be a unit: our eyes on the same goal, our hearts in the same place, our commitment at the same level. And we must love each other.

If there is anything that would keep me away from Christ these days, if I were lost, it would be the attitude Christians have toward one another. That would do it. While there is much wonderful fellowship in the church where the fire of friendship warms and affirms us, there are still too many places where for the life of me I don't know how people stay in ministry. The conditions in which some men and women labor are occasionally beyond belief.

Paul wrote to the Philippians:

> Do nothing from selfishness or empty conceit, but with humility of mind let each of you regard one another as more important than himself; do not merely look out for your own personal interests, but also for the interests of others. (Phil. 2:3–4)

Selfishness and conceit and pride are the things that break down our fellowship and erode our unity. Everything you need to know about getting along well in a family, to say nothing of getting along well in a church, is right here in these verses.

If you're on a church board and you're wondering what's going wrong, what's missing, what's happened to the unity you once had, I'll guarantee somebody isn't abiding by these verses.

You want to pull together as the family of God? It's merely a matter of obeying Philippians 2:3–4. Stop looking for credit. Stop looking for what you can get out of it. Think about the other person instead of yourself. Don't be selfish. Sounds like something a teacher would say to a roomful of kindergartners, doesn't it? Yet how many adult problems could be solved if the elementary truths woven into these two verses were the driving force in our relationships with one another? How many committees could resolve their disputes? How many couples could reconcile their marital differences?

Love: A Never-to-Be-Forgotten Command

With the teachings of Christ and Paul as a backdrop, we are better able to understand and appreciate Peter's comments about love and unity. Remember, he was writing to hurting people. They were scattered, many of them far from home (see 1 Pet. 1:1). They were "distressed," living in extreme situations (1:6). They were being "tested" by "various trials" (1:6–7). Some of them were running for their lives. With the madman Nero on the throne in Rome, it was a dangerous time to be a Christian. Some, no doubt, were tempted to conform, compromise, or give up altogether.

When I was a kid and an argument broke out in our home, my dad always used to say, "We may have a few differences inside these walls, but just remember, we're family. If your brother or your sister needs you, you take care of 'em. You love 'em. You pull for 'em." Good advice for the church as well!

When people hurt—and we've all been there—it's easy to get a little thin on love. But that's what these people needed. They needed to pull together and support each other. They needed a community where they could find acceptance and unity. They needed to conduct themselves as members of the family of God.

Following his strong words encouraging fellow believers to live holy lives, Peter gives them a pep talk, explaining exactly how they have been freed to support each other. He says, in effect, "You have everything you need that makes it possible; you don't have to live in lonely isolation." Read his counsel carefully:

> Since you have in obedience to the truth purified your souls for a sincere love of the brethren, fervently love one another from the heart, for you have been born again not of seed which is perishable but imperishable, that is, through the living and abiding word of God. (1 Pet. 1:22–23)

As we read Peter's uplifting words, we see that he specifies three things that encourage mutual support. First, obedience to the truth. Second, purity of soul. Third, a lack of hypocrisy.

Being obedient to the truth means that we don't have to look at others through the distorted lenses of our own biases. We can see them as God sees them and love them as He loves them. This has a purifying effect on us. It purges us, not only from a limited perspective, but from prejudice, resentment, hurt feelings, and grudges. Such purity of soul helps us love each other without hypocrisy and with a sincere love. It doesn't blind us to each other's faults; it gives us the grace to overlook them.

The glue—the bonding element—that holds all this together is love: "Fervently love one another from the heart." Peter writes with a strong, emotional, passionate commitment that is difficult to pick up on in the English.

Two Greek words are used predominantly in the New Testament to describe love, and Peter uses both of them here. One is *philos*, which generally refers to a brotherly love or the love of a friend. That is the word he uses for "love of the brethren." The other is *agape*, a higher form of love, a more divine type of love, which is the word he uses for "love one another." Peter then intensifies both with passionate modifiers: "sincere," "fervently," and "from the heart."

> These Christians to whom Peter was writing already had a fondness and an affection for one another. . . . But if these Christians would blend the two kinds of love, saturate the human fondness and affection with the divine love with which they are exhorted to love one another, then that human affection would be transformed and elevated to a heavenly thing. Then the fellowship of saint with saint would be a heavenly fellowship, glorifying to the Lord Jesus, and most blessed in its results to themselves. There is plenty of the *phile* fondness and affection among the saints, and too little of the *agape* divine love.[1]

Maybe it's time to pause and take a look inside your own heart. Are you "fervently loving one another from the heart"? When I am snippy or negative, judgmental or ugly toward a brother or a sister, I look at myself with honesty, shining God's light of truth on my own attitude, and I invariably find that it's my heart that's not right. The old spiritual hymn says it well:

> It's not my brother nor my sister
> but it's me, O Lord,

Standin' in the need of prayer.
It's not the preacher nor the deacon
but it's me, O Lord,
Standin' in the need of prayer.

Support: Four Much-Needed Reminders

What kind of love and support do we need? What kind of love and support do we give? What about a "love one another" support group, in which we offer—and receive from—our brothers and sisters in the family of God this same kind of love and lack of judgmental spirit, this true affection, this arm around your shoulder, saying, "I'm in your corner"?

Many churches have support groups of various kinds in which individuals are actively involved in each other's lives. Through the years I've talked with lots of individuals who say they couldn't survive without such support groups.

Some are struggling through the backwash of a divorce, trying to gain self-respect and a sense of dignity again. Aided by the support of others who are going through, or have gone through, the same turmoil, they work through their feelings of rejection, sadness, and loneliness . . . then emerge stronger and more stable.

Some attend support groups because they are in the grip of an awful addiction. Right now they're clean or dry, but they realize they're just a day away, just an hour away, from the same old habit. The support of others keeps them strong and helps them hope again.

Most of these groups are not highly visible, but they're there for those who need them, week in and week out. With consistent regularity people keep coming because they find refuge in this safe and supportive harbor. They find love, acceptance, and a lack of judgmental spirit. They find tolerance and accountability. They find care and encouragement—and a word of affirmation from a sincere heart and an arm of support around the shoulder mean more than a thousand words from some frowning preacher.

What is it about the family of God that gives us this sense of one-ness and support? Since we don't have to look alike and we don't all have the same temperament and we don't all vote the same way at election time, what is it that draws believers together?

We Are Children of the Same Father

For you have been born again not of seed which is perishable but imperishable, that is, through the living and abiding word of God. (1 Pet. 1:23)

In the human family, there are various kinds of birth experiences. But in God's family, everybody begins the same way. We are all adopted. We all have the same Father. We all come to Him the same way—through His Son, Jesus Christ. We are all members of the same family. Our background, our education, our social connec-tions, our job, or how much money we have in the bank—all these things are irrelevant. We've all been born anew. We're all brothers and sisters in the Lord.

We Take Our Instruction from the Same Source

Not of seed which is perishable but imperishable, that is, through the living and abiding word of God. For,
"All flesh is like grass,
And all its glory like the flower of grass.
The grass withers,
And the flower falls off,
But the word of the Lord abides forever."
And this is the word which was preached to you. (1 Pet. 1:23b–25)

The seed is the Word of God, our reliable source of truth, and we all get our instruction from this source. But for that seed to grow and produce fruit in our lives, it must be embraced and applied.

There's nothing automatic about being exposed to the same source of truth. We may all hear the same Sunday morning mes-sage, but unless our ears are attentive and our hearts prepared, that seed will be picked up in Satan's beak and winged right out of our lives. You can sit and listen to truth being delivered, and it can change your life in a moment's time. Yet someone sitting right next to you, hearing the same insightful information, can go right on living against the will of God.

We have a responsibility, not only to hear the truth, but to apply it. Just being exposed to the truth will not change us. You can put me in a room with a dozen beautiful Steinway pianos and leave me there for hours, but I still won't be able to sit down and play. You could put an accomplished pianist at every one and expose me to hours of exquisite music, but even in that stimulating environment I wouldn't be able to sit down and play. Bringing beautiful music from those black-and-white keys takes work—commitment, dedication, private lessons, and untold hours of practice.

We Have the Same Struggles

Therefore, putting aside all malice and all guile and hypocrisy and envy and all slander. . . . (1 Pet. 2:1)

In case you've ever wondered what breaks down the fellowship, what keeps us from pulling together, there's your list. Read each one slowly and form pictures in your mind: malice, guile, hypocrisy, envy, and slander. In weaker moments we fall back on them, but God says, "put them aside"—get rid of them. If you want to move beyond your divisions, beyond your differences, if you want to become one in the Lord, lose them. And, by His grace, let them go!

Let's return to this list and probe a little deeper.

Malice. The Greek word here is a general word for the wickedness that characterizes unbelievers entrenched in the world system. These are the sins that hurt and injure others.

Guile. The Greek word means two-facedness, deception, or trickery. In its earliest form, this word meant "to catch with bait." It refers to a deception that is aimed at attaining one's own end—a hidden agenda.

Hypocrisy. The Greek word here means to act a part, to hide behind a mask, to appear to be someone else. This is what happens when we try to be someone or something we are not.

Some family members have a tendency to be envious of those who are going through "good times." Others have a tendency to slander those who are going through a bad patch. The next two sins are kind of the flip side of each other, and we are told to put both aside.

Envy is not only hidden resentment over another's advantage, but wanting that same advantage for yourself. According to Webster, it is "painful or resentful awareness of an advantage enjoyed by another joined with a desire to possess the same advantage." In other words, someone has something you don't have and you long to have it yourself. Edward Gordon Selwyn comments on the Greek term, saying that this sin is "a constant plague of all voluntary organizations, not least religious organizations, and to which even the Twelve themselves were subject at the very crisis of our Lord's ministry."[2]

Slander is even more vicious. Literally the word means "evil speaking." It occurs most often when the victim is not there to offer a defense or set the record straight. Often disguised as rumor or bad news or just passing on information, slander is disparaging gossip that destroys one's confidence in another, discoloring or harming that person's reputation. It can be as mild as bad-mouthing or as vile as backstabbing. When the tongue is used for slander, it becomes a lethal weapon.

Peter commands us to "strip off" these five outdated garments that once belonged to our old natures! If all of us in God's family were mutually committed to such behavior, can you imagine the pleasure we could enjoy together? But it'll never happen until we "strip off" the old garments that keep us carnal.

We Focus on the Same Objectives

Like newborn babes, long for the pure milk of the word, that by it you may grow in respect to salvation, if you have tasted the kindness of the Lord. (1 Pet. 2:2–3)

What is the objective of all this? Maturity. "Grow up," Peter says. And our model? The Lord Himself.

For three and a half years Peter followed Jesus everywhere He went. Why? Because he had "tasted the kindness of the Lord."

Nourished by that kindness, Peter grew toward greater maturity, and so can we!

What do people think of after they have had a conversation or a meal with you? What do they think after they have worked alongside you? Do they think, "How kind he is. What a kind person she is"? Selflessly giving ourselves to one another is the key to unity. Our relationships with others are to be built upon the example of the selflessness Christ first demonstrated.

It's so basic, isn't it? It reminds me of Robert Fulghum's *All I Really Need to Know I Learned in Kindergarten*, which I read when it originated as an article in the *Kansas City Times*. In it he said, "Share everything. Play fair. Don't hit people. Put things back where you found them. Clean up your own mess. Don't take things that aren't yours. Say you're sorry when you hurt somebody. . . . And it is still true, no matter how old you are: When you go out into the world, it is best to hold hands and stick together."

Come on, let's pull together. Let's support each other. In doing so, remember Paul's closing words in Ephesians 4. I like the way Eugene Peterson paraphrases that final verse:

> Make a clean break with all cutting, backbiting, profane talk. Be gentle with one another, sensitive. Forgive one another as quickly and thoroughly as God in Christ forgave you. (Eph. 4:31 MSG)

Think of somebody in the family of God—just one person you know—who could really use a word of support. Then give it! Don't wait . . . give it this week. Don't just think about it or write it in your journal. Do it. *Do it today.*

Pray for that individual you were thinking about a moment ago. Ask God to give you just the right word, just the right method of approaching that person. Maybe you need to write a note. Maybe you need to make a phone call. Maybe you need to take the person out for a cup of coffee or invite him or her over for a meal. Who knows? Your action could be the catalyst that causes that individual to gain hope beyond division.

Remember, "The enemy is over *there!*" Behold! How we need to love one another!

A Prayer for Hope Beyond Division

Forgive us, oh, forgive us, our Father, for the hours we have spent in the wasteland of malice and guile, hypocrisy and envy and slander. What grimy garments we've worn! Show us the joy of kindness, the long-lasting benefits of unity, grace, and support. Remind us that it all begins with genuine love prompted by forgiveness. Start a work within us so that our love flows from a pure heart, not from a desire to win friends or impress people.

Most of all, Lord, make us like Your Son. Kind. Meek. Humble. Gracious. May we grow up into His kindness, may we model His meekness, may we walk with His humility. May we reflect His grace so that others gain new hope. What we're really asking is that You help us grow up!

We're so glad to be in Your family, so grateful for Your forgiveness. Use us this week, perhaps even today, to help someone else feel grateful that he or she, too, is a part of this family. Through Christ, who prayed for our unity.

AMEN

5

Hope Beyond Guilt

Becoming
Living
Stones

FOR SOME STRANGE REASON, those of us who have known the Lord since we were young have a tendency to outgrow a close friendship with Him. When we were children, we felt free and open with our heavenly Father. But when we became adults, we seemed to take a few giant steps backward in that relationship.

When we were young, we talked to Him freely. With a child's faith, knowing He loved us, we trusted Him with the details of our life. Nothing was too small and, for sure, nothing was too big to ask of Him. In unguarded innocence, we prayed for *anything*!

The ease with which we once approached God can be seen in the letters written to Him by children. See if the ones below don't take you back to a time of innocence and openness in your own relationship with Him.

Dear Lord,
    Thank you for the nice day today. You even fooled the TV weatherman.
Hank (age 7)

Dear Lord,
    Do you ever get mad?
    My mother gets mad all the time but she is only human.
                                    Yours truly,
                                    David (age 8)

Dear Lord,
    I need a raise in my allowance. Could you have one of your angels
tell my father?
                                    Thank you.
                                    David (age 7)[1]

Dear God,
    Charles my cat got run over. And if you made it happen you have to
tell me why.
                                    Harvey

Dear God,
    Can you guess what is the biggest river of all of them? The Amazon.
You ought to be able to because you made it. Ha, ha.
                                    Guess who[2]

Wouldn't it be interesting to compile an assortment of adult letters to God? Undoubtedly the childhood innocence would be lost as
well as the candor and ease of approach. The words would be more
guarded. We would be sophisticated. Fear and feelings of worthless-
ness would underscore the halting sentences. Shame, guilt, and regret would punctuate the paragraphs. We have lost much, haven't
we, on the road to adulthood?

We can learn a great deal from children about simple faith and
simple hope. Yet we have had years to experience those truths. We
can look back at the many times He has taken our brokenness and
made something beautiful of our lives. Our greatest failures, our
deepest sorrows, have offered opportunities for the operation of His
mercy and grace. How can we forget that?

God's Appraisal of Us

The Bible is filled with reminders of how much God cares for us, His plans for our welfare, and what our relationship with Him should be. Take, for example, the familiar words of the psalmist. Though an adult, he writes of God with free-flowing delight.

> Bless the LORD, O my soul;
> And all that is within me, bless His holy name.
> Bless the LORD, O my soul,
> And forget none of His benefits;
> Who pardons all your iniquities;
> Who heals all your diseases;
> Who redeems your life from the pit;
> Who crowns you with lovingkindness and compassion;
> Who satisfies your years with good things,
> So that your youth is renewed like the eagle. . . .

> For as high as the heavens are above the earth,
> So great is His lovingkindness toward those who fear Him.
> As far as the east is from the west,
> So far has He removed our transgressions from us.
> Just as a father has compassion on his children,
> So the LORD has compassion on those who fear Him.

> For He Himself knows our frame;
> He is mindful that we are but dust. (Ps. 103:1–5, 11–14)

What a list! What a relief! Our Lord understands our limits. He realizes our struggles. He knows how much pressure we can take. He knows what measures of grace and mercy and strength we'll require. He knows how we're put together.

Frankly, His expectations are not nearly as unrealistic as ours. When we don't live up to the agenda we have set, we feel like He is going to dump a truckload of judgment on us. But that will not happen. So why do we fear it could? Because we forget that He "knows our frame; He is mindful that we are but dust."

What, then, is God's agenda for us? What does He want for us this afternoon, tomorrow morning, or next week? Well, His plans for us are clearly set forth. He wrote them originally to Israel, but they apply to us too.

> "For I know the plans that I have for you," declares the LORD, "plans for welfare and not for calamity to give you a future and a hope. Then you will call upon Me and come and pray to Me, and I will listen to you." (Jer. 29:11–12)

Isn't that wonderful? "I have plans for you, My son, My daughter," God says. "And they are great plans. Plans for your welfare and not for your calamity. Plans to give you a future and a hope." It is God's agenda that His people never lose hope. Each new dawn it's as if He smiles from heaven, saying, "Hope again . . . hope again!"

After the fall of Jerusalem, the prophet Jeremiah reminded himself of God's hope-filled plans.

> This I recall to my mind,
> Therefore I have hope.
> The LORD's lovingkindnesses indeed never cease,
> For His compassions never fail.
> They are new every morning;
> Great is Thy faithfulness.
> "The LORD is my portion," says my soul,
> "Therefore I have hope in Him."
> The LORD is good to those who wait for Him,
> To the person who seeks Him.
> It is good that he waits silently
> For the salvation of the LORD. (Lam. 3:21–26)

Right now you may be waiting for something from the Lord. Matter of fact, most people I meet are in some sort of holding pattern. (I certainly am!) They have something on the horizon that they're trusting God for. (I certainly do!) And their hope is not misplaced. He is good to those who wait for Him. He is good to those who seek Him. We have nothing to fear. And we certainly have no reason for living each day crushed by guilt or shame.

He has redeemed us, given us an inheritance, and shown us forgiveness. The most succinct summary of God's appraisal of our relationship as His children can be found in Romans 8:31–32. Many years ago I memorized the concluding paragraph in Romans 8, which begins with these two verses. I cannot number the times I have had my hope renewed by quoting these words to myself.

> What then shall we say to these things? If God is for us, who is against us? He who did not spare His own Son, but delivered Him up for us all, how will He not also with Him freely give us all things?

Contrary to popular opinion, God doesn't sit in heaven with His jaws clenched, His arms folded in disapproval, and a deep frown on His brow. He is not ticked off at His children for all the times we trip over our tiny feet and fall flat on our diapers. He is a loving Father, and we are precious in His sight, the delight of His heart. After all, He "has qualified us to share in the inheritance of the saints in light" (Col. 1:12). Think of it! He's put us in His inheritance!

Remember that the next time you think God is coming down on you. You have reason to give thanks. You don't have to qualify yourself for His kingdom. His grace has rescued you. He has already qualified you by accomplishing a great deliverance in your life. That brings to mind another verse I love to quote:

> For He delivered us from the domain of darkness, and transferred us to the kingdom of His beloved Son, in whom we have redemption, the forgiveness of sins. (Col. 1:13–14)

He has literally transferred us from the dark domain of the Enemy of our souls into the light of the kingdom of His Son. He considers us there with Him, surrounded by love, receiving the same treatment He gives His Son.

Sometimes it's encouraging just to thumb through the Scriptures and find all the promises that tell us what God thinks of us, especially in a world where folks are continually telling us all the things they have against us and all the things they see wrong with us.

God is not only "for us," according to Romans 8, He is constantly giving great gifts to us.

> Every good thing bestowed and every perfect gift is from above, coming down from the Father of lights, with whom there is no variation, or shifting shadow. (James 1:17)

Literally, that last phrase means "shadow of turning." In other words, there is no alteration or modification in His giving, regardless of how often we may turn away. No shifting shadow on our part causes Him to become moody and hold back His gifts to us. Talk about grace!

God is for us. I want you to remember that.

God is for us. Say those four words to yourself.

God is for us.

Remember that tomorrow morning when you don't feel like He is. Remember that when you have failed. Remember that when you have sinned and guilt slams you to the mat.

God is for you. Make it personal: *God is for me!*

Never ever, ever tell your children that if they do wrong, God won't love them. That is heresy. There's no grace in that. Grace says, "My child, even though you do wrong, God will continue and I will continue to love you. God is for you, and so am I!"

I thought of this the other day as I was humming the children's tune, "Jesus loves the little children, all the children of the world." I thought, well, what about all the grownups? So I changed the words of that little song.

> Jesus loves His adult children,
> All the grownups of the world.
> Red and yellow, black and white,
> We are precious in His sight.

Jesus loves all the teens and adults of the world.
[Just thought I should include the teenagers too!]

Why do we think His love is just for the little children, innocent
and disarming as they are? He loves all of His people. Let me repeat
it once more: God is for us.

In Peter's letter, we catch a glimpse of the delight God takes in us
as the apostle paints six beautiful word pictures of us, vivid pen por-
traits of God's children.

And coming to Him as to a living stone, rejected by men, but choice
and precious in the sight of God, you also, as living stones, are being
built up as a spiritual house for a holy priesthood, to offer up spiritual
sacrifices acceptable to God through Jesus Christ. For this is contained
in Scripture:
  "Behold I lay in Zion a choice stone, a precious
      corner stone,
  And he who believes in Him shall not be disappointed."
This precious value, then, is for you who believe. But for those who
disbelieve,
  "The stone which the builders rejected,
  this became the very corner stone,"
  and,
  "A stone of stumbling and a rock of offense";
for they stumble because they are disobedient to the word, and to this
doom they were also appointed. (1 Pet. 2:4–8)

We Are Living Stones in a Spiritual House

The metaphor woven through the fabric of this passage is that of a
building, Christ being the cornerstone and we, His children, being
the living stones that make up the building. (The apostle Paul uses
this same image in Ephesians 2:19–22.)

Each time someone trusts Christ as Savior, another stone is quarried out of the pit of sin and fitted into the spiritual house He's build-

ing through the work of the Holy Spirit. And carefully overseeing the construction is Christ, who is the hands-on contractor of this eternal edifice.

We are His living stones, being built up as a spiritual house.

Think of it this way. There's a major construction project going on through time as Jesus Christ builds His family. It's called the *ekklesia*, the "church," those who are called out from the mass of humanity to become a special part of God's forever family. And you, as a Christian—a follower of Christ—have been picked, chosen, and called out to be one of them.

He has quarried you from the pit of your sin. And now He is chiseling away, shaping you and ultimately sliding you into place. You are a part of His building project.

All kinds of prophets of doom wonder about the condition of God's building. They see it as condemned property, worn out, dilapidated, and derelict rather than as a magnificent edifice that is being constructed on schedule. The truth is, God is the master architect, and every stone is being placed exactly where He designed it to fit. The project is right on schedule. Never forget, even on those blue days, we are living stones in a spiritual house. But there's more. . . .

We Are Priests in the Same Temple

Peter refers to us both as a "holy priesthood" and as a "royal priesthood." It's true that we're not all preachers or evangelists or gifted teachers. But we *are* all priests, belonging to a kingly order that has been set apart by God.

The role of priest implies more than meets the eye, for priests have specific responsibilities delineated in Scripture. Priests offer up prayers, bring spiritual sacrifices, intercede to God on behalf of others, and stay in tune with the spiritual side of life. All this applies to every believer, regardless of age, regardless of sex, regardless of social standing. Perhaps you never thought of this before, but it's really true; we are priests in the same temple. But there's more. . . .

We Are a Chosen Race

Our heads might have a tendency to swell at being chosen to be on God's team, so it might behoove us to take a quick glance at exactly why God chose the Hebrews to be His people. This will help us put the whole idea of being chosen by God into perspective. Here Moses is addressing the nation Israel, preparing them to enter the Promised Land.

> For you are a holy people to the LORD your God; the LORD your God has chosen you to be a people for His own possession out of all the peoples who are on the face of the earth. The LORD did not set His love on you nor choose you because you were more in number than any of the peoples, for you were the fewest of all peoples, but because the LORD loved you and kept the oath which He swore to your forefathers, the LORD brought you out by a mighty hand, and redeemed you from the house of slavery, from the hand of Pharaoh king of Egypt. (Deut. 7:6–8)

Why did God choose Israel? Because of their strength? No. Because of their numbers? Because of their mental or moral superiority? No. He chose them not because they deserved it, but simply because of His grace—a kindness shown to them entirely without merit on their part. Simply "because the Lord loved you."

Why did God choose us? For the same reason. Not because we did anything that impressed Him. It wasn't the size of our faith . . . or the sincerity. It wasn't the goodness of our heart . . . or the greatness of our intellect. It certainly wasn't because we first chose Him. It was entirely by grace. Grace prompted by love.

The Lord chooses us because He chooses to choose us. Period. He sets His love upon us because out of the goodness and grace of His own heart He declares, "I want you to be Mine."

I love that! Not only because it exalts the grace of God, but because God gets all the glory in it. We won't walk around heaven with our thumbs under our suspenders outbragging one another. Instead, we'll be absolutely amazed that we are privileged to be there.

John 15:16 says, "You did not choose Me, but I chose you." We didn't hunt Him down. He hunted us down. He is the eternal Hound of Heaven. We didn't work half our lives to find Him; He gave His life to find us. Being chosen by God says a lot more about Him than it does about us! He is the Good Shepherd who gives His life for the sheep. When you find yourself slumping in shame or giving way to guilt, remind yourself of this: You have been chosen by the Good Shepherd. He wants you in His flock. But there is more. . . .

We Are a Holy Nation

Holy can be an intimidating word. Though meant to be sacred, it can seem scary. Remember, earlier we explained that the word means "to be set apart." But let's look at it another way.

I'm sitting in my study right now, and I'm wearing a suit and a tie because I'm going to an important meeting in a couple hours. This morning when I was getting dressed, I looked on my tie rack and I selected a tie. I had a number to choose from, but I chose this particular one. I pulled it off the rack, put it around my neck, and tied the knot, and at that moment the tie became holy. Doesn't look holy. I can assure you, it doesn't feel holy. (As a matter of fact, I can see a small spot on it. Must have gotten some gravy on it when I wore it last.) But it's still the tie I set apart for this particular purpose. In the broadest sense of the word, the tie I'm wearing is "holy." It's set apart for a special purpose.

You and I are a holy nation. We make up a body of people set apart for a special purpose: to be ambassadors for Jesus Christ, the King of the church. We are a people set apart for His special purpose and glory.

If we seem out of step with the rest of the world, it is because we march to the beat of a different drummer. We sing a different national anthem and pledge our allegiance to a different flag—because our citizenship, our true citizenship, is in heaven. You and I are parts of His holy nation. But there's more . . . .

We Are God's Own Possession

Possessions of the powerful, wealthy, or famous, no matter how common, can become extremely valuable, even priceless. Napoleon's toothbrush sold for $21,000. Can you imagine—paying thousands of dollars for someone's cruddy old toothbrush? Hitler's car sold for over $150,000. Winston Churchill's desk, a pipe owned by C. S. Lewis, sheet music handwritten by Beethoven, a house once owned by Ernest Hemingway. At the Sotheby's auction of Jackie Kennedy Onassis's personal belongings, her fake pearls sold for $211,500 and JFK's wood golf clubs went for $772,500. Not because the items themselves are worthy but because they once belonged to someone significant.

Are you ready for a surprise? We fit that bill too. Think of the value of something owned by God. What incredible worth that bestows on us, what inexplicable dignity! We belong to Him. We are "a people for God's own possession" (1 Pet. 2:9).

I love that expression—"a people for God's own possession." And I'm glad this verse is correctly translated in the version of the Bible I'm using. For the longest time I used a version that said, "We are a peculiar people." (Actually, I saw all kinds of evidence of that around me, as if Christians were supposed to be odd or weird or strange.) But the correct rendering is far more encouraging. Weird or not, we're His possession . . . owned by the living God.

The price paid for us was unimaginably high—the blood of Jesus Christ—and now we belong to Him. We have been bought with a price. That's enough to bring a smile to anyone's face. But there is more . . . one more.

We Are a People Who Have Received Mercy

Have you lived so long in the family of God that your memory has become blurred? Have you forgotten what it was like when you weren't?

> . . . for you once were not a people, but now you are the people of God; you had not received mercy, but now you have received mercy. (1 Pet. 2:10)

As a result of God's mercy, we have become a people who are uniquely and exclusively cared for by God. The fact that we are the recipients of His mercy makes all the difference in the world as to how we respond to difficult times. He watches over us with enormous interest. Why? Because of His immense mercy, freely demonstrated in spite of our not deserving it. What guilt-relieving, encouraging news!

Of all the twelve disciples, none could have been more grateful than Peter . . . or, if he had allowed it, none more guilt-ridden. Called to serve his Savior, strong-hearted, determined, zealous, even a little cocky on occasion, the man had known the heights of ecstasy but also knew the aching agony of defeat.

Though warned by the Master, Peter announced before His peers, "Even though all may fall away . . . I will never fall away" (Matt. 26:33). And later . . . "Lord, with You I am ready to go both to prison and to death!" (Luke 22:33). Yet only a few hours later he denied even knowing Jesus . . . three times!

What bitter tears he wept when the weight of his denials crushed his spirit. But our Lord refused to leave him there, wallowing in hopeless discouragement and depression. He found the broken man and forgave him . . . and used him mightily as a leader in the early church. What grace . . . what mercy!

Charles Wesley beautifully captures the theology of such mercy in the second stanza of his magnificent hymn, "And Can It Be?"

> He left His Father's throne above,
> So free, so infinite His grace!

Emptied Himself of all but love,
And bled for Adam's helpless race!
'Tis mercy all, immense and free,
For, O my God, it found out me

Our Lives Are Being Watched

Beloved, I urge you as aliens and strangers to abstain from fleshly lusts, which war against the soul. Keep your behavior excellent among the Gentiles, so that in the thing in which they slander you as evildoers, they may on account of your good deeds, as they observe them, glorify God in the day of visitation. (1 Pet. 2:11–12)

Peter begins his practical summary of this section with the words, "Beloved, I urge you." He feels passionate about this—and there's a warning here. Peter is telling us that in light of all that we are as God's children, in light of our roles as living stones in a building that will never be destroyed, and in light of our being these things he's described—a royal priesthood, a chosen race, a holy nation, a people for His own possession, those who have received mercy, we are to live in a certain way. Our earthly behavior is to square with our divinely provided benefits.

For unbelievers, earth is a playground where the flesh is free to romp and run wild. But for believers, earth is a battleground. It's the place where we combat the lusts that wage war against our souls. For the brief tour of duty we Christians have on this earth, we cannot get stalled in sin or, for that matter, incapacitated by guilt. To live the kind of life God requires, Peter offers four suggestions.

First, live a clean life. Don't think for a moment that it makes no difference to unbelievers how Christians live. We live out our faith before a watching world. That's why Peter urges us to abstain from fleshly lusts, "in order to get their attention" and to prove that what we believe really works.

You and I don't know how many non-Christians are watching us is very day, determining the truth of the message of Christianity strictly on the basis of how we live, how we work, how we respond to life's tests, or how we conduct ourselves with our families.

Every time I hear of a pastor or Christian leader or well-known Christian artist who has failed morally, it breaks my heart. Not just because it scandalizes the church and possibly destroys his or her family, although those are certainly tragedies enough. But I think of what it says to unbelievers who read it in the headlines or hear it joked about on television talk shows. Living a clean life isn't merely a nice option to consider; it's the least we can do to demonstrate our gratitude for God's deliverance.

Second, leave no room for slander. When the ancient Greek philosopher Plato was told that a certain man had begun making slanderous charges against him, Plato's response was, "I will live in such a way that no one will believe what he says."[3]

The most convincing defense is the silent integrity of our character, not how vociferously we deny the charges.

Third, do good deeds among unbelievers. It's easy for Christians to have such tunnel vision that we limit all of our good deeds to the family of God. But if you're driving along and see someone with a flat tire, you don't roll down your window and say, "Hey there . . . you with the flat tire! Are you a Christian?" . . . then determine if you should help. We would do well to extend our good deeds to those outside the family.

What makes the story of the Good Samaritan so compelling? The merciful deeds were done on behalf of a total stranger. That is how we win the right to be heard—not by a slick mass-advertising campaign but by our compassionate and unselfish actions.

Notice that Peter says, "on account of your good *deeds*," not your good *words*. The unsaved are watching our lives. When our good deeds are indisputable the unbeliever says, "There must be something to it." Chances are good that at that point the person will hear what we have to say.

Fourth, never forget—we are being watched. The world is watching us to see if what we say we believe is true in our lives. Warren

74

Wiersbe tells a brief but powerful story that illustrates this beautifully.

> In the summer of 1805, a number of Indian chiefs and warriors met in council at Buffalo Creek, New York, to hear a presentation of the Christian message by a Mr. Cram from the Boston Missionary Society. After the sermon, a response was given by Red Jacket, one of the leading chiefs. Among other things, the chief said . . .
>
> "Brother, we are told that you have been preaching to the white people in this place. These people are our neighbors. We are acquainted with them. We will wait a little while and see what effect your preaching has upon them. If we find it does them good, makes them honest and less disposed to cheat Indians, we will then consider again what you have said."[4]

Whew! That's laying it on the line. I wonder how many people are looking at us and saying to themselves, "I hear what he's saying. Now I'm going to watch how he lives. I'll see if what he says is what he does."

Let's Not Forget—God Is for Us

This has been a searching chapter to write. I've not attempted to soften Peter's words, lest we miss the punch in his points. For whatever it's worth, I've felt a few stinging reproofs as well. Sometimes an author has to swallow some of his own medicine . . . except in this case, God is giving the medicine through Peter's pen, not mine! And so, you and I both have taken it on the chin. Hopefully, it will make a difference.

But let's not forget the good news: There is hope beyond guilt! May I remind you of that oft-repeated line from Romans 8? "God is for us." In devoted love He chose us. In great grace He stooped to accept us into His family. In immense mercy He still finds us wandering, forgives our foolish ways, and (as He did with Peter) frees us to serve Him even though we don't deserve such treatment.

So . . . away with guilt! If you need a little extra boost to make that happen, read Eugene Peterson's paraphrase of Romans 8:31–19. Read it slowly, preferably *aloud*. As a good friend of mine once put it, "If this don't light your fire, you got wet wood!"

So, what do you think? With God on our side like this, how can we lose? If God didn't hesitate to put everything on the line for us, embracing our condition and exposing himself to the worst by sending his own Son, is there anything else he wouldn't gladly and freely do for us? And who would dare tangle with God by messing with one of God's chosen? Who would dare even to point a finger? The One who died for us—who was raised to life for us!—is in the presence of God at this very moment sticking up for us. Do you think anyone is going to be able to drive a wedge between us and Christ's love for us? There is no way! Not trouble, not hard times, not hatred, not hunger, not homelessness, not bullying threats, not backstabbing, not even the worst sins listed in Scripture:

"They kill us in cold blood because they hate you.
We're sitting ducks; they pick us off one by one."

None of this fazes us because Jesus loves us. I'm absolutely convinced that nothing—nothing living or dead, angelic or demonic, today or tomorrow, high or low, thinkable or unthinkable—absolutely *nothing* can get between us and God's love because of the way that Jesus our Master has embraced us. (Rom. 8:31–39 MSG)

A Prayer for Hope Beyond Guilt

*Father . . . dear gracious Father, we're our own worst enemy.
We focus on our failures rather than on Your rescues . . . on
our wrongs rather than on Your commitment to making us
right . . . on our puny efforts rather than on Your powerful*

plans for our good. Even our attempts at being devoted to You can become so self-centered. Turn our attention back to You.

- *Remind us of our exalted position in Christ.*
- *Refresh us with frequent flashbacks—"God is for us."*
- *Renew our spirits with the realization that we're your possession.*

Then, with those joyful thoughts to spur us on, slay the dragon of guilt within us so we might enjoy, as never before, your ultimate embrace. Through Christ I pray.

AMEN

6

Hope Beyond Unfairness

Pressing on
Even Though
Ripped Off

EVER BOUGHT A LEMON of a used car? Ever sent away for some marvelous $16.95 gadget displayed on an infomercial and ended up with about 85 cents worth of plastic?

Who hasn't been hoodwinked by a smooth-talking salesman with styled hair and patent-leather shoes? Who hasn't been burned by a glitzy ad campaign that promises more than it delivers? Who hasn't, at some point, been taken advantage of or "ripped off"?

Yet we recover relatively easily and quickly from ripoffs like those. What's really difficult to endure is the kind of abuse or victimization that gets personal—when someone slanders our reputations, pulls the economic rug out from under us, or even threatens our lives. It's hard enough to deal with the consequences of our own missteps, miscalculations, and stupid mistakes. But it seems unbearable to suffer the consequences of something that wasn't our fault or that we didn't deserve.

If you've ever been treated like that, you're in good biblical company. David was ripped off by Saul, Esau was duped by Jacob, Joseph was mistreated by his brothers, and Job was victimized by the Sabeans and Chaldeans.

David, as a young shepherd boy, killed Goliath and helped rout the Philistine enemy. After that, David became overwhelmingly popular among the people. He also became the object of King Saul's rage. David had done only good for Saul and his people. Therefore, the people appropriately sang their praises to David: "Saul has slain his thousands, and David his ten thousands" (1 Sam. 18:7). That popular song sent Saul into such a revengeful rage against the young hero that for more than a decade David ran for his life while Saul hunted and haunted him. David didn't deserve this, but it happened.

Joseph didn't ask to be his father's favorite, but when Jacob showed favoritism to his youngest son, Joseph's brothers, in a moment of absolute hatred, sold him into slavery. Although Joseph triumphed over his circumstances, he was initially ripped off by his brothers.

Earlier, Joseph's father, Jacob, had cheated his own brother, Esau, out of his birthright. Admittedly Esau was rash and irresponsible, but Jacob took advantage of his brother in a vulnerable moment.

And what about that good man Job? According to the Scriptures, he was "blameless" and "upright" and had taken unfair advantage of no one . . . but because Satan used him as a guinea pig, Job lost all his land, servants, possessions, and above all, his ten children.

While God ultimately used all these circumstances for the believers' good and His honor, initially all of these men could have said, "What is happening here? This is unfair! I don't deserve this!"

So while we may be in good company—and misery does love company—company doesn't alleviate the pain of unfair treatment.

Natural Reactions to Unfair Treatment

It's been my observation that when we're treated unfairly, we respond with three common, knee-jerk reactions.

First, there is the aggressive pattern: we blame others. This reaction not only focuses on the person who ripped us off and keeps a running tally of wrongs done against us, it also engineers ways to get back. This reaction says, "I don't just get mad, I get even." In the process, aggression grows from simple anger all the way to rage. It starts with the seed of resentment, germinates into revenge, and in the process nurtures a deep root of bitterness that tenaciously wraps around our hearts. When allowed to grow to full size, it leaves us determined to get back at *every* person who has done anything against us.

It's like the fellow who was bitten by a dog and was later told by his physician, "Yes, indeed, you do have rabies." Upon hearing this, the patient immediately pulled out a pad and pencil and began to write.

Thinking the man was making out his will, the doctor said, "Listen, this doesn't mean you're going to die. There's a cure for rabies."

"I know that," said the man. "I'm making a list of people I'm gonna bite."

It is probable that a few who read these words are making lists right now of people you're gonna bite the very next chance you get. Some of you are already engaged in doing just that. The blame game may temporarily satisfy an aggressive inner itch, but it doesn't lead to a lasting solution. Small wonder God warns us: "Never take your own revenge . . . 'Vengeance is Mine, I will repay,' says the Lord" (Rom. 12:19).

Second, there is the passive pattern: we feel sorry for ourselves. We throw a pity party, complaining to anyone who will lend a sympathetic ear. "Life just isn't fair," we whine. But if we wallow in this slough of despondency too long, we become depressed and immobile, living the balance of life with the shades drawn and the doors locked. Like quicksand, feeling sorry for ourselves will suck us under.

Though you may be holding back, there's a lot of anger in this passive pattern as well. Give in to this temptation, and I can assure you, you'll not be vulnerable to anybody ever again.

Reminds me of some fellows in the military who were stationed in Korea during the Korean War. While there, they hired a local boy to cook and clean for them. Being a bunch of jokesters, these guys soon took advantage of the boy's seeming naiveté. They'd smear Vaseline on the stove handles so that when he'd turn the stove on in the morning he'd get grease all over his fingers. They'd put little water buckets over the door so that he'd get deluged when he opened the door. They'd even nail his shoes to the floor during the night. Day after day the little fella took the brunt of their practical jokes without saying anything. No blame . . . no self-pity . . . no temper tantrums.

Finally the men felt guilty about what they were doing, so they sat down with the young Korean and said, "Look, we know these pranks aren't funny anymore, and we're sorry. We're never gonna take advantage of you again."

It seemed too good to be true to the houseboy. "No more sticky on stove?" he asked.

"Nope."

"No more water on door?"

"No."

"No more nail shoes to floor?"

"Nope, never again."

"Okay," the boy said with a smile . . . "no more spit in soup."

Even in a passive mode, you can spit in somebody's soup.

Third, there is the holding pattern: we postpone or deny our feelings. We might call this the Scarlett O'Hara syndrome: "I'll think about it tomorrow." Every boiling issue is left to simmer on the back burner over a low flame. On the surface all seems calm—"Doesn't bother me"—but underneath, our feelings seethe, eating away at us like acid. This failure to deal with the problem forthrightly leads only to doubt and disillusionment and weakens the fiber of our lives. Furthermore, it's physically unhealthy to sustain feelings of resentment.

An Alternative That Honors God

Though they are all very common, don't expect to find any of these reactions in Peter's wonderful letter where he informs us how to have hope beyond unfairness. Expect instead an alternative reaction to unfair treatment.

The Command

Submit yourselves for the Lord's sake to every human institution, whether to a king as the one in authority, or to governors as sent by him for the punishment of evildoers and the praise of those who do right. (1 Pet. 2:13–14)

It's important to understand the historical context of this command. The Roman Empire, throughout which the readers of Peter's letter were scattered, was not a benevolent monarchy. It was a dictatorship ruled by the insane demagogue Nero, who was especially notorious for his wickedness and his cruelty to Christians. Many of the believers who received Peter's letter had suffered persecution. The bodies of their friends and loved ones had bloodied the sand of the Roman coliseum. Their corpses, soaked in oil, had lit that vast stadium. So it was altogether natural and fitting that Peter would address the subject of unfair treatment. These believers had been the target of the grossest kind of mistreatment by government, by their fellow citizens, and by their neighbors.

Should these Christians pick up arms and resist a government with such a leader at its helm? No, said Peter. Incredibly, in the midst of all this, he had the audacity to say, "Submit."

God does not promote anarchy. Jesus said, "Render to Caesar the things that are Caesar's and to God the things that are God's" (Matt. 22:21). And Paul exhorts us to pray for those who are in authority over us (see 1 Tim. 2:1–2). Nowhere in Scripture is overt insurrection against the government recommended. The believer was not put on earth to overthrow governments but to establish in the human heart a kingdom not of this world.

There may be instances, of course, when we must stand our ground, when we must stand firm and disobey a law that is disobedient to the law of God. We are not to buckle under by compromising our convictions or renouncing our faith. But those are the exceptions, not the normal rule. Whenever possible we are to render unto Caesar the coin of civil obedience, pray for those in authority, pay our taxes, obey the laws of the land, and live honorably under the domain of earthly elected leaders.

The way to live honorably, Peter says, is to "submit." The Greek word is *hupotasso*, a military term that means "to fall in rank under an authority." It's composed of two words: *tasso*, meaning "to appoint, order, or arrange," and *hupo*, meaning "to place under or to subordinate." In this particular construction it conveys the idea of subjecting oneself or placing oneself under another's authority.

This recognition of existing authority, coupled with a willingness to set aside one's own personal desires, shows a deep dependency upon God. This submission to authority is not only in respect to God, the foremost human authority, but to lesser officials as well, such as kings and governors as well as law officers and teachers.

I'm convinced in my heart that if we were good students of submission we would get along a lot better in life. But I am also convinced that it is the one thing, more than any other, that works against our very natures, which argue, "I don't want to submit. I don't want to give in. I won't let him have his way in this." And so we live abrasively.

Let's get something very clear here. Our problem is not understanding what submission means. Our problem is doing what it says.

Because submission is so difficult, we need to look at the reason behind Peter's command.

The Reason

> For such is the will of God that by doing right you may silence the ignorance of foolish men. (1 Pet. 2:15)

The Greek word translated "silence" here means "to close the mouth with a muzzle." You see, Christians in the first century were the targets of all kinds of slanderous rumors. "They're a secret sect," people said. "They are people of another kingdom." . . . "They follow another god." . . . "They have plans to overthrow us." Throughout the Roman Empire people gossiped about their secret meetings, their subversive ideologies, their loyalty to another kingdom, their plans to infiltrate, indoctrinate, and lead an insurrection. This kind of paranoia was common, all the way to Nero. To muzzle these rumors, Peter encouraged submission to the powers that be. By submitting, Peter said, by doing right before God, they would muzzle the mouths of those passing around such rumors.

Let's translate it into today's terms. We live in a city where the government is run by civil authorities. Our church building is located in that city. Now, those civil authorities have no right to tell us what to preach, what to teach, or which philosophy to adopt as a church. If they attempt to do that, we have a right—in fact, it's a duty—to rebel, because there is a higher law than their law, the higher law relating to the declaration of truth. However, they do have the right to say, "In this room you may put 150 people and no more. If you go beyond that you are violating the fire code and will be subject to a fine and possibly other penalties." It is neither right nor wise for us to break this civil law. It does not violate God's law and is, in fact, there for our protection. So we must submit to that law.

In the church I pastored in Fullerton, California, we had to abide by local laws, one of which stated that we could not use folding seats in the worship auditorium; the seats had to be fixed to the floor. Also, the local law mandated a certain predetermined ratio between how many cars were parked in a parking lot measured against how many people could sit in an auditorium. Any church that constructed a worship center had to provide parking for "X" number of people in the worship gathering. We agreed to cooperate with that.

By submitting to this civil authority, we muzzled any rumors that we were just a maverick group, that we did as we pleased, thank you. We would have gained nothing by rebelling against the civic authorities. In fact, we would have lost in many ways by doing so.

The Principle

Act as free men, and do not use your freedom as a covering for evil, but use it as bondslaves of God. Honor all men; love the brotherhood, fear God, honor the king. (1 Pet. 2:16–17)

It's important that we keep the right perspective on the principle here. We do not submit because we necessarily agree. We do not submit because deep within we support all the rules, codes, and regulations. At times they may seem petty and galling, terribly restrictive, and even prejudicial. We submit because it is the "will of God" and because we are "bondslaves of God."

Now, you see, the principle comes to the surface: "Do not use your freedom as a covering for evil." Do not use or abuse grace so that your freedom becomes a cloak for evil.

In little staccato bursts, Peter gives us several commands in verses 16 and 17: act as free men; honor all men; love the brotherhood; fear God; honor the king. And wrapped around the commands is that main principle: "Do not use your freedom as a covering for evil."

We must forever be aware of the temptation to abuse liberty. It's so easy to stretch it; so easy to make it work for ourselves rather than for the glory of God.

An Example and *the* Example

Servants, be submissive to your masters with all respect, not only to those who are good and gentle, but also to those who are unreasonable. For this finds favor, if for the sake of conscience toward God a man bears up under sorrows when suffering unjustly. For what credit is there if, when you sin and are harshly treated, you endure it with patience? But if when you do what is right and suffer for it you patiently endure it, this finds favor with God. For you have been called for this purpose. (1 Pet. 2:18–21a)

To understand the full import of what Peter is saying we must understand something of the nature of slavery in the time of the early church. William Barclay sheds some historical light on this.

In the time of the early church . . . there were as many as 60,000,000 slaves in the Roman Empire.

It was by no means only menial tasks which were performed by slaves. Doctors, teachers, musicians, actors, secretaries, stewards were slaves. In fact, all the work of Rome was done by slaves. Roman attitude was that there was no point in being master of the world and doing one's own work. Let the slaves do that and let the citizens live in pampered idleness. The supply of slaves would never run out.

Slaves were not allowed to marry; but they cohabited; and the children born of such a partnership were the property of the master, not of the parents, just as the lambs born to the sheep belonged to the owner of the flock, and not to the sheep.

It would be wrong to think that the lot of slaves was always wretched and unhappy, and that they were always treated with cruelty. Many slaves were loved and trusted members of the family; but one great inescapable fact dominated the whole situation. In Roman law a slave was not a person but a thing; and he had absolutely no legal rights whatsoever. For that reason there could be no such thing as justice where a slave was concerned. . . . Peter Chrysologus sums the matter up: "Whatever a master does to a slave, undeservedly, in anger, willingly, unwillingly, in forgetfulness, after careful thought, knowingly, unknowingly, is judgment, justice and law." In regard to a slave, his master's will, and even his master's caprice, was the only law.[1]

That was the reality of the first-century world when Peter addressed slaves and told them to "be submissive" to their masters. It would have been easy for slaves who became Christians to think that their Christianity gave them the freedom to break with their masters. Peter, under the Holy Spirit's inspiration, stated that this was not so.

Centuries later, Christianity pervaded the culture and overcame slavery, but it didn't happen in the first century. This is a good lesson for us regarding God's timing versus our timing, even when it comes to adversity. While He certainly commands us to be salt and light and thus bring about justice and change in our culture, His ultimate priority is changing the individual human heart.

It's difficult for us in America to read some of these verses. Our frame of reference is so different—so Western, so twentieth century—that we sometimes try to rewrite God's Word to make it fit us. We can't do that. We must let it speak for itself.

"Well, that's great if you have a good master," you say. It's wonderful if you're a slave of Saint Francis of America . . . or Mother Teresa of your community. If you're working for some marvelous, saintlike boss, everything is cool. You're happy to submit. But what if your taskmaster fits the description in the last part of the verse—what if you work for "those who are unreasonable"?

Do you have an uncaring boss? Do you have a supervisor or a manager who isn't fair? Do you have to deal with unreasonable people? You may not want to hear this today, but there is a lot of truth for you in verses 18 and 19, none of which will ever appear in your local newspaper or on a television talk show.

The natural tendency of the human heart is to fight back against unfair and unreasonable treatment. But Peter's point is that seeking revenge for unjust suffering can be a sign of self-appointed lordship over one's own affairs. Revenge, then, is totally inappropriate for one who has submitted to the lordship of Jesus Christ. Christians must stand in contrast to those around them. This includes a difference in attitude and a difference in focus. Our attitude should be "submissive," and our focus should be "toward God." And how is this change viewed by God? It "finds favor" with Him.

Our focus, then, should not be consumed with getting the raise at the office but with getting the praise from God, not with getting the glory for ourselves but with giving the glory to Him.

> For what credit is there if, when you sin and are harshly treated, you endure it with patience? But if when you do what is right and suffer for it you patiently endure it, this finds favor with God. (1 Pet. 2:20)

The contrast is eloquent. There's no credit due a person who suffers for what he has coming to him. If you break into a house and steal, you will be arrested, and you could be incarcerated. And if you patiently endure your jail sentence, no one is going think you are wonderful for being such a good and patient prisoner. You won't get elected "Citizen of the Year."

But if you are a hard-working, faithful employee, diligent, honest, productive, prompt, caring, working for a boss who is belligerent, stubborn, short-sighted, and ungrateful, and if you patiently endure that situation—aha! That "finds favor" with God! (I told you this wasn't information generally embraced by the public!) Actually another meaning for the word translated "favor" is *grace*. So when you endure, you put grace on display. And when you put grace on display for the glory of God, you could revolutionize your workplace or any other situation.

Can you see why the Christian philosophy is absolutely radical and revolutionary? We don't work for the credit or the prestige or the salary or the perks! We work for the glory of God in whatever we do. The purpose of the believer in society is to bring glory and honor to the name of Christ, not to be treated well or to have life be easy or even to be happy, as wonderful as all those things are. Again, this is not promoted in today's workplace.

> For you have been called for this purpose, since Christ also suffered for you, leaving you an example for you to follow in His steps. (1 Pet. 2:21)

You are "called for this purpose." That's the reason you're in that company. That's the reason you're filling that role. That's the reason these things are happening to you. Why? So that you might follow in the steps of our Lord Jesus, who suffered for us.

I deliberately left Christ off the list of biblical examples at the beginning of the chapter because I wanted to mention Him here. No one was ever more "ripped off" than our Savior. Absolutely no one. Jesus of Nazareth was the only perfect Man who ever lived, yet He suffered continually during His brief life on this planet. He was misunderstood, maligned, hated, arrested, and tortured. Finally, they crucified Him.

And Peter says we are to walk in the steps of Jesus.

> Since Christ also suffered for you, leaving you an example for you to follow in His steps, who committed no sin, nor was any deceit found in His mouth; and while being reviled, He did not revile in return; while

suffering, He uttered no threats, but kept entrusting Himself to Him who judges righteously; and He Himself bore our sins in His body on the cross, that we might die to sin and live to righteousness; for by His wounds you were healed. (1 Pet. 2:21b–24)

In these verses Peter shifts from *an* example of unfair treatment to *the* example we should follow—from that of a servant to that of the Savior.

John Henry Jowett writes of Jesus' perfection.

The fine, sensitive membrane of the soul had in nowise been scorched by the fire of iniquity. "No sin!" He was perfectly pure and healthy. No power had been blasted by the lightning of passion. No nerve had been atrophied by the wasting blight of criminal neglect. The entire surface of His life was as finely sensitive as the fair, healthy skin of a little child. . . . There was no duplicity. There were no secret folds or convolutions in His life concealing ulterior motives. There was nothing underhand. His life lay exposed in perfect truthfulness and candour. The real, inner meaning of His life was presented upon a plain surface of undisturbed simplicity. "No sin!" Nothing blunted or benumbed. "No guile!" Therefore nothing hardened by the effrontery of deceit.[2]

That's the sinless Christ. But still they mocked Him and bruised Him and beat Him and *crucified* Him. When Peter tells us He is our example, that's saying something!

Consider His focus. He "kept entrusting Himself to Him who judges righteously."

That's a good thing to do throughout your day. "Lord, this is a hard moment for me. I'm having a tough time today. Here I am again, dealing with this unreasonable person, this person who is treating me unfairly. Lord, help me. I entrust myself to You. I give You my struggle. Protect me. Provide the wisdom and self-control I need. Help me do the right thing."

We must understand that the purpose of Jesus' suffering was different from ours. I know there comes a point where subjection to certain situations can become absolutely unwise and unhealthy. No argument there. But most of us don't get anywhere near that. We are so quick to defend ourselves. We are a fight-back generation. We know our lawyers' phone numbers better than we know verses of Scripture on self-restraint. Quick to get mad! Quick to fight back! Quick to answer back! Quick to threaten a lawsuit! "Don't you DARE step across that line . . . I've got my rights!"

When was the last time you deliberately, for the glory of Christ, took it on the chin, turned the other cheek, kept your mouth shut, and gave Him all the glory?

A Benefit That Accompanies Such Obedience

For you were continually straying like sheep, but now you have returned to the Shepherd and Guardian of your souls. (1 Pet. 2:25)

Staring in horror at the cross, one can't help but become dizzy from a swarm of questions. Why? Why should this innocent man endure such unjust suffering? Why should we? Why shouldn't we resist the thorns and the lash we are forced to bear? Why should we submit to the hammer blows, to the piercing nails, to the cross of unjust suffering?

Because it causes us to return to our Savior for protection rather than defending ourselves or fighting for "our rights." That kind of reaction has become so much a part of our lifestyle and culture that we don't even realize it when we react that way. We don't even recognize that we should be different from those around us.

By the way, see the words, "by His wounds you were healed"? Talk about vivid! Peter had seen firsthand the yoke of unjust suffering placed upon Jesus' shoulders. No doubt he was remembering. He could see it as clearly as though it were yesterday—that moment when he saw his Master's bruised and bleeding body staggering along the narrow streets of Jerusalem on the way to Golgotha. And as he remembered that scene, he said, "by that He heals us."

Are you feeling the splinters of some cross of unjust suffering? Has a friend betrayed you? Has an employer impaled you? Has a disaster dropped on your life that's almost too great to bear? If so, don't fight back. Unjust suffering can be a dizzying experience. To keep your balance in those times when things are swirling around you, it's important to find a fixed reference point and focus on it. Return to the protection and guardianship of the Good Shepherd who endured the cross and laid down His life . . . for you.

It was because David refused to take vengeance on King Saul that we remember his story to this day. It was because Joseph was so willing to forgive his brothers that we admire him to this day. And it was because Job did not waver in his faith, in spite of all those unfair calamities, that we are impressed to this day.

If you'd just as soon be forgotten because you lived consumed with blame and self-pity, keep fighting back. Get even. Stay angry.

But if you hope to be remembered, admired, and rewarded, press on even though you've been ripped off.

A Prayer for Hope Beyond Unfairness

Dear Lord, find within us a yielded and quiet spirit of submission. To make that happen, we need You to come in like a flood. Occupy us as water finding empty spaces. Occupy reserved portions of our lives where anger is festering and the secret places where grudges are being stored. Sweep through our houses . . . don't miss one room or a single area—cleanse every dark closet, look under every rug. Let nothing go unnoticed as You take full control of our motives as well as our actions. Deep within our hearts we pray that You would sweep us clean of blame and revenge, of self-pity and keeping score. Enable each one of us to be big enough to press on regardless of what unfair treatment we've had to endure. Take away the scars of ugly treatment and harsh words. Forgiveness comes hard . . . but it's essential. Help us forgive even those who never acknowledge their wronging and hurting us! Give us peace in place of turmoil and erase the memories that keep us offended. We need fresh hope to go on! I ask this in the name of Him who had no sin and did no wrong, but died, the just for the unjust: Jesus Christ our Lord.

AMEN

7

Hope Beyond "I Do"

The Give-and-Take
of
Domestic Harmony

A WEDDING IS ONE thing. A marriage is another. What a difference between the way things start in a home . . . and the way they continue.

In his book *Secrets to Inner Beauty*, Joe Aldrich humorously describes the realities of married life.

> It doesn't take long for the newlyweds to discover that "everything in one person nobody's got." They soon learn that a marriage license is just a learner's permit, and ask with agony, "Is there life after marriage?"
>
> An old Arab proverb states that marriage begins with a prince kissing an angel and ends with a bald-headed man looking across the table at a fat lady. Socrates told his students, "By all means marry. If you get a good wife, twice blessed you will be. If you get a bad wife, you'll become a philosopher." Count Herman Keyserling said it well when he stated that "The essential difficulties of life do not end, but rather begin with marriage."[1]

Marriage begins like a romantic, moonlight sleigh ride, smoothly gliding over the glistening snow. It's living together after the honeymoon that turns out to be rough backpacking across rocks and hot sand. For two people to live in domestic harmony, it takes a lot of give-and-take. If you need any confirmation of this outside your own life, just look at the statistics. No, forget statistics. Just look about you. On the job. In the office. Around your neighborhood. At church. Broken marriages. Separations. Divorces. Fractured homes. Some children have so many stepparents they can't keep track of them.

A wedding is one thing. A marriage is something else entirely.

I am a realist, not an idealist. I've been married for forty-one years, and they have been years of learning and growth, years of difficulty and ecstasy, years of delight and discovery, years of heartache and hardship, years of having children and losing children (two miscarriages), years of growing together and, I must confess, some days in which it seemed we were growing apart.

At first, of course, deceived by the rose-colored glasses of romantic love, we didn't see any of this. And looking back through the fog of disappointment, we see very few things clearly.

In an essay on the theme of "arranged marriages," writer Philip Yancey offers these insights.

> In the U.S. and other Western-style cultures, people tend to marry because they are attracted to another's appealing qualities: a fresh smile, wittiness, a pleasing figure, athletic ability, a cheerful disposition, charm. Over time, these qualities can change; the physical attributes, especially, will deteriorate with age. Meanwhile, surprises may surface: slatternly housekeeping, a tendency toward depression, disagreements over sex. In contrast, the partners in an arranged marriage [over half of all marriages in our international global village fit this description] do not center their relationship on mutual attractions. Having heard your parents' decision, you accept that you will live for many years with someone you now barely know. Thus the overriding question changes from "Whom should I marry?" to "Given this partner, what kind of marriage can we construct together?"[2]

Truthfully, that is the kind of attitude we need if we are going to move beyond romance into reality to build a strong and lasting life together. The apostle Peter gives us some helpful advice. He offers hope beyond "I do."

Tucked away in the heart of his letter is a little gem of truth, like a diamond in a ring. Without the right setting to enhance its beauty, this little gem would get lost; but viewed in its proper setting it becomes a sparkling delight. In the Bible, this setting is called the scriptural context.

The overall setting begins at 1 Peter 2:13 and continues through the end of chapter 3. These many verses challenge us to respond correctly, even in unfair circumstances. Some of those circumstances are briefly illustrated: citizens in various situations (2:13–17), slaves with unjust masters (2:18–20), wives with unfair husbands (3:1–6), and Christians in an unchristian society (3:13–17).

The key term in this context is the word *submit*, which we defined and analyzed in the previous chapter. You'll recall it is translated from a Greek military term meaning "to fall in rank under the authority of another . . . to subject oneself for the purpose of obeying or pleasing another." Some men have taken this word to the extreme in marriage, promoting cowering and servile behavior by women in the face of the worst kinds of abuse. Others have gone to the opposite extreme and labeled these passages dated and therefore culturally obsolete, saying that they apply only to the era in which they were originally written. The balance of the biblical position lies somewhere between these two poles.

Wise Counsel to Wives

The first six verses of our "gem of truth" passage refer to wives, and the seventh verse refers to husbands. One New Testament scholar gives a good explanation of this seeming inequity.

It may seem strange that Peter's advice to wives is six times as long as that to husbands. This is because the wife's position was far more difficult than that of the husband. If a husband became a Christian, he would automatically bring his wife with him into the Church. . . . But if a wife became a Christian while her husband did not, she was taking a step which was unprecedented and which produced the acutest problems.[3]

Despite that explanation, I know this passage is probably one of the hottest potatoes in Scripture, especially for women. Let me put some of you at ease. I do not believe this or any other part of Scripture admonishes a wife to stay in a situation where her health is being threatened or where her life—or the lives of her children—is in danger. That is not what submission is all about. So please don't run to that extreme and hide there, thinking you can avoid or deny the importance of submission in every other area or at any other level.

I find no fewer than three implied imperatives woven into the fabric of these important verses. They are reasonable and doable commands. They aren't culturally irrelevant. Best of all, they work!

Analyze Your Actions

> In the same way, you wives, be submissive to your own husbands so that even if any of them are disobedient to the word, they may be won without a word by the behavior of their wives, as they observe your chaste and respectful behavior. (1 Pet. 3:1–2)

Many wives tend to view their roles as conditional; their behavior depends on the behavior of their husbands. "Sure, I'll be the kind of wife I should be if he's the kind of husband he should be." On the surface, that sounds great. Turnabout is fair play. There's only one problem: This passage isn't written just to wives who have husbands who play fair. Peter doesn't let us off the hook that easily. The passage is written to all wives, even those whose husbands are "disobedient to the word." In fact, by implication this paragraph is directed to women who live with disobedient husbands—husbands who are going their own way, husbands who care little about the things of God, husbands who would even mock the things of Christ. In short, these are husbands who aren't measuring up to God's standard.

Having to exhibit godly behavior under such circumstances can, however, cause wives to substitute secret manipulation for a quiet spirit. This may take many forms: pouting, sulking, scheming, bargaining, nagging, preaching, coercing, or humiliating. Wives who use this strategy are not trusting God to change their husbands' lives. They're trusting themselves.

You see, a wife is not responsible for her husband's life. She is responsible for her life. You cannot make your husband something he is not. Only God can do that.

I think it was the evangelist's wife, Ruth Graham, who once said, "It is my job to love Billy. It is God's job to make him good." I'd call that a wonderful philosophy for any wife to embrace.

Wife, it is your job to love your husband. It is God's job to change his life.

And wives who are truly obedient to Christ will find that He will honor their secure spirit. Yes, submission is a mark of security. It is not a spineless cringing, based on insecurity and fear. It is a voluntary unselfishness, a willing and cooperative spirit that seeks the highest good for one's husband.

"Well, that sounds like a dead-end street, Chuck," some of you might be saying. "If you only knew what I am living with, what a rascal, what a reprobate, what an ungodly man he really is."

But notice what Peter says: "they may be won without a word by the behavior of their wives, *as they observe your chaste and respectful behavior.*" The Greek term for *observe* suggests that this is a keen and careful observation, not a casual glance. As a "disobedient" husband observes his wife's godly behavior, his heart will eventually soften toward spiritual things. Such a lifestyle has been called "the silent preaching of a lovely life."

Watch Your Adornment and Your Attitude

And let not your adornment be merely external—braiding the hair, and wearing gold jewelry, or putting on dresses, but let it be the hidden person of the heart, with the imperishable quality of a gentle and quiet spirit, which is precious in the sight of God. (1 Pet. 3:3–4)

Obviously Peter is drawing a sharp contrast between inner beauty and outer beauty, or as Peter puts it, between outer adornment (verse 3) and inner adornment (verse 4).

It's easy in our shop-'til-you-drop culture to get carried away with the externals, ladies. Catalogs for every conceivable item of clothing pour into our homes, with their 800 numbers eager to take your order at any hour of the day or night. If that isn't convenient enough, we have entire television channels devoted to shopping and stores available on the Internet. Ready . . . set . . . *charge!*

The point of the contrast here is to restore the balance. Peter isn't prohibiting the braiding of hair or the wearing of jewelry any more than he's prohibiting the wearing of dresses. He merely wants to put those things in the background and bring the woman's character into the foreground. Perspective is the key.

Taken to an unrealistic extreme, you can really miss the mark in your external adornment. I have seen some women who think that it is a mark of spirituality to look like an unmade bed. That is not what God has in mind. On the other hand, if externals get overemphasized, appearance, cosmetics, and clothing take on too much significance. You can become preoccupied with your external adornment, and you can begin judging yourself and others solely by appearance, which is often what our culture does.

External beauty is ephemeral. Internal beauty is eternal. The former is attractive to the world; the latter is pleasing to God. Peter describes this inner beauty as "a gentle and quiet spirit." This might be paraphrased "a gentle tranquility." Without question, this is any woman's most powerful quality—true character. And such character comes from within—from the hidden person of the heart—because you know who you are and you know who you adore and serve, the Lord Christ. God values this kind of inner beauty as "imperishable" and "precious."

Outward adornment doesn't take a great deal of time. I've seen women do it in a few minutes on their way to work in the morning. (Ever been driving behind a woman putting on her makeup in the car as she's driving to work? It's an amazing process! And dangerous. I always cringe and wonder—what happens if she hits a pothole?) It may take only a few hours to prepare yourself for the most elegant of evenings, but it takes a lifetime to prepare and develop the hidden person of the heart.

Adornment is important but not nearly as important as attitude. If the internal attitude is right, it's amazing how much less significant one's external appearance becomes. Wise is the wife who watches both.

Evaluate Your Attention

For in this way in former times the holy women also, who hoped in God, used to adorn themselves, being submissive to their own husbands. Thus Sarah obeyed Abraham, calling him lord, and you have become her children if you do what is right without being frightened by any fear. (1 Pet. 3:5–6)

The fact that Sarah called her husband her lord (Gen. 18:12) reveals much about their relationship. It shows that she respected him, was attentive to his needs, cooperated with his wishes, and adapted herself to his desires.

Wives, are you patterning yourself after Sarah's role model? Take a look at where you place most of your attention, where you spend your time, what the focus of your prayer life is. Is your husband at the top of your earthly list?

I would encourage you wives to evaluate where you place most of your attention, and this is especially true for women who are busy raising a family. It is so easy in the press of caring for the constant needs of your children to put the needs of your husband on hold. Experience has taught me that is often where a breakdown in a marital relationship begins.

Peter says, "Sarah obeyed Abraham." A good paraphrase might be, "She paid attention to him."

*

Strong Commands to Husbands

You husbands likewise, live with your wives in an understanding way, as with a weaker vessel, since she is a woman; and grant her honor as a fellow heir of the grace of life, so that your prayers may not be hindered. (1 Pet. 3:7)

The final verse in this section turns the spotlight on husbands. It's short, but penetrating. I find that it is packed with three strong imperatives.

First, live with your wife. The Greek term here is a compound word composed of *sun* (with) and *oikeo* (to dwell / abide); put together they obviously mean "to dwell together." Now, you're probably thinking, "Well, certainly, I live with my wife. I'm *married* to her." But that is not what Peter is talking about. He's talking about a "close togetherness." *Sunoikeo* suggests much more than merely living under the same roof. There is a depth, a sense of intimacy, in the word. He is saying that husbands are responsible for that in the relationship. Providing a good living should never become a substitute for sharing deeply in life. The husband needs to be "at home with" his wife, understanding every room in his wife's heart and being sensitive to her needs. "Dwelling together" definitely means more than eating at the same table, sharing the same bed, and paying for the same mortgage.

Second, know your wife. Peter exhorts husbands to live with their wives "in an understanding way." That phrase literally means, "according to knowledge"—not an academic knowledge, but a thorough understanding of how your wife is put together.

"Oh, I know my wife," you may say. "Brown hair. Blue eyes. Weight. Height. I know what she likes for supper. Her favorite color is blue. I know where she likes to go for dinner." It's not that kind of knowledge either. Any man can know those things about her!

Your wife is a unique vessel, carefully crafted and beautifully interwoven by her Creator. To "know your wife" means you know the answers to those complex questions about her. What is her innermost makeup? What are her deepest concerns and fears? How do you help her work through them in the safety and security of your love? What does she need from you? Why does she respond as she does?

There's no handbook for those insights into her life. Even your father-in-law can't give you this inside information. You have to find it out in the intimacy of marriage and in the process of cultivating your life together. It takes time. It takes listening. It takes paying attention, concentrating, praying for insight, seeking understanding. Most wives long for that. Some of them die longing for it. Few things give a woman more security than knowing that her husband really knows her. That's what results in intimacy. That's what turns romance into a deep, lifelong love. That's what keeps her focused on and committed to you, longing to have you there, delighting in your presence, your words, your listening ear.

By the way, we need to address another phrase that occurs here: "living with your wife in an understanding way, *as with a weaker vessel.*" Now a word of caution: This has nothing to do with weakness of character or intelligence.

> The woman is called the "weaker vessel" (*skeuos*, lit., "vessel"); but this is not to be taken morally, spiritually, or intellectually. It simply means that the woman has less physical strength. The husband must recognize this difference and take it into account.[4]

Sometimes this is a bit difficult to comprehend when we consider what a woman goes through in bearing children. There's no doubt about the kind of strength women have within them when it comes to enduring pain. When my daughter gave birth to her second child, our fourth grandchild, she had natural childbirth. (Seemed strange to me—"natural" childbirth—and I was thankful I never had to go through that. I've never heard of anybody having a natural appendectomy or requesting a natural root canal!) What strength she demonstrated!

But when it comes to actual physical strength, Dr. Robert Kerlan, orthopedic surgeon and sports medicine specialist, says: "If the battle of the sexes was reduced to a tug-of-war with a line of 100 men on one side of the trench and 100 women on the other, the men would win." What makes the difference, he says, is muscle makeup.[5]

God's goal for us as husbands is to be sensitive rather than to prove how strong and macho we are. We need to love our wives, listen to them, adapt to their needs. We need to say no to more and more in our work so we can say yes to more and more in our homes . . . so we can say yes to the needs of our children and our families. (How else will your children learn what it means to be a good husband and father?)

Mind you, this is not to be a smothering kind of attention—the kind that says a husband is so insecure he cannot let his wife out of his sight. Instead, this is the kind of love that means your wife can't come back fast enough to your arms. Which brings us to the third imperative.

Third, honor your wife. To "grant her honor" is to assign her a place of honor. The same word translated "honor" here in 3:7 refers to the blood of Christ as "precious" in 1:19. I'd call that a rather significant analogy, wouldn't you?

Authors Gary Smalley and John Trent define this word well in their book *The Gift of Honor.*

> In ancient writings, something of honor was something of substance (literally, heavy), valuable, costly, even priceless. For Homer, the Greek scholar, "The greater the cost of the gift, the more the honor." . . .
>
> Not only does it signify something or someone who is a priceless treasure, but it is also used for someone who occupies a highly respected position in our lives, someone high on our priority list.[6]

That's how husbands are to treat their wives—to honor them by assigning them the top priority on their list of human relationships . . . in their schedules . . . and most importantly, in their hearts.

May I ask a few very personal questions? How do you treat your wife on an average day? Do you honor her? Do you give her a place of significance? Does she know she's your "top priority"? And do you communicate that in both actions and words? Honoring another is never something we keep to ourselves.

This is a magnificent truth, and you'll only get it from the Scriptures. It revolutionized my home. That's why I know it works. I didn't come from a model home and my wife didn't come from a home where her mother was honored. Cynthia and I knew that if we were going to make our marriage work, we had to go God's way, which meant we both had to be willing to change. We determined to do just that. And I'll freely admit, of the two of us, I have had to change more. About the time I think I've got things in good shape, another area emerges, and I have to deal with that! The journey toward marital maturity is a long one! And each year there are always some changes that must occur.

Let me summarize what Peter has written. Wives, your actions, your adornment, your attitudes, your attention are crucial in your marriage. Husbands, living with your wife, getting to know your wife, and honoring your wife are imperative if your marriage is going to be what it should be in God's eyes. Marriage is a two-way street. Both sides must be maintained.

A Promise to Both Partners

To seal this "heavenly bargain," Peter closes with a promise to both partners: "So that your prayers may not be hindered." This is an added incentive for husband and wife to live together in domestic harmony.

If you and your mate hope to cultivate an effective prayer life, the secret lies in your relationship with each other. Your prayers will not be hindered if you cultivate a close and caring relationship. Could that explain why your prayers are not being answered now?

A Project to Add Hope to Your Home

During the next week I'd like you to work on a very practical project. It will involve your doing two things. *First*, write down four qualities you appreciate most about your mate. After thinking them through, tell your spouse what they are and why they come to mind. Give examples. Take your time. Spell them out. Genuinely affirm your partner. *Second*, using this section of 1 Peter as your guide, admit the one thing you would most like to change about yourself. Don't be afraid to be vulnerable. Your mate will appreciate your willingness to be transparent.

Now don't get those two reversed. Don't mention four things you want your partner to change and the one thing you like most about yourself!

Talk truth. Refuse to blame. Guard against this becoming an evening of confrontation. Make it an evening of getting back together. Go ahead . . . be willing to risk.

You may be amazed to discover how quickly new hope for your marriage can return. The secret isn't that profound. A good marriage isn't so much finding the right partner as it is being the right partner.

And that starts with you.

A Prayer for Hope Beyond "I Do"

Lord, marriage was Your original idea. You hold the patent on this one. You brought the first couple together and gave Adam and Eve wise instruction on how to make their marriage flourish.

I believe You are still bringing men and women together . . . all around this big world. But today I pray specifically for those who read this chapter. For some, their hopes are dim. They don't know where to start or how to rekindle the flame that once burned brightly. For others, starting over seems too great a hurdle . . . too huge a mountain to climb . . . too much to face.

Somehow, Lord, break down the barriers. Bring back the "want to." Restore a glimmer of hope, especially in the lives of that one couple who think they will never make it. May Your Spirit miraculously renew their hope at this moment. I ask this in the name of Christ, in whom nothing is impossible.

AMEN

8

Hope Beyond
Immaturity

Maturity
Checkpoints

DURING MY MOST obnoxious years as a teenager I frequently received two admonitions. The first one was an abrupt, "Shut up!" The second was, "Grow up!"

Though I found it difficult on occasion, I usually managed to accomplish the first rather quickly. But I must confess, there are still days when I struggle with the second piece of advice.

En route to maturity, we all spill our milk, say things we shouldn't, and fail to act our age. At times we act like a two-year-old throwing a temper tantrum. At other times we pout like a pubescent child or go through sweeping mood swings like an awkwardly adjusting teenager.

This process is called "growing up." Let's not minimize the truth—it's painful. We struggle through it more by trial and error than by unfaltering charm-school grace. Consequently, every now and then we skin an elbow, bruise a knee, or bloody a nose from falling on our faces.

Growing up. Sooner or later we all have to do it. The sooner we do, the easier it will be to walk the uneven and sometimes uncertain sidewalks of faith.

Problem is, how do we determine whether we are grown up? Does it mean our hair starts to turn gray? No, that means we're growing older but not necessarily wiser. I've met people with snow-white hair who are still immature. Signs of aging do not necessarily mean we are showing signs of maturity.

If you think it's easier to tell from the inside out, forget it. How do you know that you are more mature this year than you were last year? Has living twelve months longer made any difference? We know we're growing older, but how do we know we're growing up? And is growing up something God even requires of us? Maybe He just wants us to live in His family, sort of exist between now and eternity, then He's planning to take us home. No, that's not the way it works. Growing up is a stated objective for every member of God's family. God says so in His Word.

The writer of Hebrews addresses this very matter when he takes his readers to task for their lack of maturity. They had grown older in the faith, but they had not yet grown up. Instead of building on the foundation laid by the apostles, they were still playing with blocks.

> For though by this time you ought to be teachers, you have need again for someone to teach you the elementary principles of the oracles of God, and you have come to need milk and not solid food. For everyone who partakes only of milk is not accustomed to the word of righteousness, for he is a babe. But solid food is for the mature, who because of practice have their senses trained to discern good and evil.
>
> Therefore leaving the elementary teaching about the Christ, *let us press on to maturity,* not laying again a foundation of repentance from dead works and of faith toward God, of instruction about washings, and laying on of hands, and the resurrection of the dead, and eternal judgment, and this we shall do, if God permits. (Heb. 5:12–6:3, italics added)

Do you notice the Lord's concern that some seem perpetually immature? "You have need *again* for someone to teach you the elementary principles of the oracles of God," says the writer (italics added). "You have come to need milk and not solid food." How interesting that he puts it like that. We would say, "You're back on baby food."

I've had grocers tell me that they sell more baby food to the aging than to the parents of infants in their community. As we get older, in many ways we revert back to childhood. Physically that can't be helped—as we age and grow infirm, our bodies deteriorate. But spiritually, immaturity is something we must not allow. God wants us to get beyond the elementary matters of the faith and set out on a life-long pursuit of maturity. He longs for us to grow up in the faith.

Leave behind elementary teachings, says the letter to the Hebrews. Press on to maturity.

By "elementary teachings," the writer is very likely referring to the Old Testament signs and sacrifices. "We've gone beyond that now," he says. In today's terms we could say, "Move beyond the gospel. You have heard the gospel, you have responded to the gospel, you have believed the gospel, now go on. Grow up. Get into areas of teaching and learning that probe much deeper into your life." That kind of solid food results in spiritual strength. In fact, I've heard it rendered, "We are to leave the ABCs of the faith." In other words, we need to quit playing blocks and sucking milk from a bottle and wanting to be entertained. Leave the things that characterize infancy and get on with a grown-up lifestyle.

Few things are more pathetic to behold than those who have known the Lord for years but still can't get in out of the rain doctrinally and biblically. To put it succinctly, they have grown old, but they haven't grown up.

Do you feed yourself regularly on the Word of God or must you have the teaching of someone else to keep growing? Now, don't get me wrong; I don't decry teaching and preaching. How could I? That's my job security! All of us have a need for someone to instruct and exhort us in the things of God. But it isn't because we have no way of taking it in on our own. Teaching and preaching are more like nutritional food supplements.

Let me ask you several penetrating questions. Are you digging into the Word of God? Are you truly searching the Scriptures on your own? Are you engaged in a ministry of concerted and prevailing prayer? Can you handle pressure better than you could, say, three years ago? Are you further along on your own growth chart than you were a year ago, two years ago, five years ago?

Checkpoints for Maturity

How can we know we're growing up? Outwardly we have various signs of physical growth and aging. But when it comes to spiritual maturity, we need another kind of growth chart, and Peter, in his letter of hope, offers us a series of checkpoints to help us know we're growing up and getting on in spiritual life.

In the past three years I have flown on more airplanes than ever before in my life, commuting from California to Texas and back again, plus dozens of other destinations. When people ask Cynthia and me where we live, I sometimes reply, "Seats 16C and D, American Airlines." We're now on a first-name basis with many of the airline personnel.

As a result of this unusual transitional lifestyle, I have had ample occasions to watch the procedure pilots go through as they prepare for an upcoming flight. You may have observed it as well. The next time you're taking a trip, stand in the terminal and look out the windows into the cockpit of the airplane parked at the gate. You'll see the pilot sitting there with a clipboard, checking off all the instruments and systems. He'll also get out and check the outside of the aircraft, walking all around it. This is a seasoned pilot, with perhaps tens of thousands of hours in the air. Still, every time, before he takes that airplane up, he runs through his preflight checklist. We're thankful he does!

Look at 1 Peter 3:8–12, and you'll find another kind of checklist—a checklist for spiritual maturity. It helps us evaluate how we're doing on this pilgrimage from earth to heaven.

To sum up, let all be harmonious, sympathetic, brotherly, kind-hearted, and humble in spirit; not returning evil for evil, or insult for insult, but giving a blessing instead; for you were called for the very purpose that you might inherit a blessing. For,

> "Let him who means to love life and see good days
> refrain his tongue from evil and his lips from speaking guile.
> "And let him turn away from evil and do good;
> let him seek peace and pursue it.
> "For the eyes of the Lord are upon the righteous,
> and his ears attend to their prayer,
> but the face of the Lord is against those who do evil."
> (1 Pet. 3:8–12)

If I count correctly, there are no fewer than eight checkpoints in this section of Scripture. They help us determine how we're doing in our growth toward maturity.

Unity

The first checkpoint is unity: "Let all be harmonious." This refers to a oneness of heart, a similarity of purpose, and an agreement on major points of doctrine.

Please remember, this quality is not the same as *uniformity*, where everyone must look alike and think alike, form identical convictions and prefer the same tastes. That's what I call a cracker-box mentality. Peter isn't promoting uniformity. Nor is he referring to *unanimity*, where there is 100 percent agreement on everything. And it is not the same as *union*, where there is an affiliation with others but no common bond that makes them one at heart.

The secret to this kind of harmony is not to focus on petty peripheral differences but to concentrate on the common ground of Jesus Christ—His model, His message, and His mission.

How mature are you in the area of unity? Are you at harmony with other believers in the family of God? Are you one who works well *with* others?

Mutual Interest

The second checkpoint is mutual interest: "Let all be . . . sympathetic." The Greek root gives us our word *sympathy*, meaning "to feel with."

This means that when others weep, you weep; when they rejoice, you rejoice. It connotes the *absence* of competition, envy, or jealousy toward a fellow Christian.

Romans 12:15–16 states it well: "Rejoice with those who rejoice, and weep with those who weep. Be of the same mind toward one another. . . ." Believers who are growing toward maturity share in mutual feelings—mutual woes and mutual joys.

This is one of the best benefits of being part of the body of Christ and a major reason why we need to be involved in a local church. In that local community we have a context in which we can rejoice with each other and weep with one another. Think what happens when you move to a new community, a new home. Sadly you leave the church that has been your home, your spiritual family, where God has used you and encouraged you. But then He leads you to another. When you move to a new town or city, as a Christian one of the first things you do is search for a new church home, one where your new brothers and sisters welcome you and receive you into their fellowship and life. Right away you're surrounded by a family.

How's your maturity level on this second checkpoint? Can you truly say you enter the feelings of the other person? When others hurt, do you hurt? When they enjoy life, do you really enjoy it with them? When God blesses them with material prosperity or some significant award or promotion, do you rejoice with them or do you envy them? When they lose, do you feel the loss with them, or do you feel just a tiny pinprick of satisfaction?

I've heard it said, "Maturity begins to grow when you can sense your concern for others outweighing your concern for yourself."

Maturing believers care very much about the things others are experiencing.

Affectionate Friendship

The third checkpoint is friendship and affection: "Let all be . . . brotherly."

The word translated here as "brotherly" is from the Greek word *philos*, which has in mind the love of an affectionate friend. The poet Samuel Coleridge once described friendship as "a sheltering tree." When you have this quality, the branches of your friendship reach out over the lives of others, giving them shelter, shade, rest, relief, and encouragement.

Much has been written about the importance of friendship. James Boswell said, "We cannot tell the precise moment when friendship is formed. As in filling a vessel drop by drop, there is at last a drop which makes it run over; so in a series of kindnesses there is at last one which makes the heart run over." Longfellow wrote, "Ah! How good it feels, the hand of an old friend." Isn't that true!

Friends give comfort. We find strength near them. They bear fruit that provides nourishment and encouragement. When something troublesome occurs in our life, we pick up the phone and call a friend, needing the comfort he or she provides. I think there are few things more lonely than having no friend to call. Friends also care enough about us to hold us accountable . . . but we never doubt their love or respect.

Are you cultivating such friends? Are you being a friend? Are there a few folks who will stand near you, sheltering you with their branches?

Jay Kesler, my long-time friend and currently the president of Taylor University, has said that one of his great hopes in life is to wind up with at least eight people who will attend his funeral without once checking their watches. I love it! Do you have eight people who'll do that?

As we mature, it is healthy for us to have a circle of friends who lovingly hold us close, regardless . . . who care about our pain, who are there for us when we can't make it on our own. The flip side of that is equally healthy—our being friends like that to others. Works both ways. As we mature our friendships deepen.

Kindheartedness

The fourth checkpoint is kindheartedness: "Let all be . . . kindhearted." The Greek term here can also be translated "compassionate," and it is used in the Gospels to describe Jesus.

> And seeing the multitudes, He *felt compassion* for them, because they were distressed and downcast like sheep without a shepherd. (Matt. 9:36, italics added)

As a good shepherd, Jesus looked at humanity's lost sheep who were scattered, frightened, and hungry. What He saw pulled at His heartstrings. He was full of tenderness for them. He had compassion for them. Just as these hurting people touched the heart of the Savior, so should hurting people today touch our hearts. If they do, it's a definite sign of spiritual growth. No one who is mature is ever so important that the needs of others no longer matter.

I've just finished reading a fascinating volume, *Character Above All.* It is a compilation of ten essays on the ten United States presidents from Franklin Roosevelt in the 1930s to George Bush in the 1990s, each written by people who knew those presidents well—friends, speechwriters, fellow politicians, and other colleagues who worked alongside them.

My favorite was the chapter on Ronald Reagan, who served our country from 1981–1989. His speechwriter, Peggy Noonan, wrote the piece and captured the essence of his character in twenty-two pages. Wonderful reading!

She concludes with a story about, in her words, "the almost Lincolnian kindness that was another part of Reagan's character . . . everyone who worked with Reagan has a story about his kindness." Before I retell that story, go back and read those eleven words. Wouldn't it be great if that could be said about each of us? Wouldn't it be wonderful to be remembered for our kindness?

In highlighting this quality in Reagan's character, Noonan tells the story of Frances Green, an eighty-three-year-old woman who lived by herself on social security in a town just outside San Francisco. She had little money, but for eight years she'd been sending one dollar a year to the Republican National Convention.

Then one day Frances got an RNC fund-raising letter in the mail, a beautiful piece on thick, cream-colored paper with black-and-gold lettering. It invited the recipient to come to the White House to meet President Reagan. She never noticed the little RSVP card that suggested a positive reply needed to be accompanied by a generous donation. She thought she'd been invited because they appreciated her dollar-a-year support.

Frances scraped up every cent she had and took a four-day train ride across America. Unable to afford a sleeper, she slept sitting up in coach. Finally she arrived at the White House gate: a little elderly woman with white hair, white powder all over her face, white stockings, an old hat with white netting, and an all-white dress, now yellow with age. When she got up to the guard at the gate and gave her name, however, the man frowned, glanced over his official list, and told her that her name wasn't there. She couldn't go in. Frances Green was heartbroken.

A Ford Motor Company executive who was standing in line behind her watched and listened to the little scenario. Realizing something was wrong, he pulled Frances aside and got her story. Then he asked her to return at nine o'clock the next morning and meet him there. She agreed. In the meantime, he made contact with Anne Higgins, a presidential aide, and got clearance to give her a tour of the White House and introduce her to the president. Reagan agreed to see her, "of course."

The next day was anything but calm and easy at the White House. Ed Meese had just resigned. There had been a military uprising abroad. Reagan was in and out of high-level secret sessions. But Frances Green showed up at nine o'clock, full of expectation and enthusiasm.

The executive met her, gave her a wonderful tour of the White House, then quietly walked her by the Oval Office, thinking maybe, at best, she might get a quick glimpse of the president on her way out. Members of the National Security Council came out. High-ranking generals were coming and going. In the midst of all the hubbub, President Reagan glanced out and saw Frances Green. With a smile, he gestured her into his office.

As she entered, he rose from his desk and called out, "Frances! Those darn computers, they fouled up again! If I'd known you were coming I would have come out there to get you myself." He then invited her to sit down, and they talked leisurely about California, her town, her life and family.

The president of the United States gave Frances Green a lot of time that day—more time than he had. Some would say it was time wasted. But those who say that didn't know Ronald Reagan, according to Peggy Noonan. He knew this woman had nothing to give him, but she needed something he could give her. And so he (as well as the Ford executive) took time to be kind and compassionate.[1]

In our high-tech, cyberspace era it is so easy to become distant. We can live our lives untouched and untouchable. In a fast-lane world it isn't difficult to become uncaring and preoccupied with our own agendas. The freeway of life requires that we keep moving, no matter what we see happening around us. The pace at which we travel does not allow us to stop easily. And even if we could, we've seen the stories in the news about people who stopped to help and were rebuffed, mugged, or carjacked—even murdered. So we learn to keep our eyes straight ahead and keep going . . . fast! The homeless person on the sidewalk? The mentally disturbed stranger at the mall? Hurry past. Just keep looking straight ahead, moving past them, down the road of life.

Of course, we need to be wise; we must use discernment. Still, is there no place for kindheartedness and compassion in our world? Is there no time for tender mercies?

Read again the words that appear at the end of Ephesians 4:

And be kind to one another, tender-hearted, forgiving each other, just as God in Christ also has forgiven you. (Eph. 4:32)

Maturing people are tender people. How valuable they are in a busy society like ours!

Humility

The fifth checkpoint is humility: "Let all be . . . humble in spirit." The phrase "humble in spirit" literally means "lowly" or "bowed down" in mind. It speaks of an internal attitude rather than an external appearance. Humility isn't a show we put on; in fact, if we think we're humble, we're probably not. And in our day of self-promotion, self-assertion, spotlighting "celebrities of the faith," and magnifying the flesh, this quality—so greatly valued by the Lord Jesus—is a rare commodity indeed. Oswald Chambers writes of this so insightfully:

> We have a tendency to look for wonder in our experience, and we mistake heroic actions for real heroes. It's one thing to go through a crisis grandly, yet quite another to go through every day glorifying God when there is no witness, no limelight, and no one paying even the remotest attention to us. If we are not looking for halos, we at least want something that will make people say, "What a wonderful man of prayer he is!" or "What a great woman of devotion she is!" If you are properly devoted to the Lord Jesus, you have reached the lofty height where no one would ever notice you personally. All that is noticed is the power of God coming through you all the time.
>
> We want to be able to say, "Oh, I have had a wonderful call from God!" But to do even the most humbling tasks to the glory of God takes the Almighty God Incarnate working in us.[2]

If you are blessed with abilities, if you are gifted, if you are used by God, it is easy to start believing your own stuff. Yet one of the marks of a truly mature life is humility of spirit.

> It can be said without qualification that no human being can consider himself mature if he narrows the use of his efforts, talents, or means to his own personal advantage. The very concept of maturity rests on the degree of inner growth that is characterized by a yearning within the individual to transcend his self-concentration by extending himself into the lives of others. In other words, maturity is a stage in his development when to live with himself in a satisfying manner it becomes imperative for him to give as well as to receive.[3]

A truly humble person looks for opportunities to give himself freely to others rather than holding back, to release rather than hoarding, to build up rather than tearing down, to serve rather than being served, to learn from others rather than clamoring for the teaching stand. How blessed are those who learn this early in life.

Carl Sandberg once related the story about a mother who brought her newborn son to General Robert E. Lee for a blessing. The southern gentleman tenderly cradled the lad in his arms then looked at the mother and said, "Ma'am, please teach him that he must deny himself."[4]

Forgiveness

Thus far, Peter has written about how maturity affects how we think and how we feel. In his last three checkpoints, found in verses 9 through 11, he tells us how maturity affects *what we do and what we say.* In verse 9 he tells us not to return evil for evil. In other words, be willing to forgive.

> . . . not returning evil for evil, or insult for insult, but giving a blessing instead; for you were called for the very purpose that you might inherit a blessing. (1 Pet. 3:9)

Isn't that a great statement? It touches all the important bases regarding forgiveness. Just look at the four steps in it; observe the process.

First, when we have true forgiveness in our hearts, we refuse to get back or get even.

Second, we restrain from saying anything ugly in return.

Third, we return good for evil, "giving a blessing instead [of evil or insult]."

And fourth, we keep in mind that we were called to endure such harsh treatment.

It's easy to miss that last one, isn't it? I thought at first I was misreading it, and then I went back to chapter 2 and found that's what Peter says over there too. So he must mean it. Do you remember his earlier comment?

What credit is there if, when you sin and are harshly treated, you endure it with patience? But if when you do what is right and suffer for it you patiently endure it, this finds favor with God. For you have been called for this purpose. (1 Pet. 2:20–21a)

What is a sure sign that I'm growing up? When I stop fighting back. When I take the chip off my shoulder. When I stop working on my clever answer so I can punch back with a sarcastic jab.

Whenever the urge to get even comes over us, it's important for us to realize that retaliation is a sign of adolescence while restraint is a mark of maturity.

A Controlled Tongue

> "Let him who means to love life and see good days
> refrain his tongue from evil and his lips from speaking guile."
> (1 Pet. 3:10)

You knew we'd get around to this one, didn't you? The tongue . . . what a battle! Warnings about the tongue are threaded throughout the Bible. In fact, in this verse and the one that follows Peter is quoting from Psalm 34:12–16.

Here he says to "refrain" your tongue from evil. Actually the psalmist used a little more forceful language: "Keep your tongue from evil." The idea is to get control of your tongue, or, as James puts it, put a bridle on it. It's the idea of holding it back from galloping headlong into greater evil (see James 3:1–10). Control your tongue!

Show me a person who has learned to refrain from gossip, to refrain from passing on confidential information, to refrain from making an unverified comment, and I'll show you somebody who is well on his or her way to maturity.

You really want to love life? You want to see good days? Gain better control of your tongue. Life will be happier for you. It'll even be easier for you. You'll see better days.

Some never learn this lesson. Remember the classic grave marker from jolly old England?

Beneath this sod,
this lump of clay,
lies Arabella Young,
who, on the 24th of May
began to hold her tongue.

Will it take death to control your tongue? It need not! Pray that God will control your tongue, starting today! Pray that He will muzzle your mouth when someone says, "Please don't share this with anyone else." When someone speaks to you in confidence, seal the information in the secret vault of your mind.

Believe me, I'm a preacher, and I know how tempting it is to use real-life examples in my sermon illustrations, especially family-related examples. I heard recently about a preacher up in the Northwest who pays his kids a royalty of a dollar every time he uses them in an illustration! He asks permission, they approve, he tells the story, they get a buck. That'll curb a loose tongue real quick!

A mark of maturity is a controlled tongue.

A verse in Psalm 141 puts all of this so clearly. It's from the ancient writings of David, and I've often thought of it as a great prayer with which to begin each day.

Set a guard, O Lord, over my mouth;
Keep watch over the door of my lips. (Ps. 141:3)

How are you doing on the checklist so far? Unity. Mutual interest. Friendship and affection. Kindheartedness and compassion. Humility. Forgiveness. A controlled tongue. Pretty convicting list, isn't it? But if we wish to have hope beyond our immaturity, these qualities are worth our time and attention. And there's one more twofold checkpoint.

Purity and Peace

"And let him turn away from evil and do good;
let him seek peace and pursue it.
"For the eyes of the Lord are upon the righteous,

And his ears attend to their prayer,
But the face of the Lord is against those who do evil."
(1 Pet. 3:11–12)

Look again at Peter's counsel. "Turn away from evil and do good."
That's purity. "Seek peace and pursue it." That's peace. And then he
tells us that the Lord is watching us and listening to us. Why? Because He cares about our modeling these qualities.

The eyes and ears of the Lord are emblematic of God's providential care for His people. What a wonderful reason for pursuing purity
and peace—the promise of God's providential care!

A Final Glance at the Checklist

That's quite a checklist, isn't it? Eight distinct notches to mark our
Christian maturity. How do you measure up?

We're told to grow up. We're told to press on to maturity. But
growing up is never easy. We all have areas of trouble, setbacks,
stumbling points along the way. (I don't know of one item on this list
that isn't a struggle for me at various times in my own life.) So those
are the things that we pray about, for "His ears attend to our
prayers."

Here's a practical suggestion. Go over that list at the end of every
month. Write it out and stick it where you will see it. Put it under a
refrigerator magnet. Tape it to your mirror. Ask God for strength in
these eight areas.

As children of God moving toward maturity, let's be committed to
harmony, to a spirit of unity. Let's engage in a mutual interest in
each other's lives. Let's develop friendships marked by affection, by
"touchable love"—love that is genuine and demonstrative. Let's be
kindhearted and compassionate. Let's exhibit humility of spirit and
a mind that is concerned about others instead of ourselves. Finally,
let's forgive, control our tongues, and pursue purity and peace.

I am grateful airline pilots take the time to check their lists before
we take off. I'm especially glad they don't shrug their shoulders when

they see a bulge on one of the tires and say, "Well, we'll just hope for the best." I'm glad they don't ignore the smallest detail, even though they've gone down the same list hundreds of times in their careers. I'm glad they don't take my life and safety for granted. That's why they are willing to return to that list again and again and again.

We dare not take our Christian maturity for granted either. That's why we must return to God's checklist again and again and again.

We dare not do any less if we hope to get beyond a life of immaturity.

A Prayer for Hope Beyond Immaturity

Father, thank You for the reminder today of things that are such an important part of our lives. Though none of these qualities is new, we continue to need the reminder. How often we have come asking for help in one or more of these areas. You've heard our pleas on many occasions. We so want to be growing toward maturity . . . but the journey takes forever! And so, this very moment, we thank You for the Lord Jesus Christ, our model and our master, who fulfilled each of these marks of maturity and dozens of other character qualities to perfection, though fully man. Thank You for the hope we have that Your Holy Spirit will be with us each step of our way on our road to maturity. We certainly need His empowerment to keep us going and growing.

I would ask, finally, that You give us hope beyond our immaturity. Guard us from discouragement as we look back over the checklist and realize how far we have to go. Remind us that we've come a long way toward the goal, by Your grace. Through Jesus Christ I pray.

AMEN

9

Hope Beyond Bitterness

When Life
"Just Ain't Fair"

AN OLD FRENCH fairy tale tells the story of two daughters—one bad and the other good. The bad daughter was the favorite of her mother, but the good daughter was unjustly neglected, despised, and mistreated.

One day, while drawing water from the village well, the good daughter met a poor woman who asked for a drink. The girl responded with kind words and gave the woman a cup of water. The woman, actually a fairy in disguise, was so pleased with the little girl's kindness and good manners that she gave her a gift.

"Each time you speak," said the woman, "a flower or jewel will come out of your mouth."

When the little girl got home, her mother began to scold her for taking so long to bring the water. The girl started to apologize, and two roses, two pearls, and two diamonds came out of her mouth.

Her mother was astonished. But after hearing her daughter's story and seeing the number of beautiful jewels that came out in the telling, the mother called her other daughter and sent her forth to get the same gift. The bad daughter, however, was reluctant to be seen performing the lowly task of drawing water, so she grumbled sourly all the way to the well.

When the bad daughter got to the well, a beautiful queenly woman—that same fairy in another disguise—came by and asked for a drink. Disagreeable and proud, the girl responded rudely. As a result, she received her reward too. Each time she opened her mouth, she emitted snakes and toads.[1]

How's that for poetic justice!

There's something in each one of us that longs for circumstances to be fair, isn't there? Maybe that's why fairy tales are so appealing. Good people receive their rewards and "live happily ever after" while bad people are soundly punished. Life works out, justice is done, and fairness reigns supreme.

Unfortunately, real life doesn't usually turn out that way. Every child needs to be taught, "Fairness is rare." Every epitaph could read, "Life is difficult."

Our lives are haunted by unfairness when we want fairness. Instead of justice we are surrounded by injustice. We want deceit exposed, dishonesty revealed, and truth rewarded. But things don't work out that way. At least not as we perceive them.

Some families have been racked by unfairness. A mate leaves a loving, faithful partner. Disease steals a loved one prematurely. An unfair situation at work or at school keeps escalating.

Life just doesn't turn out fair for some . . . for most!

Truly, life *is* difficult. But therein lies some of life's best lessons.

I was reminded of those words when I read this astonishing statement by a well-known British writer and radio personality:

> Contrary to what might be expected, I look back on experiences that at the time seemed especially desolating and painful with particular satisfaction. Indeed, I can say with complete truthfulness that everything I have learned in my seventy-five years in this world, everything that has truly enhanced and enlightened my existence, has been through affliction and not through happiness. In other words, if it ever were to

be possible to eliminate affliction from our earthly existence by means of some drug or other medical mumbo jumbo . . . the result would not be to make life delectable, but to make it too banal and trivial to be endurable. This, of course, is what the Cross signifies. And it is the Cross, more than anything else, that has called me inexorably to Christ.[2]

Now it is one thing to read those words from a man like Malcolm Muggeridge and almost be moved to tears. It's another thing to embrace them in our own lives. I know there isn't a person reading this who hasn't, at some point, had reason to become bitter because of the way you were treated by someone or because of some "unfair" affliction or experience. Everyone can blame someone for something!

As Christians we know that, ultimately, good will triumph over evil and that our God is just and kind and fair. But what can we do with the injustices and unfairnesses in the meantime? How can we keep pressing on in spite of such mistreatment?

Two Different and Distinct Perspectives

Our response to unfairness, as with all other issues, is based on our perspective—the particular vantage point from which we look at life. Basically, in this case, we have two perspectives to choose from: the human perspective or the divine.

The Human Perspective

Our natural, human perspective contends, "Since life isn't fair, I'm going to get my share. I'm going to look out for number one. I'm going to spend my energy getting my own back or setting things straight or making it right. I'm not going to take it any longer."

Our world is full of literature and counselors who will help you carry out this agenda. The problem is, you may get even but you won't get peace. You may feel better for the short term, but you won't get lasting satisfaction. You may find a way to channel your anger, but if retaliation is your major goal, you will not glorify God. Those who live their lives from this perspective are more likely to end their lives as bitter, cynical, hostile people. Tragically, I have just described how the majority of Americans choose to live.

The Divine Perspective

Fortunately, we do have another option, and we find it clearly spelled out for us in 1 Peter.

> "For the eyes of the Lord are upon the righteous,
> And His ears attend to their prayer,
> But the face of the Lord is against those who do evil."
> (1 Pet. 3:12)

The principle that Peter gives us is this: God misses nothing. He's looking out for us. He's listening to our prayers. And He is completely aware of the evil that is happening to us.

Don't ever think He has missed the evil. He sees, and He remembers. He may be long-suffering, but He doesn't compromise His justice. Not only is His eye on the righteous, His face is against evil. Ultimately, good will overcome evil. In the end, God wins!

But if this is true, we wonder, why doesn't He do something about evil? Why does He let it go on so long? Because God's time line is infinite—He doesn't close His books at the end of the month. It may take a lifetime—or longer—before justice is served. But in the end, count on it, *God will be just*. In the end, He will "work everything together for good" and for His glory.

That thought gives us hope beyond bitterness. If we don't believe that and if we don't focus on that, we become the loser. We spend our years like a rat in a sewer pipe, existing in the tight radius of cynicism and bitterness. Ultimately, we become, in our aging years, angry old men and jaded old women.

★

Some Helpful Insights and Techniques to Keep Hope Alive

Building on this divine perspective, Peter gives us five ways we can live in an unfair and inequitable world. But first there's a general principle we need to underscore.

A General Principle

> And who is there to harm you if you prove zealous for what is good? (1 Pet. 3:13)

If we were to paraphrase this verse, we could say that those who live honest lives will not usually suffer harm. *Usually.* There are exceptions, of course, to almost every rule, as we will see below. But as a general rule, if you live a life of purity and integrity, in the long run you usually won't suffer as much as those who habitually traffic in evil.

For example, if you pay your debts, chances are good that you won't get into financial trouble. If you pay all your taxes on time, you probably won't have the IRS on your case. If you take care of your body—get sufficient exercise and sleep, watch your diet and your stress level—chances are good that you will live a healthier life than those who don't. If you help others, chances are good that when you are in need someone will be there to help you. To paraphrase Peter's principle, those who do what is right are usually not in harm's way. *Usually* that's the rule.

Occasional Inequities

However, to return to reality, because life is difficult, there are times when life "just ain't fair." So there will be are times when, despite that general principle, despite your righteous life, despite your faithful walk with God, situations turn on you. And it's these exceptions to the rule that Peter is addressing in chapter 3, verses 11 through 17. He begins with a general summation of the condition.

> But even if you should suffer for the sake of righteousness, you are blessed. (1 Pet. 3:14a)

Before going on, notice the words, "But even if you should." In New Testament Greek, there are four conditions introduced by the word *if*. Three were quite common. The first-class condition, meaning "assumed as true," was a common usage (see Matt. 4:3, 6); the second-class condition, meaning "assumed as not true," was also commonly used (see Gal. 1:10); the third-class condition, meaning "maybe, maybe not," was frequently employed by writers (as seen earlier in 1 Pet. 3:13). The fourth-class condition, meaning "unlikely but possible," is rarely used in Scripture. Interestingly, this is the condition Peter uses here in verse 14. It could be paraphrased, "It is unlikely that you should suffer for the sake of righteousness, but if you should. . . . " That, alone, ought to give us a boost of fresh hope!

Then Peter goes on to suggest five ways you and I should respond if this happens. Remember, this is not my advice; this is God's advice. Human advice says, "Kick 'em in the teeth. Get even." That's not good advice, but it's often heard. So we need to know what God has to say about how to respond when we have done what is right but wrong is done to us in return.

It might help if you wrote these responses down on a three-by-five card and keep them handy. I'd suggest that you look at the card at least once a day. You might want to stick it on your bathroom mirror or slide it under the glass of your desktop.

How are we to respond when the exception to the rule occurs? *First, consider yourself uniquely blessed by God.*

As far as the injustice itself is concerned, Peter's surprising advice is, "Be happy! Consider yourself blessed!" James tells us something similar in the first chapter of his letter.

When all kinds of trials and temptations crowd into your lives, my brothers, don't resent them as intruders, but welcome them as friends! (James 1:2 PHILLIPS)

Sure sounds nice, you may say, but honestly now, how can we be happy and consider ourselves blessed when we've just been punched in the eye with the fist of injustice?

Well, we can do this by remembering two things: first, as we saw in chapter 6, we are called to patiently endure unfair treatment (see 1 Pet. 2:21; 3:9) so that when it comes we can know we're still experiencing God's plan and fulfilling our calling. Such treatment reminds us that God's hand is still on our lives. And second, someday we will be rewarded for our endurance of these undeserved trials (see Matt. 5:10–12; James 1:12).

Anybody can accept a reward graciously, and many people can even take their punishment patiently when they have done something wrong. But how many people are equipped to handle mistreatment after they've done right? Only Christians are equipped to do that. That is what makes believers stand out. That's our uniqueness. And, yes, there are occasions in life when we will be called for that very purpose. In the mystery of God's sovereign plan, we will be singled out. Then later, like Job, we will be rewarded for enduring those trials we did not deserve.

Remember Jesus' instruction?

"Blessed are those who have been persecuted for the sake of righteousness, for theirs is the kingdom of heaven. Blessed are you when men cast insults at you, and persecute you, and say all kinds of evil against you falsely, on account of Me. Rejoice, and be glad, for your reward in heaven is great, for so they persecuted the prophets who were before you." (Matt. 5:10–12)

Because of these promises (there are many similar ones throughout the Scriptures) Christians can do something different from all the rest of humanity. We can respond to injustice with a positive attitude. When we do, mouths drop open . . . and we're frequently given an opportunity to explain why we're not eaten up with revenge.

Second, don't panic and don't worry.

And do not fear their intimidation, and do not be troubled. (1 Pet. 3:14b)

It doesn't take a linguistic scholar to interpret that counsel. Peter puts his finger on two common responses. Panic and worry. I do both of those things when I operate in the flesh, don't you? But observe what Peter says.

First, look at the word *fear*. It comes from the original term *phobos*, from which we also get our word *phobia*. This kind of fear is the fear that seizes us with terror and causes us to take flight, running away from the pressure. Peter says, "Don't do that. There's no reason to run. Don't attempt to escape the trial. Don't panic."

In the second phrase he tells us that we don't need to "be troubled." The word *troubled* in Greek means "to be agitated, uneasy," the idea of feeling inner turmoil or agitation. Remember John 14:1, "Let not your heart be troubled"? Same root word here.

The energy and effort we expend worrying never solves a thing. In fact, it usually makes the situation worse for us, creating a terrible inner turmoil which, if allowed to intensify, can paralyze us.

Peter's counsel to us is that, even when trials are pressing in and people are trying to intimidate us, we can have a calmness of spirit. As far as the persecutor or instigator is concerned, we can be free from panic and worry. How? Why? Because we know that God is on our side.

Third, acknowledge Christ as Lord even over this event.

But sanctify Christ as Lord in your hearts . . . (1 Pet. 3:15a)

We often overlook the first phrase of this verse in our concentration on the second part:

. . . always being ready to make a defense to everyone who asks you to give an account for the hope that is in you. (1 Pet. 3:15b)

We usually apply those words to some public defense of the faith. While they may be used in that way, the verse actually appears in a context of wrong having come to us as a result of our doing what is right. And it says, "Do not fear . . . but in your hearts set apart [sanctify] Christ as Lord" (NIV).

You and I can do that in prayer. When we think a wrong has been done to us that we don't deserve, we can respond, "Lord, You're with me right now. You are here, and You have Your reasons for what is happening. You will not take advantage of me. You're much too kind to be cruel. You're much too good to be unjust. You care for me too much to let this get out of hand. Take charge. Use my integrity to defend me. Give me the grace to stay calm. Control my emotions. Be Lord over my present situation." In such a prayer, we "set apart Christ as Lord" in our hearts.

If I have prayed that sort of prayer once, I must have prayed it dozens of times. "Lord, there is no way I can set the record straight, it seems. It's getting more complicated and I find myself completely at Your disposal . . . at Your mercy. Take over, Lord. You be the sovereign Master over this moment. I can't change this person . . . I can't alter these circumstances. You be the Lord over this scene."

When our older daughter, Charissa, was in high school, she was on the cheerleading squad. One day at the church office I got an emergency call from her school. She had accidentally fallen from the top of a pyramid of the other cheerleaders during practice and landed on the back of her head. To her and everyone else's amazement, she couldn't move. It took me about fifteen minutes to drive from my study at the church to the school campus. I was praying that kind of prayer all the way. "Lord, You are in charge of this situation. I have no idea what I'm going to face. You be the Lord and Master. I am trusting You in all this."

When I got to the school, they already had Charissa immobilized on a wrap-around stretcher. I slipped to my knees beside her.

"Daddy, I can't move my fingers. My feet and legs are numb," she said. "I can't feel anything in my body very well. It's kind of tingling."

At that moment, I confess I had feelings of fear. But I leaned closer to Charissa and whispered in her ear, "Sweetheart, I will be with you through all of this. But more importantly, Jesus is here with you. He is Lord over this whole event."

Her mother and I were totally helpless. We had absolutely no control over the situation or over the healing of our daughter's body. She was at the mercy of God. I can still remember the deliberateness with which I acknowledged Christ as Lord in my heart and encouraged her to do the same. Cynthia and I waited for hours in the hospital hallway as extensive X-rays were taken and a team of physicians examined our daughter. We prayed fervently and confidently.

Today, Charissa is fine. She recovered with no lasting damage. She did have a fracture, but thankfully it wasn't an injury that resulted in paralysis. Had she been permanently paralyzed, we would still believe that God was in sovereign control. He would still be Lord!

A good example of someone who sanctified Christ as Lord in his heart is Stephen. When he gave an eloquent and penetrating defense of Jesus before the Jewish Sanhedrin, this infuriated many who heard him. Their hatred raged out of control. Do you remember his response?

> But being full of the Holy Spirit, he gazed intently into heaven and saw the glory of God, and Jesus standing at the right hand of God; and he said, "Behold, I see the heavens opened up and the Son of Man standing at the right hand of God." (Acts 7:55–56)

They wouldn't listen to him. They covered their ears and rushed upon him. They drove him out of the city and violently stoned him to death.

As Stephen died, "he called upon the Lord and said, 'Lord Jesus, receive my spirit!' And falling on his knees, he cried out with a loud voice, 'Lord, do not hold this sin against them!'" (Acts 7:59–60). And then he died.

Stephen didn't deserve their savage attack. He certainly didn't deserve death. Because of that, he could have died in bitterness and cynicism. He could have died with curses on his lips. Instead, he sanctified the moment to God and died with a prayer on his lips, asking forgiveness for those who so mercilessly killed him. When those men looked into Stephen's face, they didn't find their own hatred reflected back at them; they saw the reflection of the Savior's grace and love.

Like Stephen, we need to acknowledge Christ's control over our unfair circumstances and do our best to see that He is glorified in them. That is the only thing that will bring us lasting, peaceful satisfaction.

Fourth, be ready to give a witness.

> . . . . always being ready to make a defense to everyone who asks you to give an account for the hope that is in you, yet with gentleness and reverence. (1 Pet. 3:15b)

I'm intrigued by this. Some of us are so anxious to give a witness that we press it on others even when it isn't appropriate or when the timing isn't right. But this says we are to be ready *when they ask us* to give an account. And believe me, if you are handling mistreatment or unfairness or suffering for the glory of God, people will ask.

"How do you do it?" . . . "How do you handle this?" . . . "How do you live with it?" . . . "Why is it you haven't lost your joy?" . . . "What keeps you on your feet?" . . . "Why haven't you just turned tail and run?" . . . "Why haven't you fought back?" Common questions from curious onlookers.

"Be ready to make a defense . . . to give an account." The word *defense* comes from the term *apologia*. We get our word *apology* from this Greek word. It refers to making a verbal statement of defense. And *account* comes from the word *logos*, translated elsewhere in Scripture, "the word." At such times we are to be ready to give a verbal witness . . . a gentle and yet pointed declaration of the truth.

Stop and consider. Mistreatment is a perfect platform for a witness. Your neighbors will want to know how you stay calm in the midst of it, how you go through it without strongly reacting. Your friend at work will want to know, "How do you pull it off?"

Be ready to make a defense, to give an answer, to witness to anyone who asks. Seldom will there be a more opportune time to share your faith than when you are suffering and glorifying Him through it. Others who know what you are enduring will listen. You have earned the right to be heard. But don't miss the way you should testify: "with gentleness and reverence." Wise counsel from Peter, a man who had been broken.

William Barclay gives an excellent explanation of what our "defense" and "account" should be like.

> It must be *reasonable*. It is a *logos* [account] that the Christian must give, and a *logos* is a reasonable and intelligent statement of his position. . . . To do so we must know what we believe; we must have thought it out; we must be able to state it intelligently and intelligibly. . . .
>
> His defence must be given with *gentleness*. . . . The case for Christianity must be presented with winsomeness and with love. . . . Men may be wooed into the Christian faith when they cannot be bullied into it.
>
> His defence must be given *with reverence*. That is to say, any argument in which the Christian is involved must be carried on in a tone which God can hear with joy. . . . In any presentation of the Christian case and in any argument for the Christian faith, the accent should be the accent of love.[3]

And fifth, keep a good conscience.

Here Peter digs below the surface, turning up the rich soil of inner character. And what is the precious gem he is trying to unearth? *Integrity.*

> And keep a good conscience so that in the thing in which you are slandered, those who revile your good behavior in Christ may be put to shame. (1 Pet. 3:16)

Nothing speaks louder or more powerfully than a life of integrity. Absolutely nothing! Nothing stands the test like solid character. You can handle the blast like a steer in a blizzard. The ice may form on your horns, but you keep standing against the wind and the howling, raging storm because Christ is at work in your spirit. Character will always win the day. As Horace Greeley wrote: "Fame is a vapor, popularity an accident, riches take wing, and only character endures."

There is no more eloquent and effective defense than a life lived continually and consistently in integrity. It possesses invincible power to silence your slanderers.

The Underlying and Unwavering Principle

For it is better, if God should will it so, that you suffer for doing what is right than for doing what is wrong. (1 Pet. 3:17)

Simply stated, the principle is this: Unjust suffering is always better than deserved punishment. And sometimes—though we cannot fully explain why—it is God's will that His people should suffer for doing what is right.

An old Hebrew story tells of a righteous man who suffered undeservedly. He was a man who had turned away from evil, took care of his family, walked with God, and was renown for his integrity. But suddenly, without warning, and seemingly without reason, he lost everything he had: his flocks, his cattle, his servants, his children, and finally his health. This old Hebrew story is no fairy tale. It is the real account of a real person—Job.

Though he suffered terribly, and though he could never have foreseen it himself or understood it when it happened, Job has been remembered down through the ages and to this very day as a model of patient endurance. "The patience of Job" remains one of our axiomatic phrases.

I would not wish the life of Job on anyone. But, then, I'm not God. I've never been too good at directing anyone else's life. I have a hard enough time keeping my own on track. But I have observed a few "Jobs" in my years in ministry. They come under that fourth-class condition: "If He should will it so . . . it's unlikely but possible."

If you are one of those modern-day "Jobs," don't waste your time trying to figure out *why*. Someday all will be made clear. For now, follow the five responses outlined by Peter.

Dr. Bruce Waltke was my Hebrew professor during three of my years at Dallas Seminary. He has since become something of a mentor and friend. He is a brilliant man with a tender heart for God. When I was going through a very difficult time in my senior year in seminary and wanted some answers to the *whys*, Bruce said something like this: "Chuck, I've come to the place where I believe only on very rare occasions does God tell us why, so I've decided to stop asking." I found that to be very helpful counsel. From that point on, I began to acknowledge that I am not the "answer man" for events in life that don't make logical, human sense. I'm now convinced that even if He did explain His reasons, I would seldom understand. His ways are higher and far more profound than our finite minds can comprehend. So I now accept God's directions, and I live with them as best I can. And frankly, I leave it at that. I've found that such a response not only relieves me, it gives me hope beyond bitterness.

If God has called you to be a Job—a rare calling—remember that the Lord is not only full of compassion, He is also in full control. He will not leave you without hope. He offers us His promises:

"For My thoughts are not your thoughts,
Neither are your ways My ways," declares the LORD.
"For as the heavens are higher than the earth,
So are My ways higher than your ways,
And My thoughts than Your thoughts." (Isa. 55:8–9)

When a man's ways are pleasing to the LORD,
He makes even his enemies to be at peace with him. (Prov. 16:7)

Listen to the counsel of Peter. Calmly and quietly let these five bits of counsel sink in.

- Consider yourself uniquely blessed by God.
- Do not run in panic or sit and worry.

- Acknowledge Christ as Lord even over this event.
- Be ready to give a witness.
- Keep a good conscience.

A Prayer for Hope Beyond Bitterness

Our Father, as we acknowledge Your Son as Lord, it is with a sigh, because we cannot deny the pain or ignore the difficulty of earthly trials. For some who read these words, the reality of this is almost unbearable. But being sovereign and being the One with full capacity to handle our needs, it is not beyond Your strength to take the burden and, in return, to give us the perspective we need.

Quiet our spirits. Give us a sense of relief as we face the inevitable fact that life is difficult and that there will be those rare moments when it will not be at all fair. Erase any hint of bitterness. Enable us to see beyond the present, to focus on the invisible, and to recognize that You are always there. Remind us, too, that Your ways are higher and far more profound than ours.

Thank You for the joy of this day. Thank You for the pleasure of a relationship with You and a few good, caring, loving friends. And especially, Father, thank You for the truth of Your Word that lives and abides forever. In the strong name of Him who is higher, Jesus the Lord.

AMEN

10

Hope Beyond the Creeds

Focusing Fully
on
Jesus Christ

WHEN I WAS a little boy, my family moved to Houston, where my father had been hired to work at what was called, in those days during World War II, a "defense plant." Houston is a city of industry, and during those war years many of the industries retooled in order to manufacture implements, ammunition, and equipment for the war. The particular place where my father worked built transmissions for the rugged Sherman tank and landing gears for the powerful B-17 "Flying Fortresses."

We didn't see much of my dad during those five years because he was working ten to fifteen, sometimes even eighteen, hours a day, from six to seven days a week. Since our family had only one car, which Dad used each day to drive himself and several coworkers to the shop, the rest of our family had to walk to the grocery store, to school, and to church.

The closest church was a Methodist church at the end of our street. I still remember sitting in those wooden pews almost every Sunday. And every Sunday, as part of the worship-service liturgy of that particular Methodist church, we recited the Apostles' Creed.

I don't remember one sermon that was preached during those five years. I cannot recall any church-sponsored event that made an impact on me. But I clearly remember repeating the Apostles' Creed. In fact, I memorized that statement of faith in a matter of months simply because we repeated it Sunday after Sunday. You, too, may know these words well:

> I believe in God the Father Almighty, maker of heaven and earth;
> And in Jesus Christ, His only begotten Son, our Lord, who was conceived by the Holy Spirit, born of the Virgin Mary, suffered under Pontius Pilate, was crucified, dead and buried; He descended into hell; the third day He rose again from the dead; He ascended into heaven, and sits at the right hand of God the Father Almighty; from thence He shall come to judge the living and the dead.
> I believe in the Holy Spirit, the holy catholic church, the communion of saints, the forgiveness of sins, the resurrection of the body, and the life everlasting. Amen.

Even though I was only a small boy when I recited the creed, there were two statements in it that troubled me. My first concern was, "I believe in the holy catholic church." I knew our family wasn't Catholic, so how could I keep saying I believed in the Holy Catholic Church? Then, at some point, a youth worker explained to me that catholic (small "c") really meant "universal," so what we were really saying was, "I believe in the universal church." No problem.

More difficult to resolve, however, was the part where we said that Jesus Christ "descended into hell." That troubled me. There was nobody around who could answer that for me, not even my mother. Interestingly, it was almost twenty years later in a Greek class in seminary that I experienced a flashback to those days as a little boy in the Methodist church. We were digging into the text at the end of 1 Peter 3, and I came across the verse that described in Scripture what I had stated as a little boy but had never understood.

Let me remind you of the last five verses in 1 Peter 3:

For Christ also died for sins once for all, the just for the unjust, in order that He might bring us to God, having been put to death in the flesh, but made alive in the spirit; in which also He went and made proclamation to the spirits now in prison, who once were disobedient, when the patience of God kept waiting in the days of Noah, during the construction of the ark, in which a few, that is, eight persons, were brought safely through the water. And corresponding to that, baptism now saves you—not the removal of dirt from the flesh, but an appeal to God for a good conscience—through the resurrection of Jesus Christ, who is at the right hand of God, having gone into heaven, after angels and authorities and powers had been subjected to Him. (1 Pet. 3:18–22)

Isn't that a grand statement of faith? It's almost like another creed that we might recite in church from Sunday to Sunday.

Our Example

I have found in my study of the Bible that one of the best rules to follow if I'm going to understand any particular section of Scripture is to look at the whole scene (the context) before I try to work my way through each verse. Sort of like looking at the forest before examining the trees.

Following that rule, we first need to answer a primary question: What's the main subject of this paragraph? As you may recall from the subject we dealt with in chapter 9, it is unjust suffering. Remember the words of Peter?

For it is better, if God should will it so, that you suffer for doing what is right rather than for doing what is wrong. (1 Pet. 3:17)

If unjust suffering is the main subject, what's the point of the whole paragraph? Clearly, it is this: blessings follow suffering for well-doing.

Now at this point, immediately after Peter has written verse 17, the Spirit of God prompts him to mention the One who best exemplifies that truth. Who in every believer's mind would best exemplify blessing following unjust suffering? Obviously, Christ. And that's why Peter at verse 18 says, "For Christ." He doesn't say so, but we could insert in parentheses, "As an example."

> For Christ (as an example) also died for sins . . . the just for the unjust, in order that He might bring us to God . . . .

What is the blessing that came to us following Christ's unjust suffering? Our salvation. And what was the blessing for Him, personally, following His unjust suffering? His resurrection. That is stated at the end of verse 20.

The focus of attention here is Jesus Christ, not the recipients of the letter or those who would read it centuries later. It is Jesus Himself. He alone is the focal point. Look at this great statement of faith regarding the Lord Jesus.

Verse 18: He "died for sins." That's His *crucifixion*.

Verse 19: "He . . . made *proclamation*."

Verse 21: "through the *resurrection* of Jesus Christ."

Verse 22: "who is at the right hand of God . . . after angels and authorities and powers had been subjected to Him." That's *exaltation*.

What we have here, in brief, is a survey of the crucifixion, proclamation, resurrection, and exaltation of the Lord Jesus Christ. Peter is clearly and openly highlighting some major doctrines related to Jesus Christ. So far, so good. But the paragraph also includes a digression (see verses 19–21).

Sometimes while writing a letter you'll mention a subject that is important to you, which reminds you of something not as pertinent as the subject but since it completes the picture, you add it. It might take another paragraph to do so, or it might just take a sentence or two. In this instance, Peter completes the overall thought regarding Christ by adding some details . . . things seldom mentioned elsewhere in the Bible. In fact, there are two knotty issues here that every serious student of the New Testament struggles with. One of them has to do with Christ's "descent into hell" (see verses 19–20), and the other has to do with what appears to be an affirmation of baptismal regeneration, "baptism now saves you" (verse 21)—more about these later.

Our Entree

Having considered the overall context, then, let me come to the central theme of the passage. Look back again at verse 18. This is one of those all-encompassing verses that states the gospel in its briefest and most concentrated form. That concentrated statement concerning the Lord Jesus is beautiful: "Christ also died for sins once for all." We don't have to relive or redo the death of Christ. We don't have to anticipate His dying another time or several other times. He has died "once for all." It was the death of all deaths, permanently solving the sin problem.

When Christ came, He was the perfect substitute for sin. And as a lamb without spot and without blemish, He hung on the cross and died. His blood became the one-and-only, all-sufficient payment to God for sins. The anger of God was satisfied, because Christ's payment for sin settled the account, once for all. Furthermore, all the debt against us was wiped away as Christ's righteousness was credited to our account. It wasn't fair for Him to die. He was just. He died, "the just for the unjust."

You may not know it, but you're mentioned (by implication) in Scripture on a number of occasions. And here is one of those times. Your name could appear in the place of the words "the unjust."

Let me state it in my case: "For Christ also died for sins once for all, the just for Chuck Swindoll. . . ."

Or you could put *your* name there: "The just for [your name]."

Why did He do it? "In order that He might bring us to God." One very careful student of the New Testament calls this "an entree." Our Lord Jesus Christ, in dying on the cross, provided us with "an entree" into heaven. He gave us access. As a result of His death, the access to heaven is now permanently paved. It is available to all who believe in the Lord Jesus Christ.

He "was put to death in the flesh, but made alive in the Spirit." So what is He doing now? "He is at the right hand of God." Maybe you didn't know that—a lot of people don't know what Christ is currently doing. He has ascended from this earth, and He has gone back to the place of glory in bodily form. (He is the only member of the Godhead who is visible. God the Father is in spirit form. God the Spirit is in spirit form. The only visible member of the Trinity is the Lord Jesus Christ.) He sits at the right hand of God making intercession for us. He's praying for us. He is moved by our needs; He is touched with the feelings of our infirmities. He is there for us, His people, and He is interceding for us. Since He is at the right hand of God, there is no question of His place of authority.

The Apostles' Creed is correct when it says, "He ascended into heaven and sits at the right hand of God; from thence He shall come to judge the living and the dead." He will come to judge both, and that judgment awaits His return to this earth. What powerful truths are here! Peter knew his theology!

His Proclamation

All that is fairly clear . . . now the tough part. First of all, let's address the subject of Jesus' descent, as the creed calls it, "into hell." Referring to the Lord Jesus Christ, Peter tracks His itinerary following His crucifixion.

> . . . in which also He went and made proclamation to the spirits now in prison, who once were disobedient, when the patience of God kept waiting in the days of Noah, during the construction of the ark, in which a few, that is, eight persons, were brought safely through the water. (1 Pet. 3:19–20)

What in the world does that mean? When exactly did this occur? Who were these spirits that He visited? And what is the "proclamation" that He made? Good questions.

Let me draw upon your knowledge of the Scriptures and ask you to remember a scene back in the days before the Flood. It's recorded in the sixth chapter of Genesis. (When you have time, you may want to go back and read it.) We are told that during this period the depravity of men and women reached an all-time high. Their wickedness was so severe that it grieved the heart of God—He was sorry He had even created humanity!

> Then the LORD saw that the wickedness of man was great on the earth, and that every intent of the thoughts of his heart was only evil continually. And the LORD was sorry that He had made man on the earth, and he was grieved in His heart. (Gen. 6:5–6)

If you read this in the context of the first four verses of Genesis 6, you learn of an amazing and seldom-mentioned series of events that had happened. There was sexual cohabitation at that time between spirit beings and women on this earth. It is believed that during the antediluvian era—the time prior to the Flood—these spirits came in bodily form and somehow had intercourse with human women. As a result, a generation of supernatural beings were born—admittedly a strange phenomenon rarely mentioned by preachers and therefore seldom taught to Christians.

When the Flood came, it put an end to that heinous lifestyle and that freakish generation. Also, God's judgment fell upon those spirits who cohabited with women, and He placed them in a location called, in the original, *Tartarus*. It was a special place, described here as "a prison." It was there Jesus made His victorious proclamation.

What was this proclamation? I find it helpful to know that this is not the word used for proclaiming the gospel. Rather, it is a word, *kerusso*, used to describe someone "heralding" a statement. It denotes one who proclaims that the king has made a decision or that someone is declaring a certain edict—actually, it can refer to a proclamation of any kind. Jesus openly and forthrightly proclaimed that He had fulfilled His mission. He had died for the sins of the world. The work of salvation was accomplished.

When I put all of this together, I come to the following conclusion. I believe verses 19 and 20 describe the time immediately after Jesus died. His body was taken down from the cross and placed in a grave, but His inner being, His soul and spirit, descended into the shadowy depths of the earth, into the place of Tartarus (the creed calls it "hell"), where the antediluvian wicked spirits were imprisoned. Once there, He proclaimed to them His victorious death over sin and His power over the enemy, Satan himself. It was this proclamation that caused them to realize their work of attempting to corrupt and confuse the human race had been in vain. All of their attempts to sabotage the cross, to keep it from happening, were null and void. He went to that place to proclaim His victory at Calvary.

Our Faith

That brings us to the second question raised by verse 21, where we read: "Baptism now saves you." What does this mean?

Again, we can't ignore the context. First, we must understand that the Flood is in Peter's mind. He has just said so (verse 20). It was the Flood that brought death and destruction to those who didn't believe. It was also the water that brought deliverance to those who did—eight of them. Imagine that. Though there were multiple millions of people, only eight got in the ark. Along with the animals, only eight human beings believed and lived!

It was the ark floating on the water that got them through the Flood, which became a beautiful picture to the early church. In fact, the ark was frequently used to describe salvation. Today, we see the cross as our ark. It is our way to life. It is the way we get through the death-like world about us. Thus, baptism became another beautiful expression or picture of just such a deliverance from death—through the water.

Baptism symbolizes deliverance, just as the ark did. In fact, look at the words in parentheses, which in my Bible, the New American Standard version, are placed between dashes:

And corresponding to that, baptism now saves you—not the removal of dirt from the flesh, but an appeal to God for a good conscience—through the resurrection of Jesus Christ. (1 Pet. 3:21, italics added)

Baptism doesn't cleanse anyone, either literally or symbolically. It does not cleanse us externally, as a bath does; nor does it cleanse us within. But, indeed, it is our appeal to God for a good conscience. That which saves us is faith in the Lord Jesus Christ, and this is what is illustrated beautifully in baptism as we come out of the water. The Living Bible, in 1 Peter 3:21, offers a fine paraphrase of this parenthetical section.

(That, by the way, is what baptism pictures for us: In baptism we show that we have been saved from death and doom by the resurrection of Christ; not because our bodies are washed clean by the water, but because in being baptized we are turning to God and asking Him to cleanse our *hearts* from sin.)

Now you understand why in a baptismal service each candidate testifies personally to his or her faith in Jesus Christ. Nothing in the waters of baptism cleanses the flesh or the soul, but the water does illustrate what has already happened in the life of the redeemed.

Practical Principles

As we wrap up our thoughts here, let me mention a couple of very practical principles we can draw from this section of Peter's letter.

First, when unjust suffering seems unbearable, remember the crucifixion. I know you've heard that before, but it is something we cannot be reminded of too often. It can be a wonderful comfort. It is remarkable how focusing on the Lord Jesus Christ's body hanging on the cross as a payment for sin really does help alleviate the pain in my life. About the time I start thinking my suffering is terribly unjust I turn my attention to what He endured; that does a lot to ease or even erase any sense of bitterness or resentment within me. And so, when unjust suffering seems unbearable, remember the crucifixion.

Second, when the fear of death steals your peace, remember the resurrection. There is nothing quite like the hope we derive from our Lord's resurrection. Every Easter we celebrate it. In fact, every Lord's Day we're to be reminded of it. Certainly the Apostles' Creed reinforces it. Which brings us back to where we began.

I believe in God the Father Almighty, maker of heaven and earth;

And in Jesus Christ, His only begotten Son, our Lord, who was conceived by the Holy Spirit, born of the Virgin Mary, suffered under Pontius Pilate, was crucified, dead and buried; He descended into hell; the third day He rose again from the dead; He ascended into heaven, and sits at the right hand of God the Father Almighty; from thence He shall come to judge the living and the dead.

I believe in the Holy Spirit. . . .

Despite the all-encompassing truths contained in these concise words, the most personal and crucial part of the creed is the first two words, "I believe." Without them, it's just a statement someone originated—a statement many worshipers recite every week without ever having any kind of personal relationship with Christ. A body of bright, godly, religious-minded men honed that statement to put in simple form the salient features of our faith. But without our faith, it's still just a creed—a statement of *their* faith. What we need most is a firm hope beyond any creed we may recite.

The question is, do I *believe* the truth of that statement? Do you *believe* it? If you do, there is hope for you beyond it or any other creed. And that hope is a heavenly home reserved for you.

A Prayer for Hope Beyond the Creeds

*Father, thank You for the truth of Your Word, for its clarity
and its simplicity. And, Lord, because it is so exact, there isn't*

any reason to doubt. We do believe. Freely and willingly and gratefully, we believe.

But our belief goes beyond any creed . . . far beyond any statement originated by humans, no matter how godly or sincere. With great faith, our Father, we believe in the Lord Jesus Christ who died for us. We believe He suffered unjustly. We believe His payment was sufficient to wash away sins. Our sins. And now that He has been raised and ascended, our Father, we believe that He is alive, interceding for us, and is coming again.

Because of Christ's crucifixion, proclamation, resurrection, and exaltation, give us a sense of peace when we face death. Give us a sense of hope when we suffer unjustly. Remind us that heaven is our ultimate hope. I pray in His matchless name, with great anticipation.

AMEN

Hope Beyond the Culture

How to
Shock the
Pagan Crowd

STEPPING ONTO FOREIGN soil and into the midst of another language and culture for the first time in one's life can be an uneasy experience.

It happened to me while I served in the Marine Corps in the late 1950s. Our troopship had carried us across the Pacific, and my comrades and I were about to step onto Japanese soil. We eagerly anticipated being on land after such a long time at sea. For many of us, it was our first visit to a foreign country. We were surging with excitement, imagination, and every other emotion you could think of due to those seventeen days on the same ship. We were ready!

Before we left the ship, however, our company commander called all of us together. He stood in front of us, looked around at the group, and then, staring deeply into our eyes, he said loudly and sternly, "I want all of you men to remember that for the first time in your lives, *you are the foreigners*. This is not your country or your culture. Now you are the minority. These are not your fellow citizens. They do not speak your language. They know nothing of your homeland except what they see in you."

It was one of those "behave yourself" pep talks, but it went beyond that. Our commander was also saying, "You, as individuals, are representing the entire United States. Don't blow it! Don't become another example of 'the ugly American.' Act in such a way that the Japanese people will gain a good impression of your country and what America must be like. Make us proud, not ashamed." Those words rang in my ears for many days.

As Christians, we face a similar situation. Since our citizenship is in heaven, planet Earth is really not our home. For us, it is foreign soil. We are citizens of another realm. We belong to the kingdom of God. Consequently, we need to be on our best behavior; otherwise, people will get a distorted perception of what our homeland is like. As a result of our behavior, they will either be attracted to or repelled by heaven, the place we call home.

The old gospel song is still right on target.

> This world is not my home.
> I'm just a passin' through.
> My treasures are laid up
> Somewhere beyond the blue.[1]

It's true! But it's easy to forget. Maybe this is a good time to be reminded . . . we live in a pagan culture, surrounded by people who embrace a pagan philosophy and a pagan way of life.

Just consider the latest Broadway fare being ecstatically hailed as "the breakthrough musical of the nineties" . . . "the most exuberant and original American musical to come along this decade." The play, *Rent*, is set "among the artists, addicts, prostitutes, and street people of New York City's East Village." The leading characters are "a drug-addicted dancer in an S&M club who is suffering from AIDS" and a rock singer who is HIV positive. "AIDS is the shadow hovering over all the people in *Rent*, but the musical doesn't dwell on illness or turn preachy; it is too busy celebrating life and chronicling its characters' effort to squeeze out every last drop of it." Those characters are a gay teacher, a transvestite, and a lesbian attorney, among others.[2]

A friend of mine would call that "being mugged by reality," but that's the world we live in. Our earthly culture is pagan to the core. Let's not forget that God has left us here on purpose. We're here to demonstrate what it is like to be a member of another country, to have a citizenship in another land, so that we might create a desire for others to emigrate. Our mission is to create a thirst and an interest in that land "beyond the blue."

In 1 Peter 4:1–6, the apostle gives some marching orders to Christian soldiers who are stationed on this foreign soil. He opens the subject by addressing a Christian's behavior before a watching world with the connective word, *therefore*.

> Therefore, since Christ has suffered in the flesh, arm yourselves also with the same purpose. (1 Pet. 4:1a)

Careful students of the Scriptures pay close attention to words, especially words that connect main thoughts. The word *therefore* is a word of summary that connects what the author is about to write with what he has just written. And what has he just written? Look back at 3:18 and 22.

> For Christ also died for sins once for all, the just for the unjust, in order that He might bring us to God, having been put to death in the flesh, but made alive in the spirit . . . . who is at the right hand of God, having gone into heaven, after angels and authorities and powers had been subjected to Him. (1 Pet. 3:18, 22)

Christ has suffered and died on our behalf, the just for the unjust. *Therefore* . . . Do you see how it all ties together? Since Christ has died for our sins, the just for the unjust, and since He has been seated at the right hand of God, and since all authorities have been subjected to Him, and since He has suffered in the flesh, *therefore*, we should arm ourselves with the same purpose He had when He was on this earth.

I like the way one scholar amplifies what was meant by "arm yourselves."

> [Peter] exhorts the saints to arm themselves with the same mind that Christ had regarding unjust punishment. . . . The Greek word translated "arm yourselves" was used of a Greek soldier putting on his armor and taking his weapons. The noun of the same root was used of a heavy-armed footsoldier who carried a pike and a large shield. . . . The Christian needs the heaviest armor he can get to withstand the attacks of the enemy of his soul.[3]

This word picture offers a blunt reminder that we Christians are not living on this earth as carefree tourists. We are not vacationing our way to heaven. We are soldiers on raw, pagan soil. Everywhere around us the battle rages. The danger is real, and the enemy is formidable. Christ died not only to gain victory over sin's dominion but to equip us for that fight—to give us the inner strength we need to stand against it. Therefore . . . we are to arm ourselves with the strength that Christ gives because our purpose in life is the same as His.

Martyn Lloyd-Jones's warning bears repeating:

> Not to realize that you are in a conflict means one thing only, and it is that you are so hopelessly defeated . . . you do not even know it—you are unconscious! It means that you are completely defeated by the devil. Anyone who is not aware of a fight and a conflict in a spiritual sense is in a drugged and hazardous condition.[4]

Transformation: Remarkable Difference in the Christian Life

Several years ago when I was preaching on First Peter, a man called me and said, "I just want to let you know, Chuck, that the message of First Peter is happening in my life." When I asked what he meant, he went on to describe some difficulties he'd been going through. As he did, he said, "The things you've been talking about recently came back to my mind."

He said he had felt a heaviness in his spirit . . . he called it "a dark oppression." We prayed together about his situation. A few days later when I saw him after the Sunday morning service, he said, "I just want you to know the cloud has lifted." He had sensed the beginning of deliverance from his private war in the realm of darkness.

Many of you live in the competitive jungle of the business world, and some of you may work for a boss who asks you to compromise your ethics and integrity. Pressured by the tension between pleasing your boss, who can fire you or demote you or just make your life difficult, and your commitment to Christ, you need the inner resources to stand firm. "Arm yourselves with the same purpose" is certainly applicable for you. The good news is this: you have it! The provision Christ gives will be sufficient for such a stress test.

> Therefore, since Christ has suffered in the flesh, arm yourselves also with the same purpose, because he who has suffered in the flesh has ceased from sin, so as to live the rest of the time in the flesh no longer for the lusts of men, but for the will of God. For the time already past is sufficient for you to have carried out the desire of the Gentiles, having pursued a course of sensuality, lusts, drunkenness, carousals, drinking parties and abominable idolatries. (1 Pet. 4:1–3)

Fortunately those who are "in Christ" have been transformed. This transformation brings with it at least four benefits that Peter mentions. We no longer serve sin as our master (verse 1b); we don't spend our days overcome by desires as we once did (verse 2b); we now live for the will of God (verse 2b); we have closed the book on godless living (verse 3).

We've sowed our wild oats. Most have had enough time to see the end result of this lifestyle of loose living. Peter calls that lifestyle "the desire of the Gentiles."

Before Christ entered our lives, we had no power to withstand sin. When temptation came along, we yielded. We were unable to do otherwise. When the weakness of the flesh appeared, we fell into its trap. Though we may have looked strong on the outside, we had no inner stability. But when Christ took up residence in our lives, He gave us strength so that we could cease serving sin as a master. (Romans 6 is a wonderful section of scripture on this subject.) Because Christ now lives within us, we have been released from sin's control. We are no longer enslaved to sin. We've been freed!

Observe how "the will of God" (verse 2) is contrasted with "the desire of the Gentiles" (verse 3). Notice, too, how "the desire of the Gentiles"—the old habits, practices, associations, places of amusement, evil motives, and wicked pastimes—are all scenes from the past. The list sounds like your average *Animal House* on some college campus:

- sensuality
- lusts
- drunkenness, carousals, and drinking parties.

The original terms are vivid. *Sensuality* refers to actions that disgust and shock public decency. *Lusts* go beyond sexual promiscuity and involve sinful desires of every kind, including the lust for revenge and the lust for money (greed). *Drunkenness, carousals, and drinking parties* describe a whole miserable spectrum of pleasure-seeking consumption, from wanton substance abuse to wild sexual orgies. And we thought these things represented twentieth-century wildness! When it comes to a shameless, pagan lifestyle, nothing is new.

What is so liberating about our relationship with Christ is that He fills the void in our lives that we once tried to fill with all that garbage. With the void filled, the gnawing emptiness that accompanied it is gone too. And with the emptiness gone, we no longer crave the things we used to crave.

That's where Christians are different from the world. That's where we stand out. That's where the light shines in the darkness. And invariably the darkness reacts to such a light.

★

Reaction: Angry Astonishment from the Unsaved World

While we may live in this foreign land, far from our ultimate home, we live for the will of God. As a result, there is a marked contrast between our lifestyle and the lifestyle of the pagans—people who do not know the Lord—around us. And when we don't partake of that lifestyle, we are considered "weird."

Make no mistake about it. If we don't participate in that lifestyle, you and I are weird. *We are really weird!* And they notice it. Again, Peter's words are as relevant as this morning's newspaper. Look how he describes the reaction of the unsaved world.

> And in all this, they are surprised that you do not run with them into the same excess of dissipation, and they malign you. (1 Pet. 4:4)

Talk about the relevance of Scripture! Peter sounds like he is alive today! Any lifestyle of restraint, no matter how tactful we try to be, makes unbelievers uncomfortable. Sometimes it makes them defensive and angry, causing them to lash out at us as though in living our lifestyle we were judging theirs. I experienced this among fellow marines on numerous occasions—those who spent their lives in a realm of lustful drives and carousals and one drinking party after another. We see the same thing today in the after-hours of the corporate world. It's all part of the so-called "happy hour."

Beyond their discomfort and defensiveness, of course, is the inner emptiness they live with, day in and day out, the natural result of a life of lust and debauchery. What emptiness there is when the party's over and everybody goes home! They're left with the horrors of the sunrise and a head-splitting hangover, the guilt and even some shame as they crawl out of somebody else's bed, wondering what disease they might have gotten this time. And there's always that dark-brown taste in their mouth.

It's a horrible lifestyle! I don't care how beautiful the commercials look, it stinks! It doesn't last an hour, and it's anything but "happy!" But if they haven't any power to overcome it, the only thing they have to look forward to is the next "happy hour." And if they play the music loud enough and if there's enough booze and drugs, they think they can drown their troubles. Another lie of the Enemy. He's got a thousand of them.

Do you get the picture? The time already past is sufficient for you to have had your fill of "the desire of the Gentiles." You've tasted it. You've known it firsthand. But when Christ transformed your life, He filled the void and took away a lot of that drive. It's borderline miraculous, in fact, especially if He's enabled you to quick-kick an addiction.

But when that happens, you stand out like a sore thumb in your neighborhood . . . in your university dorm . . . at the office party. You're noticed. Even without saying a word, you're noticed. Even if you very quietly and graciously request a 7-Up instead of a cocktail, the word gets out.

Why? Because you've been transformed. You're no longer a helpless slave to sin. You're not overcome by your glandular drives. You are now interested in God's will; you have closed the door on godless living. And the pagan sits up like a doberman, eyes open, ears perked. "What in the world is wrong with Sam? Remember when we used to run around together? Now he's got religion." Or, "Suzy's gotten really weird . . . became a Bible-thumper. She was once a ton o' fun. Now she's Miss Goody Two Shoes. Next thing we know she'll become a televangelist!"

Brace yourself for such reactions if you're getting serious about Jesus and you've just broken off from a wild bunch of friends. The fact is, He is transforming you. Your old friends will not only be surprised, even shocked, at your new lifestyle, they might also actively ridicule and unjustly judge you for it as well. Expect it . . . it'll keep you from being "mugged by reality." You've just begun to experience hope beyond the culture.

Sometimes I wonder if they are really saying, "Look, misery loves company. If I'm gonna be this miserable, then you need to be miserable with me—like you used to. I don't want to do this alone."

The terrible irony of our unsaved friends' judgment is that they will themselves face the ultimate judgment . . . but that's the *last* thing they want to hear. Nevertheless,

> . . . they shall give account to Him who is ready to judge the living and the dead. (1 Pet. 4:5)

Some of you have discovered that your close friends have changed now that you're in Christ. Regarding that, let me first warn you, and then I want to commend you.

First, I want to warn you about spending all of your time with Christians. If your entire circle of friends and acquaintances is nothing but Christian people, you will really get idealistic and unrealistic about the world. You really will get weird! Furthermore, how are the lost going to hear the gospel if all the saved stay clustered, sipping their 7-Ups and reviewing Bible verses together? We need to guard against our tendency to be with believers exclusively. The lost, deep down, are curious . . . and we need to be nearby when they start asking questions.

Second, I commend you for changing your circle of close friends. Some of your former friends do you no good, especially if you cannot withstand the lifestyle temptations they bring your way. Most people who fall into gross sensuality do not do it alone. They're usually prompted or encouraged by other people. You need to be wise and tactful about it . . . but before long, your change in lifestyle needs to be communicated.

There's a line in a country-western song sung by Alabama, "I'm Not That Way Anymore," that says it well: "Time has closed yesterday's door."

That's the way it is with Christians. You're not like that anymore. The fact is, my friend, Christ has closed yesterday's door. The way you are is different from the way you *were*. You won't be able to hide it . . . nor should you want to. Hopefully, however, you'll become a magnet of understanding, drawing others to the Savior rather than an offensive porcupine, driving them away.

Ideally, we want to be a fragrant aroma of Christ, winsomely attracting the unsaved to Jesus, the Savior. But Scripture, as well as our own experience, teaches us that what is fragrant to some is occasionally fetid to others.

Live an Authentic Lifestyle

The point of all of this? Once again we're back to the theme of Peter's letter: finding hope beyond unjust suffering. Enduring hardship. Seeing the reasons behind unfairness. Simply because you desire to live for Christ you will have people who once really enjoyed your company now talking about you behind your back, wondering if you've lost it . . . gone over the deep end. That is tough to take, because you know they aren't representing you fairly. But it's to be expected, looking at life strictly from their pagan perspective.

In fact, the longer I live, the more I see the value of having a thick skin but a tender heart. If you do, their cutting comments won't get to you. Furthermore, you won't feel the need to "set the record straight." Those maligning and ugly words kind of glance off, freeing you from an attack-back reaction.

Let me tell you what's happening. The pagan crowd will never tell you this, but down deep inside, many of them envy you. They wonder, *How does she do that?* . . . *How can he no longer do these things?* . . . *I'm not able to stop.* . . . *What in the world has made the difference?* And when you get them alone, it's remarkable how many of them will really listen as you tactfully and graciously tell them what has transformed your life. That's the joy of being left on foreign soil. You get to acquaint them with a life that is now yours and can be theirs, if only they'll genuinely and completely turn their lives over to Christ.

But let me warn you: Don't beat them up for their lifestyle. Nobody ever got saved because he was rebuked for his drinking or shamed for taking drugs or sleeping around. To tell you the truth, I'm surprised more in the pagan world don't do more of that to fill the void. So don't make an issue of their lifestyle. They can't help it.

They have no power to stop. Let grace and mercy flow. Relax . . . and leave the rebuking to the Lord.

Admittedly, there will be times that it will get to you . . . and you'll find yourself reaching the end of your tether.

One of the Bible teachers who used to lecture at Dallas Seminary when I was a student on campus was as tough as nails yet pure in heart. On one occasion while he was in the city to deliver a series of lectures, he went to a local barbershop to get a haircut. (A friend of mine happened to work there and overheard this conversation.) The barber, who didn't have the faintest idea who the man was, began talking about various issues of the day, giving his opinion, as barbers usually do. He peppered every phrase with an oath or a four-letter word. The teacher bit his lip as long as he could. Finally, he grabbed the barber's arm, pulled him around to the side of the chair, and looked the man right in the eye. Quietly but firmly he pulled on his own earlobe and said to the barber, "Does that look like a sewer?" The rest of the haircut was done in absolute silence.

I realize that such a reaction may not win many friends . . . but I understand the frustration.

Sometimes I just get my fill of it, too, don't you? Especially something as prevalent as blasphemous profanity. Throughout my months in the marines, I listened to that stuff till I thought I'd scream, so it's not that I haven't heard it before or that I can't handle it. I just occasionally reach the place where I have to say something. If it's handled right, even *that* can result in an opportunity to witness.

But in the final analysis, you cannot clean up anybody's lips until you've cleaned up his or her heart. And, ultimately, that's Christ's job. He's a master at it. So you stand it as best you can, realizing these are all simply signs of being lost. Such habits make the inhabitants of this pagan culture appear rough and rugged, but down inside they're often frightened little children. And they're scared to DEATH of death and what it might mean—whether they believe that to be nothingness or judgment.

Thankfully, the believer doesn't have to fear any of that. Our judgment is behind us . . . but their judgment is in front of them. Christ took our judgment, and He bore it on a cross. And He's given us the power He had now that we're in Christ. Remember the words of Isaac Watts?

> Am I a soldier of the cross?
> A follower of the Lamb?
> And shall I fear to own His cause
> Or blush to speak His name?

> Sure I must fight if I would reign:—
> Increase my courage, Lord!
> I'll bear the toil, endure the pain,
> Supported by Thy Word.

It's a great hymn. Even though it is almost 275 years old it is really up to date! It applies to businessmen and women who are facing verbal from their fellow employees. It applies to athletes today who refuse to live the lifestyle of the others on the team. It applies to those in the military service who love Christ but serve alongside those who don't. You're a soldier of the cross. What more can you expect? You're not a martyr. You're just taking a few verbal punches. It's good for you and me to be talked about like that. It drives us back to our knees before Christ and reminds us of our dependence on Him.

All believers owe it to themselves to read at least a portion of *Foxe's Book of Martyrs*, which traces the martyrdom of Christians throughout the centuries and demonstrates how viciously the world can act in its attempt to extinguish the light of Christlike character. There are some scenes that will make you shake your head. Talk about paying a price for one's faith!

Do you, like the brave saints of old, want to stand out like a bright light against the darkness of your world? Do you want to shock the pagan crowd? You don't need flamboyance or fanaticism. You don't need to fly a giant JESUS SAVES flag over your house or to wag your finger and rail against others' lifestyles. You don't need put-down bumper stickers or T-shirts with big, bold messages. You certainly don't need to rely on sermons or shame. What you do need to do is live differently. And you need to be aware of the consequences of Christlike living. For some it may mean persecution; for others, it could mean death . . . as it did for John Hus, a Bohemian Reformer accused of heresy.

Prior to his appearance before the Council of Constance in 1414, Hus wrote to one of his friends,

> I shall not be led astray by them to the side of evil, though I suffer at His will temptations, revilings, imprisonments, and deaths—as indeed He too suffered, and hath subjected His loved servants to the same trials, leaving us an example that we may suffer for His sake and our salvation. If He suffered, being what He was, why should not we?[5]

I love that last sentence: "If He [Christ] suffered, being what He was [perfect, the ideal model], why should not we?"

You want to know how to really shock the pagan crowd? *Live an authentic Christian life.* No fanfare, of course. No need to wave John 3:16 signs at a ball game . . . or embarrass your colleagues by loudly spouting Bible verses to your unsaved friends at work. That's offensive, not winsome. They're lost, but they're not ignorant or beyond feelings. Just keep three things in mind—three simple but workable suggestions, not at all complicated.

First, continue living for Christ. That means being different on purpose. Let your integrity speak for itself. When opportunities occur for you to speak of your faith, do so graciously and kindly.

Second, expect to be misunderstood. Don't be surprised when ugly things are said or false accusations are made or twisted statements are passed along about your life. Your life will prove that they're wrong. Relax . . . and let the Lord defend you.

Third, keep your eyes fixed on Christ. Stay on a steady course. Keep on being different. Live an authentic godly life, and you'll blow the world away. This is especially true if you keep a healthy sense of humor! They will not be able to stay quiet about the difference between your life and theirs.

Never forget, this world is not your home . . . you're just passin' through.

A Prayer for Hope Beyond the Culture

Lord God, Your Son has closed yesterday's door, and we don't live like that anymore. Not because we've been strong and good and noble but because You have transformed our lives, Lord. You've changed our course of direction. Even though You've left us on foreign soil, we have a home in the skies. And sometimes we get pretty homesick!

Hear the prayers of Your people as we call out to You. Give us self-control on those occasions when we're tempted to moralize and put people down. Make us aware that a godly life, alone, preaches the most unforgettable message the unsaved can be exposed to. Help us remember that we're soldiers away from home, living in a culture that's lost its way and is in desperate need of Jesus Christ. Keep us easy to live with, strong in faith, unbending in our convictions, yet full of grace toward those who are bound by sin and captured by habits they cannot break. Enable us to shock this pagan culture with lives that are real, that still have fun, and that ultimately glorify You, O God . . . as Jesus did. In His name I pray.

AMEN

12

Hope Beyond Extremism

Marching Orders for Soldiers of the Cross

WHEN TIME IS short, things get urgent. And simplified. Something about the brevity of time introduces both urgency and simplicity to the equation of life.

When a friend or family member tells you he or she hasn't long to live, your time together becomes more urgent and your discussions return to the basics. When a hurricane is blowing in or the black funnel of a tornado looms on the horizon, you don't pull out a Monopoly game or begin preparing a gourmet meal. It's all about survival, and survival calls for simplicity. If you're driving to church and you see an accident happen and you are the only one there to assist, you don't worry about being late or about getting your Sunday clothes dirty or bloody. The situation is urgent. The mission is simple.

Jesus Himself modeled this for us. As long as there was time, He took time—to eat with His disciples, to train His disciples, to minister to individuals whenever and whatever their need. He would linger over a meal with friends. He would sit back and enjoy relaxed moments with close friends like Mary and Martha and Lazarus. But when the hour of the cross drew near, urgency gripped His voice and His attention focused on those few priorities that were in front of Him.

> From that time Jesus Christ began to show His disciples that He must go to Jerusalem, and suffer many things from the elders and chief priests and scribes, and be killed, and be raised up on the third day. (Matt. 16:21)

At that point, Peter—the same disciple who had just given a wonderful statement of faith—rebuked Jesus, saying, "God forbid it, Lord!" (v. 22), telling Him not to talk like that—that such things should never happen to Him.

Such audacity! Peter was planning on a kingdom. He was not planning on a cross.

But Jesus turned and said to Peter,

> Get behind Me, Satan! You are a stumbling block to Me; for you are not setting your mind on God's interests, but man's. (Matt. 16:23)

And then Jesus said to His disciples, in effect, "Let's get down to basics. Let's get down to the essentials, the simple requirements of discipleship."

> If anyone wishes to come after Me, let him deny himself, and take up His cross, and follow Me. (Matt. 16:24)

He was down to urgent, simple demands. Why? Because the hour was short.

During World War II, Winston Churchill encouraged and supported the people of Britain through endless dark hours. He made many memorable statements and speeches, but one rings particularly apt here. He was speaking to Parliament just after London had been bombed to smithereens, and he sensed the people were losing heart. It seemed as though Churchill never did. He must have had low moments, but his speeches don't reveal it. So he said to those people in Parliament, who were probably quaking in their spirits, "This is not the end. This is not even the beginning of the end. But it is, perhaps, the end of the beginning."

Jesus said the same sort of thing to His disciples, telling them, in essence, "When you see these things occurring, it isn't the end."

> And you will be hearing of wars and rumors of wars; see that you are not frightened, for those things must take place, but that is not yet the end. (Matt. 24:6)

If you live in the light of Christ's return each day of your life, it does wonders for your perspective. If you realize that you must give account for every idle word and action when you stand before the Lord Jesus, it does amazing things to your conduct. It also makes you recognize how many needless activities we get involved in on this earth. Sort of like rearranging the deck chairs on the *Titanic*. Don't bother! Don't get lost in insignificant details! He's coming soon! Recognize the urgency and the simplicity of the hour!

Peter seems to have gotten the message. He was a practical man. Prior to following Christ, his life consisted of very tangible, practical things: boats, nets, fish, supporting a family, hard work. And then he met the hard realities of the Master. Consequently, we should not be surprised that his personality and his prose followed suit.

Being neither scholarly nor sophisticated, Peter had little interest in theoretical discussions. Life was not meant to be talked about but lived out. If an urgent situation demanded action, Peter wasn't one to call for a committee to study the alternatives. He cut through the bureaucratic red tape and got down to business.

So when the big fisherman took up his pen to write about suffering saints, he cut to the chase. And when he addressed the reality of the end times, he summed up a game plan in a one-two-three fashion rather than waxing eloquent on the options. Pragmatic Peter at his best offers four commands and one goal to those of us who live nearer than ever to Jesus Christ's return. Simple. Direct. No beating around the bush.

Marching Orders for Soldiers of the Cross

Now remember, Peter is dealing with suffering saints, men and women who are being taken advantage of, men and women who can see no relief in sight. During days of suffering we often become even more intensely aware of the end—the final outcome, whatever that may be. And in writing to his brothers and sisters suffering in the trenches of persecution, Peter himself intensified his focus as he deployed the troops and briefed them for battle.

Observe the urgency and the simplicity in the words that follow.

> The end of all things is at hand; therefore, be of sound judgment and sober spirit for the purpose of prayer. Above all, keep fervent in your love for one another, because love covers a multitude of sins. Be hospitable to one another without complaint. As each one has received a special gift, employ it in serving one another, as good stewards of the manifold grace of God. Whoever speaks, let him speak, as it were, the utterances of God; and whoever serves, let him do so as by the strength which God supplies; so that in all things God may be glorified through Jesus Christ, to whom belongs the glory and dominion forever and ever. Amen. (1 Pet. 4:7–11)

Suddenly, with no relief in sight, Peter introduces the one thought that always helps people hope again: *the end of all things.* In doing so, he not only adds urgency to the moment, he also simplifies the game plan. He leaves his reader with four direct commands to obey and one clear goal to pursue in the midst of it all.

Four Commands to Obey

First, he says: *Use good judgment and stay calm in a spirit of prayer.*

> The end of all things is at hand; therefore, be of sound judgment and sober spirit for the purpose of prayer. (1 Pet. 4:7)

Be of sound judgment. Be of sober spirit. Be calm. Today we might say: Stay cool. Don't be filled with anxiety. Don't panic. Face life realistically. Realize God is in control.

Sober does not mean the opposite of *intoxication*. It means the opposite of living in a frenzy, in a maddening kind of extremism. For example, don't try to set dates regarding Christ's coming. That's an extreme reaction to prophecy. Here's another. Don't panic, as if things were out of control. And another. Don't be filled with anxiety. Don't quit your job, put on a white robe, and sit on some rooftop waiting for Christ to come back. That's extremism. And don't think you have to know every detail of the end times in order to feel secure, as Warren Wiersbe, in his book *Be Hopeful*, rightly notes.

Early in my ministry, I gave a message on prophecy that sought to explain everything. I have since filed away that outline and will probably never look at it (except when I need to be humbled). A pastor friend who suffered through my message said to me after the service, "Brother, you must be on the planning committee for the return of Christ!" I got his point, but he made it even more pertinent when he said quietly, "I've moved from the program committee to the welcoming committee."

I am not suggesting that we not study prophecy, or that we become timid about sharing our interpretations. What I am suggesting is that we not allow ourselves to get out of balance because of an abuse of prophecy. There is a practical application to the prophetic Scriptures. Peter's emphasis on hope and the glory of God ought to encourage us to be faithful today in whatever work God has given us to do (see Luke 12:31–48).[1]

The secret of maintaining the balance and calmness that my friend writes about is prayer. We don't need to parade through the neighborhood wearing a big signboard that says REPENT! THE END IS NEAR! Instead, Peter says, "Be calm, use sound judgment, and do it in a spirit of prayer." Such wise, reasonable counsel from a man who once was neither. Before, Peter would panic so easily. Now . . . he urges prayer.

We don't dream our way into eternity. We pray and watch. In fact, there is nothing quite like prayer to sharpen our awareness, to keep us alert, to make us more discerning, and yet to remind us who has the controls.

When I see a person who is all out of sorts, full of anxiety, on the ragged edge of extremism, I'm looking at a person who isn't spending enough time in prayer. Prayer calms your spirit, yet it doesn't make you indifferent. On the contrary, it reminds you: He has everything in control. Use sound judgment. Stay calm.

Let me go back, again, to yesteryear . . . a dark night in a garden near the edge of Jerusalem. Peter was one of the disciples who was told by the Lord in the Garden of Gethsemane to "Wait here and pray, while I go over there to pray." But when the Lord returned to them, he found Peter asleep. Sound asleep. And He said to Peter and the others, "Couldn't you have waited with Me for this hour?" That must have stung, especially since Peter was the disciple who, a few hours earlier, had bragged about his loyalty and commitment. You think Peter doesn't write with a sense of urgency and understanding here? You think he doesn't remember that rebuke? "I left you to pray, and you fell asleep." That's why Peter could add those words to his letter with a real sense of understanding.

Prayer was what allowed Jesus to submit to His arrest, and the lack of it was what made Peter resist.

The second command is: *Stay fervent in love for one another.*

Above all, keep fervent in your love for one another, because love covers a multitude of sins. (1 Pet. 4:8)

"Fervent" speaks of intensity and determination. It comes from the Greek word *ektene*, which literally means "strained." It's used to describe athletes straining to reach the tape at the finish line or stretching high enough to clear the bar.

When lean sprinters race around that last turn and are pressing for the tape, they'll get right to the end and then they'll deliberately lean forward. I've even seen runners fall on the track because they're pushing so hard to reach the tape before their competitors. That's "being fervent." It's the idea of stretching yourself. Those who do the long jump leap into the air and throw their feet forward as they stretch every muscle of their body to reach as far as they can. The same is true with the high jump or the pole vault. Athletes stretch to the utmost to reach the limit. All those actions describe "fervent." But here Peter applies it to love, not athletic events. He tells us to have fervency in our love for one another.

If there was ever a time when we needed to stay close, it is today. Don't play into the hands of the Enemy. This is the time to stick together. Don't waste precious time criticizing other Christians. Don't waste time criticizing another church or some pastor. Spend your time building up one another, staying fervent in love.

Look at how the verse begins: "Above all"—more than anything else. And then Peter gives them a compliment. He says, "Keep fervent." This implies that they already were fervent. Keep at it, he says. You're doing it already, so stay at it.

Because my schedule is already so full of regular responsibilities connected to both Dallas Seminary and our radio ministry, Insight for Living, I rarely accept invitations to minister elsewhere. But Cynthia and I have made an exception to this when it comes to the Christian Embassy in Washington, D.C., and a retreat they sponsor for many of the flag officers in the Pentagon and various members of Congress who serve on Capitol Hill.

On several occasions we have returned to this significant group of men and women to minister to them and spend some time getting to know their world better. Most of these generals and admirals are academy graduates who have spent many years in military leadership, some of which were during wars on land and at sea. The politicians are also seasoned veterans who have invested their time and effort serving the people of their states, standing for what is right and representing causes worth fighting for. Most who attend the retreat are Christians. They operate their lives on the cutting edge of our times. What amazing, admirable people they are!

As a result of our annual reunions, my wife and I have been able to see how these men and women have grown spiritually in their Christian walk (yes, there are *many* Christians in high places!). What stands out most eloquently to the two of us is their love for the Lord and their love for one another . . . as well as for us. Rather than being sophisticated and distant, these dear folks *fervently* express their love and *fervently* demonstrate compassion.

Peter would have been proud of them. They "keep fervent"—they stay at it, year after year.

If there's ever a time to stretch our love for one another to the limit, it's during the end times—*it's now*. And what is it that reveals this love? Forgiveness.

When Peter says that "love covers a multitude of sins," he's alluding to the principle in Proverbs 10:12:

> Hatred stirs up strife,
> But love covers all transgressions.

Nothing is a more compelling witness than the love and unity that Christians exhibit toward each other, and nothing is more disturbing or disruptive to the unity of the body than Christians who are stirred up against each other and experiencing strife. Nothing is a poorer witness.

Don't think the unsaved aren't watching when we bash our brothers and smash our sisters! They *love* it when we can't get along with each other. It makes news. They love to quote one Christian who is after another Christian. It's as if the journalist or pundit leans back and says, "Aha! Gotcha!"

Mahatma Gandhi, the Indian nationalist leader, once said, "I like your Christ but I don't like your Christians. . . . They are so unlike your Christ."[2]

What a rebuke. I deeply regret that his words are so often true!

And what is Christ like? He is characterized by love and forgiveness. An insightful person once said, "We are most like beasts when we kill. We are most like men when we judge. We are most like God when we forgive."

Let me repeat something I said earlier: I have never met a person who didn't have a reason to blame someone else. Every one of us can blame somebody for something that has happened in our lives. But don't waste your time. What we need most is a steady stream of love flowing among us. Love that quickly forgives and willingly over-looks and refuses to take offense.

Moffatt states that this passage "is a warning against loving others by fits and starts. It is a plea for steady affection, persisting through the irritations and the antagonisms of common life in a society re-cruited from various classes of people."

Some people are so easy to love that you just naturally fall into their arms. But others are so hard to love, you have to work overtime at it. There's something about their natures that's abrasive and irri-tating. Some are the opposite of magnets. They repel. Yet even they need our love, perhaps more than the others. How very important that we "stretch fervently" to love each other!

The third command Peter gives is: *Be hospitable toward one another.*

Be hospitable to one another without complaint. (1 Pet. 4:9)

Underscore the words "one another." It is the same phrase Peter uses in verses 8 and 10, and it doesn't refer just to those who are lov-able or friendly or fun to be with. It refers to all who are in the body of Christ, even the unlovely and unfriendly.

Another little phrase tacked onto the end of verse 9 is a crucial one when it comes to showing hospitality—"without complaint."

What do you complain about when it comes to hospitality? About the time and trouble it takes? The energy it requires to invite some-one into your home and entertain them? The expense? The mess? The clean-up? It's true that hospitality takes effort and planning, and it interrupts your privacy. But hospitality is never a problem when our priorities are in place, when love opens the door.

"True love is a splendid host," said the famous English preacher John Henry Jowett. In his excellent volume on the epistles of Peter, he writes with eloquence:

There is love whose measure is that of an umbrella. There is love whose inclusiveness is that of a great marquee. And there is love whose comprehension is that of the immeasurable sky. The aim of the New Testament is the conversion of the umbrella into a tent and the merging of the tent into the glorious canopy of the all-enfolding heavens. . . . Push back the walls of family love until they include the neighbor; again push back the walls until they include the stranger; again push back the walls until they comprehend the foe.[3]

When was the last time you entertained someone who was once your enemy? There is something about hospitality that disarms a foe.

Since the former head coach of the Dallas Cowboys, Tom Landry, has served on our Dallas Seminary board for many years, I have had the opportunity to get to know the man. My respect for him has grown, not lessened, as time and our mutual roles have linked us together.

I was told a wonderful story about Coach Landry that illustrates the level of his Christian love for others. Years ago, the late Ohio State coach, Woody Hayes, was fired for striking an opposing player on the sidelines during a football game. The press had a field day with the firing and really tarred and feathered the former Buckeye coach. Few people in America could have felt lower than he at that time; he not only lost control in a game and did a foolish thing, but he also lost his job and much of the respect others had for him.

At the end of that season, a large, prestigious banquet was held for professional athletes. Tom Landry, of course, was invited. Guess who he took with him as his guest? Woody Hayes . . . the man everyone was being encouraged to hate and criticize.

The quality of our love is determined by its inclusiveness. At the one extreme there is self-love; but at the other extreme there is philanthropy! What is the "tense," the stretch, of my love? What is its covering power? . . . *"Love covereth a multitude of sins."* Not the sins of the lover, but the sins of the loved! Love is willing to forget as well as to forgive! Love does not keep hinting at past failures and past revolts. Love is willing to hide them in a nameless grave. When a man, whose life has been stained and blackened by "a multitude of sins," turns over a new leaf, love will never hint at the old leaf, but will rather seek to cover it in deep and healing oblivion. Love is so busy unveiling the promises and allurements of the morrow, that she has little time and still less desire to stir up the choking dust on the blasted and desolate fields of yesterday.[4]

Are you hospitable . . . I mean *really* hospitable? Do you make room in your life to be interrupted? Do you allow people to be drawn by the magnet of your love because of Christ's presence? One more question: Would you have done what Tom Landry did?

There's something about sitting down with someone over a cup of coffee or a sandwich. Something about taking time . . . making time. I am fully aware that there are times when we need to be alone. *But not all the time.*

Have you ever opened your home for a traveling college choir or other strangers who need lodging? Remember how Jesus and His disciples always stayed in private homes when they traveled and preached? Is your home open to those in need?

I can't tell you how many times people have told me what a blessing it has been to open their homes. Many of these were folks who felt a little uneasiness or apprehension at first, letting strangers invade their most private domain. But there's an unforgettable job connected with hospitality. Folks never forget the warmth of a home . . . the joy of kids around the table . . . the pleasure of meaningful conversation. A friend of mine traveled with a musical group during her college days, over thirty years ago, and she says she can still remember homes she stayed in and Christian hospitality demonstrated on her behalf. Such expressions of hospitable love gave her numerous opportunities to hope again during the three decades that followed.

From the perspective of the guest, however, hospitality is not something we should ever abuse. Apparently this was happening in the first century, largely by people who were living unbalanced lives in response to prophetic teaching. They reasoned, "Since Christ is coming soon, why bother working? Why not liquidate all assets and live off others?" The apostle Paul speaks directly to this heretical reasoning in 2 Thessalonians 3:6–15. Peter speaks to it more indirectly in the next two verses by promoting involvement in the local church and the exercise of spiritual gifts.

In fact, verses 10–11 contain his fourth command: *Keep serving one another.*

As each one has received a special gift, employ it in serving one another, as good stewards of the manifold grace of God. Whoever speaks, let him speak, as it were, the utterances of God; whoever serves, let him do so as by the strength which God supplies. (1 Pet. 4:10–11a)

Do you know, fellow Christian, that you have at least one—perhaps more than one—spiritual gift? Several sections of the New Testament talk about these gifts—special abilities God has given the body of Christ with which we minister until He returns. Each gift we have needs to be used in serving one another. That is how we become good stewards of our gifts.

Here's a list of some of the places where spiritual gifts are listed. Look them up and examine your own life in the light of them.

- Ephesians 4:11–12
- 1 Corinthians 12:28–30
- Romans 12:6–8

Make a list of these gifts and then ask yourself, where do I best fit in this list? You might approach it the way you would approach applying for a job. If you don't find your spot right away, keep pursuing it. Keep thinking about it. Ask other Christians—those who know you and have been around you during various experiences—what they think your gifts are. Then try them out. Put them into action as you serve others. You'll discover what you do well . . . then do that throughout the balance of your life.

But note the warning in verse 11 that goes along with exercising our gifts.

Whoever speaks, let him speak, as it were, the utterances of God; whoever serves, let him do so by the strength which God supplies. (1 Pet. 4:11)

When we speak, we shouldn't be voicing our own opinions and

philosophies about life; we should be speaking "the utterances of God." And when we serve, we shouldn't be doing so in our own strength but "by the strength which God supplies."

When you speak for Christ, base your words on the Scriptures, not on your own opinions. You will be forever relevant if you do. And you'll never lack for a message! When you serve, serve in His strength, not your own. That way, He gets the glory.

Many of you have the gift of teaching. You can teach children, teenagers, or adults. You can lead a Bible study at work or in your neighborhood.

Many gifted people also serve behind the scenes, doing vital but perhaps not-so-visible jobs. You help, encourage, and pray. The body would be crippled without the many parts that are able to serve, to help, to encourage.

Others have the gift of showing mercy, of ministering to those who are laid aside or suffering. You visit hospitals and nursing homes. You spend hours listening, caring.

Still others have the gift of evangelism. With ease they communicate the gospel and lead people to Christ. It's a natural part of their lives. God uses them again and again as He harvests souls for His kingdom.

But all of these gifts—there are many others—have one thing in common. They come alive in serving other people. So get out of your own tiny radius. It will do wonders for your depression, for your pity parties, for those times when you sit alone and want to sing, "Woe is me. Woe is me. Woe is me." (That's a very dull song.)

Think of it this way: When we employ our spiritual gift(s), others benefit. Others are encouraged. Others gain fresh hope. Interestingly, so do we!

A Goal to Pursue

Verse 11 ends with a purpose clause that reveals the logical reason we should obey these four commands. Why stay calm and pray? Why be fervent in love? Why demonstrate hospitality? Why serve one another?

. . . so that in all things God may be glorified through Jesus Christ, to whom belongs the glory and dominion forever and ever. Amen.

In everything, God gets the glory. How many church conflicts could be resolved if God's glory were everybody's goal? How many egos would be put in their place if God's glory—not human glory—were at stake? How much extremism would be avoided if we did all for the greater glory of God?

"But that's so basic," you may say. "Why even spend time on it?" Because without that, your teaching becomes drudgery, your helping leads to burnout, your evangelism becomes either frenetic or self-glorifying.

When we keep His glory uppermost in our minds, it's amazing how much else falls into place. Since He gets the glory, we're more comfortable leaving the results with Him in His time. Since He gets the glory, our umbrella of love expands to cover others. Since He gets the glory, it's easier for us to show hospitality to others, for we're ultimately serving Him. Since He gets the glory, exercising our gifts is not a pain but a privilege. The benefits are endless when the glory goes to God!

A Concluding Thought

Let me bring this to a close by returning to a comment I made at the beginning of the chapter: Time is short. You and I don't have forever to put these things into action. Whatever needs to be simplified, *let's simplify*! Whatever it takes to remind us of the urgency of the hour, *let's do it*! Time is short. That means we need to move the words off the pages and slide them into our lives—*now*.

Need a little boost? One of the most encouraging promises in all the New Testament comes to mind:

For God is not unjust so as to forget your work and the love which you have shown toward His name, in having ministered and in still ministering to the saints. (Heb. 6:10)

Read that again, only this time *with feeling*.

Your effort is not in vain. Your love will not be overlooked. Your ministry—whatever it includes—will be rewarded. You will maintain a wonderful balance in the process. Keep your eyes on the Shepherd as you open your heart to His flock. And remember, He gets all the glory!

> The Bride eyes not her garment,
>   But her dear Bridegroom's face;
> I will not gaze at glory
>   But on my King of grace.
> Not at the crown He giveth
>   But on His pierced hand,
> The Lamb is all the glory
>   Of Immanuel's land.[5]

A Prayer for Hope Beyond Extremism

Our Father, keep us calm and cool in a spirit of prayer. Give us a fervency in our love for one another that has a way of covering a multitude of sins. Find us to be hospitable people who take time, who are accessible, available, and caring. And, Lord, as we put our gifts into action, use us to give a hope transplant to someone really in need. And may we do it all for Your glory.

May these words make a difference in the way we live, and may the difference be so significant that it is noticed, so that others have cause to give You praise . . . for You, alone, deserve all the praise and all the glory. I pray in Jesus' wonderful name.

AMEN

13

Hope Beyond Our Trials

"When through Fiery Trials . . ."

I am progressing along the path of life in my ordinary, contentedly fallen and godless condition, absorbed in a merry meeting with my friends for the morrow or a bit of work that tickles my vanity to-day, a holiday or a new book, when suddenly a stab of abdominal pain that threatens serious disease, or a headline in the newspapers that threatens us all with destruction, sends this whole pack of cards tumbling down.

At first I am overwhelmed, and all my little happinesses look like broken toys. Then, slowly and reluctantly, bit by bit, I try to bring myself into the frame of mind that I should be in at all times. I remind myself that all these toys were never intended to possess my heart, that my true good is in another world and my only real treasure is Christ. And perhaps, by God's grace, I succeed, and for a day or two become a creature consciously dependent on God and drawing its strength from the right sources. But the moment the threat is withdrawn, my whole nature leaps back to the toys.[1]

How eloquently C. S. Lewis's words from his penetrating book, *The Problem of Pain*, describe the role of trials in our lives. Such is human nature, and such is the nature of trials and tribulations.

Remember the words from the old hymn: "When through fiery trials my pathway shall lie, Thy grace all sufficient shall be my supply"? Well, fiery trials and painful ordeals aptly describe what most of us must pass through at one time or another in life . . . some, more frequently than that.

Peter addresses Christians who are going through just such desperate circumstances.

> Beloved, do not be surprised at the fiery ordeal among you, which comes upon you for your testing, as though some strange thing were happening to you. (1 Pet. 4:12)

Ever had anything like that in your life? Not simply trials, but what Peter calls "fiery ordeals"? If so, ever heard this kind of advice on how to handle such trials?

> . . . but to the degree that you share the sufferings of Christ, keep on rejoicing; so that also at the revelation of His glory, you may rejoice with exultation. (1 Pet. 4:12–13)

Probably not!

Practical Truths about Trials

Peter was not the only apostle who wrote to Christians who were strangers and aliens in a foreign land. James addressed his letter to those who were "dispersed abroad"—another group of people far away from home, and not by choice. This also applies to those of us who are strangers in this world below and those of us forced to live in the midst of circumstances that are not our choice. To all these, James wrote:

> Consider it all joy, my brethren, when you encounter various trials, knowing that the testing of your faith produces endurance. And let

endurance have its perfect result, that you may be perfect and complete, lacking in nothing. (James 1:2–4)

From these three verses we learn a great deal about trials. Four specifics stand out.

First, trials are common for Christians to encounter.

Don't ever let anybody tell you (and don't you dare tell anybody else!) that when you become a Christian your trials are over, from then on, "you can just trust Christ and fly away like birds toward the heavens." Get real! Notice that James says *"when* you encounter," not "if." If you're experiencing trials, you're the rule, not the exception. If you have just gotten through one, take heart; there are more around the corner! Going through a trial is one thing that pulls us together. We've got that in common.

Second, trials come in various categories.

They may be physical, emotional, financial, relational, or spiritual. They may slip in unexpectedly and knock on the door of your business, your church, or your home. They may arrive at any time or at any season. They may come suddenly, like a car accident or a natural catastrophe. They may be prolonged, like a drawn-out court case or a lingering, nagging illness. Trials can be public in nature or very private. They can be directly related to our own sin, the sin of others, or not related to sin at all.

A trial can be like a rock hitting the water. You don't cause the jolt, but you're impacted by it. You're just standing there, and suddenly the smooth lake of your life surges into giant waves and almost drowns you.

Frankly, some trials seem to blow in absolutely without reason. My brother, Orville, encountered something like that when a hurricane named Andrew blew through the community where he lived in south Florida a few years ago. It tore and ripped and screamed its way through, tearing his house apart. He had a great attitude, though. He called and said, "What an experience! It really did a lot of damage. But the good news is it tore down everyone's fences, so now we'll get to meet our neighbors."

Third, trials put our faith to the test.

No matter what its source or intensity, there's something about suffering that simplifies life and draws us back to the basics. Invariably, especially during a time of intense trial, I go back to my theological roots. I go back to what I really believe. I return to the elementals such as prayer and dependence, like getting quiet and waiting on God. I remind myself, God is sovereign . . . this is no accident. He has a plan and a purpose. Those thoughts give us hope beyond our trials.

Trials put our faith to the test as well as stretch our confidence in Him. They force us back to the bedrock of faith upon which our foundation rests, and this becomes a refining and necessary process.

Fourth, without trials, there could not be maturity.

James says we experience trials so that we may be become "perfect and complete" (verse 4), like a plant that has matured to its maximum growth and fruitfulness. That, he says, is the "perfect result" of "endurance."

Most often, because of the discomfort, the pain, or the hardship, we try to cut our trials short—to put an end to them. Before long, we're resenting them to such an extreme that we'll try anything to escape, to run from them. Instead, James says, *endure* the trial; let it come to completion. When it does, you'll be a better person for it.

Remember the words of song writer Andrae Crouch? "If I'd never had a problem, I'd never know that He could solve them. I'd never know what faith in God could do."[2]

Few feelings compare with the joy of watching God step in and solve a problem that seems impossible.

Some trials are slight, brief, and soon forgotten. Others hang on and weigh heavily upon us. They leave us exhausted and sometimes bench us on the sidelines. The latter category is what Peter is talking about when he writes of "the fiery ordeal." This is no slight struggle Peter has in mind. It's an "ordeal" . . . one from which we cannot find relief.

Biblical Strength for Fiery Ordeals

What do you do when the rug is jerked out from under you? Do you panic? Do you doubt the Lord's love? Do you trust in God to get you through the tough times? Perhaps this is a good time to go back to God's truth and read His counsel written by Christ's closest companion while He was on earth.

We can learn a lot from Peter, a man who spent over three years with Christ and who, as we have seen, both pleased Him and failed Him. In fact, most of us should be able to identify with Peter. He'd been an eager disciple, defending his Master against all comers. He'd also been a failure, denying his Lord in the pinch . . . not once, but three times, back to back. Through all this, God reshaped him into a powerfully effective man of God. The vacillating, impulsive, overly zealous Simon was changed and broken, emerging as "Peter, the rock." Now, he writes out of his maturity and seasoned wisdom, under the guidance of the Holy Spirit. These are not theoretical terms the old fisherman tosses around but words shaped in the blast furnace of his own afflictions and pain. Read them again with that in mind:

> Beloved, do not be surprised at the fiery ordeal among you, which comes upon you for your testing, as though some strange thing were happening to you; but to the degree that you share the sufferings of Christ, keep on rejoicing; so that also at the revelation of His glory, you may rejoice with exultation. (1 Pet. 4:12–13)

He begins this section by addressing his letter to the "Beloved." This is truth directed to the beloved of God . . . in other words, truth for the believer only. This is information just for the Lord's people. It's got your name on it. Think of your name here in place of unnamed folks who were "beloved" to Peter.

He then goes on to tell us how to react to this more intense form of suffering.

How to React

Interestingly, our first response to an ordeal is usually surprise—"I can't believe this is happening." But Peter says, *"Don't be surprised."* The lack of surprise will enable us to remain calm.

Life is a schoolroom. In it, we encounter pop quizzes and periodic examinations. You can't have a schoolroom without tests—at least I've never seen one. I've never seen anyone earn a high school diploma or college degree without taking exams. The same is true in graduate school. Throughout the educational process our knowledge is assessed on the basis of examinations. The curriculum of Christlikeness is much the same. Our Christian maturity is measured by our ability to withstand the tests that come our way without having them shake our foundation or throw us into an emotional or spiritual tailspin.

The wonderful thing about God's schoolroom, however, is that we get to grade our own papers. You see, He doesn't test us so He can learn how well we're doing. He tests us so *we* can discover how well we're doing. So we can put our own benchmarks on our level of maturity.

Back in 1984, when you were tested, perhaps you didn't do too well. Maybe others didn't know that, but you did. In 1989, you did better. In 1993 an even tougher test confronted you, and you did rather well. As you grade your own paper, you can see the improvement. The testing of your faith reveals your increasing level of maturity.

Many years ago a good friend of mine, Dr. Robert Lightner, who is a long-time member of the theology department faculty at Dallas Seminary, was involved in a terrible plane crash. He was in a single-engine plane that flipped over during takeoff. He was badly injured and bruised beyond recognition. His wife, Pearl, said that when she first saw him at the hospital, "I looked at this black mass of flesh, and I didn't even know who he was." Thankfully, he did recover, and today he is a living testimony of the grace of God through that ordeal. "I learned things I didn't know I needed to learn," I heard him say on one occasion. Isn't that the way it usually is? What hope this should give us!

Don't be surprised when a test comes. Even though you don't know you need to learn certain things, God knows, and He sovereignly determines, "Now's the time." God is molding you into the image of His Son, and that requires trials. So, first off, don't be surprised.

But the second reaction Peter says we are to have is even more amazing: *"Keep on rejoicing."*

I hear some of you saying right now, "What! Are you kidding me? We're talking trials, right?" Right. "We're talking fiery ordeals, correct?" Correct. "And you're telling me to keep on rejoicing?" Wrong! I am not telling you this—*God* is telling you to keep on rejoicing. "To the degree that you share the sufferings of Christ, keep on rejoicing."

James put it another way: "Consider it all joy" (1:2). Why? Because trials enable us to enter into a more intimate partnership with Christ, and if we endure them faithfully, we will receive a future reward (see Phil. 3:10 and James 1:12). Along with that, our trials here give us at least a glimpse into the magnitude of Christ's suffering for us.

Trials, therefore, become a means to a greater end: a deeper relationship with Christ on earth and a richer reward from Him in heaven.

You and I would never know such fellowship were we not put to the test. Some of you are going through trials right now that have dropped you on your knees. At the same time those trials are pulling you closer to the Lord than you've ever been in your life. That ought to bring rejoicing. You'll be more closely linked to Him. Some of the mysterious themes threaded through His Word will become clearer because you have been leveled by some unexpected affliction or enduring persecution or facing misunderstanding.

Furthermore, you can rejoice because you will receive a future reward.

As I write these words, it happens to be getting close to graduation time, those days when diplomas, honors, and special awards are granted. Each year at Dallas Seminary we have a special chapel service near spring graduation during which we distribute special awards to those who have earned them. Our "Awards Chapel" is one of the highlights in our academic year.

Did you know that in the future when we stand before Christ our Lord, there will be special awards distributed by Christ Himself? They are called crowns. And did you know that there is a unique crown given to those who endure suffering? Read James 1:12:

> Blessed is a man who perseveres under trial; for once he has been approved, he will receive the crown of life, which the Lord has promised to those who love Him.

God has a crown reserved for those who endure the fiery ordeal. My brother, Orville, will have one. Bob Lightner will have one. My wife deserves one for living with me for over forty years! And many of you will have earned that crown as well.

In case you still are not convinced that trials can bring rejoicing, I want you to look at a classic case in point, recorded at the end of Acts 5. There we find that the apostles, including Peter, had just been flogged and ordered to stop preaching about Jesus. (Pause and imagine that bloody, brutal scene.) Look at what they did while they were still bleeding from the beating.

> So they went on their way from the presence of the Council, *rejoicing* that they had been considered worthy to suffer shame for His name. And every day, in the temple, from house to house, they kept right on teaching and preaching Jesus as the Christ. (Acts 5:41–42, italics added)

These men were people just like us . . . not super saints, but real-life folks. Only difference—they refused to let their "fiery ordeal" steal their joy or deter their objective. An attitude of joyful gratitude opens our minds to glean lessons from suffering we would not otherwise learn.

So much for how to react. Now let's focus on what to remember.

What to Remember

First: *Trials provide an opportunity to draw upon maximum power.*

> If you are reviled for the name of Christ, you are blessed, because the Spirit of glory and of God rests upon you. (1 Pet. 4:14)

We must remember that we are never closer to Him, never more a recipient of His strength, than when trials come upon us. This is especially true when we are reviled for the name of Christ. One of the highest privileges on earth is to suffer for His sake. At those times the Holy Spirit draws near, administers strength, and provides an abiding presence of God's glory. If you recall the account of Stephen's martyrdom in Acts 7:54–60, which we read earlier, you'll see that's exactly what happened to him.

The second thing to remember is: *Sometimes our suffering is deserved.*

> By no means let any of you suffer as a murderer, or thief, or evildoer, or a troublesome meddler. (1 Pet. 4:15)

If our "fiery ordeal" comes as a result of our own sinful behavior, then we're not suffering for the glory of God; we're merely reaping the consequences of wrongdoing we have sown. As the prophet put it, when we "sow the wind" we "reap the whirlwind" (Hos. 8:7).

Sometimes we deserve the treatment we're getting. We deserve the punishment or the loneliness, the brokenness and pain. And notice that "troublesome meddlers" are listed right along with such reprehensible sinners as murderers, thieves, and other evildoers. That ought to get our attention! The term that is translated here as "troublesome meddler" literally means "one who oversees others' affairs." In other words, a busybody. Ouch! Suffering the consequence of being a busybody brings no one applause or affirmation, only a whirlwind of anguish.

The third thing Peter wants us to remember is: *Most suffering should in no way cause us to feel shame.*

> But if anyone suffers as a Christian, let him not feel ashamed, but in that name let him glorify God. (1 Pet. 4:16)

I have met folks who are ashamed that they are going through trials. Many apologize for their tears, almost as if they are embarrassed to weep. I've even known people who felt they needed to apologize because they had sought help from a professional to get through a very personal "fiery trial." Others feel ashamed because their walk of faith has caused a negative reaction. No need!

Instead of shame, we should feel honored when we suffer for our Lord. It is a privilege to bear wounds for the One who was "pierced through for our transgressions" and "crushed for our iniquities" (Isa. 53:5). That's the way Peter and the other apostles must have felt when they left the Sanhedrin, bloody but unbowed.

Self-imposed guilt and shame can be terrible taskmasters in our souls, whipping us down and keeping our spirits from soaring. Such guilt and shame have no place in our lives!

The fourth thing we need to remember is: *Suffering is usually timely and needed.*

> For it is time for judgment to begin with the household of God.
> (1 Pet. 4:17a)

One of the most difficult things to keep in mind is that we need to be purged and purified. After the fact we usually look back on the test or trial and say, "I really needed that," or, "The benefits that came from that are incredible," and we can name three or four insights we would not have gained had we not gone through the valley. Such perspective enables us to hope again.

Purging is not only needed among individuals in the household of God, but also in the church as a whole—locally, denominationally, or otherwise. Sometimes the "house of God" needs not only daily dusting but a thorough spring cleaning. Remember this the next time a scandal surfaces in the church. Don't get disillusioned. It's just God refusing to let us sweep the dirt in His house under the rug.

Sometimes we're rolling along happily, meeting our budgets, running our programs, yet there is no sense of zeal or revival among God's people. It's sort of sit, soak, and sour time for the flock. Congregations can get spoiled. With a smug shrug, they can be saved, sanctified, galvanized, and petrified. Church attendance becomes business as usual. What a miserable existence! About then God comes in and sweeps things clean as He works *through* the church in a timely and needed way.

Now look at the perspective Peter adds:

> If it begins with us first, what will be the outcome for those who do not obey the gospel of God? And if it is with difficulty that the righteous is saved, what will become of the godless man and the sinner? (1 Pet. 4:17b–18)

The latter part of that verse is a quotation from Proverbs, which the New International Version renders this way:

> If the righteous receive their due on earth,
>   how much more the ungodly and the sinner! (Prov.11:31)

In other words, if you think your testing is tough, imagine how tough it is for the person going through trials *without* the Lord. I'll be candid with you: I am absolutely at a loss to know how the lost person makes it when the bottom drops out of his or her life. This person has no Savior. No foundation. No borders. No absolutes. No reason to go on. Nothing to hold on to . . . no one to turn to . . . no way to calm his or her fears . . . no purpose for living . . . no peace in dying. Can you imagine that kind of hopelessness? If you can't, just look at what's happening in the world around you.

Imagine being without the Lord and hearing the worst kind of news from your physician or from the policeman who knocks on your door late at night. Though we, too, are rocked back on our heels by such things, as Christians we immediately turn to our sovereign absolute, our firm foundation, and we lean hard on Him. And if these earthly trials are hard for the lost to bear, imagine their having to face *eternal* judgment!

Which brings me to the fifth thing to remember: *There is no comparison between what we suffer now and what the unrighteous will suffer later.*

If we who are justified by faith have "fiery ordeals" in our walk now, imagine the inferno the lost will face in the literal fiery future that awaits them. Turn to Revelation 20:10–15 and take a few minutes to read and then imagine the horror. Talk about fiery ordeals. Talk about a reason to give your life to Christ.

Thus far, Peter has told us how to react and what to remember when we are going through fiery trials. Now he encourages us by telling us *on whom we are to rely*.

> Therefore, let those also who suffer according to the will of God entrust their souls to a faithful Creator in doing what is right. (1 Pet. 4:19)

Entrust. What a wonderful word! It is a banking term in the original text, meaning "to deposit." One commentator has said, "The idea is that of depositing treasure into safe and trustworthy hands."[3] When it comes to trials, we deposit ourselves into God's safekeeping, and that deposit yields eternal dividends.

When you deposit money in the bank, there's a limit on how much the FDIC will insure under one account ownership; usually it's about $100,000. But our infinite God has no limits. Millions upon multimillions of Christians can deposit themselves in His care, and He will make every one of them good. He will hold every one of us securely. No one can declare Him bankrupt of compassion or care. God will never say to anyone, "Sorry. We're full up. That's the limit. We can't guarantee more." You can entrust your soul to this "faithful Creator."

Interestingly, the Greek word that is translated "entrust" here is the same one used by Jesus on the cross when He said, "Father, into Thy hands I *commit* My Spirit" (Luke 23:46, italics added). When we entrust our souls to God during our trials, we are following Jesus' example on the cross when He deposited His soul into the care of the Father. Again, I remind you, those without faith in Christ have no one in whom they can "entrust" their souls.

Personal Growth Through All the Heat

Tests are never wasted. God never says, "Oops, made a mistake on that one. I shouldn't have given you that. I meant that for Frank.

Sorry, Bob." It's as if the Lord has our name on specific trials. They are specifically designed for us, arranged with our weaknesses and our immaturity in mind. He bears down and doesn't let up. And we groan and we hurt and we weep and we pray and we grow and we learn. Through it all we learn to depend upon His Word. You see, there really is hope beyond our trials.

The furnace of suffering provides not only light by which to examine our lives but heat to melt away the dross. Just as famine and financial ruin brought the prodigal son to his senses, so our trials bring us to our senses and draw us into the embrace of our Father. The common response to trials is resistance, if not outright resentment. How much better that we open the doors of our hearts and welcome the God-ordained trials as honored guests for the good they do in our lives.

> Thus the terrible necessity of tribulation is only too clear. God has had me for but forty-eight hours and then only by dint of taking everything else away from me. Let Him but sheathe that sword for a moment and I behave like a puppy when the hated bath is over—I shake myself as dry as I can and race off to reacquire my comfortable dirtiness, if not in the nearest manure heap, at least in the nearest flower bed. And that is why tribulations cannot cease until God either sees us remade or sees that our remaking is now hopeless.[4]

As C. S. Lewis implies here, trials are not an elective in the Christian-life curriculum; they are a required course. Trials 101 is a prerequisite to Christlikeness. But sometimes the tests are so gruelingly comprehensive that our tendency is to drop the course entirely. Especially if we feel abandoned by God.

If that's how you're feeling in the test you are going through now, you need to consult the course syllabus for a few guiding principles. First, when trials come, it's important to remember that God is faithful and that you can rely on Him. Second, when trials stay, it's important to remember to do the right thing and to take refuge in Him. Rest in Him.

When the X-ray comes back and it doesn't look good, remember,

God is still faithful. When you read that heartbreaking note from your mate, remember, God is still faithful. When you hear the worst kind of news about one of your children, remember, God is still faithful. He has not abandoned you, though you're tempted to think He has.

At the height of one of his own personal tests, Hudson Taylor expressed his response in these words: "It doesn't matter how great the pressure is. What really matters is where the pressure lies, whether it comes between me and God or whether it presses me nearer His heart."

When we are pressed near the heart of God, He is faithful and He will hold us. He will hug us through it. We can entrust our souls "to a faithful Creator in doing what is right." But that doesn't mean things will calm down and start making better sense. Not necessarily! Our Lord's agenda for us is full of surprises, unexpected twists, and abrupt turns.

I like the way one fellow pastor put it:

> One of the most frustrating things about Jesus is that He just won't settle down. He is constantly moving us away from the places where we would prefer to stay . . . And moving us closer to . . . where we do not want to go.[5]

When you are tested, you will be tempted to resist such redirection, go your own way, fight in your own strength, and do what is wrong because it just comes naturally. It's called being streetwise (another word for *carnal*). You've fought your way thus far through life; you can fight your way through this test too.

But wait! Is that what God wants you to do? When trials linger on and you begin to wear down, the Enemy will be whispering all kinds of new carnal ideas. He'll even give you evidence that other people did those trials and got away with them. How much better to remember when trials *come* that God is faithful, still faithful. When trials *stay*, remind yourself to do what is right and take refuge in Him. Find your hiding place in Him.

"Suffering" and "glory" are twin truths that are woven into the fabric of Peter's letter. The world believes that the *absence* of suffering means glory, but a Christian's outlook is different. The trial of our faith today is the assurance of glory when Jesus returns . . . . This was the experience of our Lord . . . and it shall be our experience.

But it is necessary to understand that God is not going to *replace* suffering with glory; rather He will *transform* suffering into glory.[6]

When you and I take the long view, we should be grateful that Jesus just won't settle down. He's busy shaping us into His image . . . and for some of us, He's got a long way to go.

A Prayer for Hope Beyond Our Trials

Father, I pray today especially for those who find themselves in a dark place, who see no light on the horizon, who feel the hot blast from the fiery trials, with no relief in sight. Change this painful place into their hiding place where You are near, where You are real. Use this particular chapter to minister in a very special way to those chosen ones whom You are testing to prove their faith. Calm their fears. Quiet their spirits. Remind them that trials are essential if we hope to become Christlike.

This I pray through Jesus, who was, Himself, a Man of Sorrows, acquainted with grief . . . and who, though Your Son, learned obedience from the things which He suffered.

AMEN

14

Hope Beyond Religion

A Job Description
for Shepherds

OF ALL THE PREACHERS who ever lived, Charles Haddon Spurgeon was among the most colorful. He was also among the most prolific . . . and among the most controversial . . . and among the most eloquent . . . and on and on I could go. Spurgeon was one of a kind—if not the greatest preacher in the history of the church, certainly among the top ten, in my opinion. Any time the subject of preaching arises either in a classroom or among a group of pastors, the name Spurgeon will soon surface.

His works are both helpful and insightful. That is all the more re-markable because he lived over one hundred years ago, from 1834 to 1892. At the age of twenty, Spurgeon was called to the New Park Street Baptist Chapel in London, where he served his Lord until he preached his last sermon on June 7, 1891. He died the following January. During his years there, it was not uncommon for his congregation to number as many as 6,000. One biographer states that people would stand in the snow in the dead of winter waiting for the doors to open to assure themselves of a seat to hear this prince of the

pulpit preach. During his thirty-eight years at the Metropolitan Tabernacle (five years after Spurgeon began his ministry there, they had
to build a new building, which they renamed the Metropolitan Tabernacle), he was responsible for the swelling of the membership of
the church to approximately 14,500. Remarkable, remarkable man.
Although a Baptist, he was an evangelical Calvinist. Most of all, he
was a man made for the pulpit. As one biographer put it:

> Preeminently he was a preacher. His clear voice, his mastery of Anglo-
> Saxon, and his keen sense of humor, allied to a sure grasp of Scripture
> and a deep love for Christ, produced some of the noblest preaching of
> any age.[1]

Despite all his strengths and noble accomplishments, however, a
great deal of criticism was leveled against Spurgeon in his day. Like
Martin Luther, he seemed to thrive in the storm. He was a man I
would call *unflappable*. While he was criticized for a number of
things in his preaching, the two things he was criticized for in his
private life are curious.

First, he loved a good cigar. One of my favorite stories goes back
to an occasion when a man called on him and criticized his cigar
smoking. Spurgeon's response was classic: "When I take this to an
extreme, then I will stop." When the man asked, "What is an extreme?" Spurgeon replied with a twinkle in his eye, "Two cigars at
one time."

The other private criticism was leveled against him and his wife
because, out of their own funds, they purchased and enjoyed an extremely large home on a sizable acreage. Predictably, the American
press arrived on the scene and exaggerated the report of the home.
This *infuriated* Spurgeon. But he pressed on, refusing to allow petty
minds and exaggerated comments to deter him from his objectives.
While many around him were "religious" and tried very hard to
squeeze him into their proper religious mold, Spurgeon remained a
maverick at heart, fiercely independent yet Christian to the core, thor-
oughly committed to Christ and His Word but unmoved by the pressure in Victorian England to fall in line and blend in with his peers.

The longer I live, the greater my admiration grows for this unique vessel so mightily used of God yet so vehemently criticized by others—especially other Christians. Though dead, he still speaks. His volumes continue to stimulate and instruct those of us in vocational Christian service. Anyone who enters the ministry owes it to himself or herself to read Spurgeon and to do so at least once a month. I especially recommend his book, *Lectures to My Students*. In it he writes:

> Every workman knows the necessity of keeping his tools in a good state of repair. . . . If the workman lose the edge . . . he knows that there will be a greater draught upon his energies, or his work will be badly done. . . .
>
> . . . It will be in vain for me to stock my library, or organize societies, or project schemes, if I neglect the culture of myself; for books, and agencies, and systems, are only remotely the instruments of my holy calling; my own spirit, soul, and body are my nearest machinery for sacred service; my spiritual faculties, and my inner life, are my battle axe and weapons for war. . . .
>
> [Then, quoting from a letter of the great Scottish minister, Robert Murray McCheyne, he concludes,] "Remember, you are God's sword, His instrument—I trust a chosen vessel unto Him to bear His name. In great measure, according to the purity and perfection of the instrument, will be the success. It is not great talent God blesses so much as likeness to Jesus. A holy minister is an awful weapon in the hand of God."[2]

There is every temptation for God's people (especially God's *ministers!*) to fall in line, get in step, and follow the cadence of our times . . . and in so doing, we will become unauthentic, boring, predictable, and, well, "religious." We need to be warned against that! While we cannot be Spurgeons (one was enough), there is much we can learn much from this model of clear thinking, passionate preaching, creative writing, and unbending determination. It is nothing short of amazing that a man of his stature and gifts remained at the same church almost four decades . . . especially since he was such a lightning rod, drawing criticism for so long from so many people.

One Practical Guideline for All to Remember

Let me begin with a few practical words of exhortation about sustaining a long-term ministry. My comments here have to do with unrealistic expectations—and they occur on both sides of the pulpit. A young minister comes to a church and has expectations of the flock. On the other side, the flock contacts and calls a man to pastor the church, and they also have their expectations. Both sets of expectations are so idealistic they're usually off the graph. This has the makings of early madness in any ministry.

One of the secrets of a long-term pastorate is clear-thinking realism on the part of both the pastor and the congregation. Let's understand, most churches will never be anything like a Metropolitan Tabernacle . . . and none of us in ministry will ever be a Spurgeon. My opening illustrations in this chapter are examples of the extreme. But the fact is, most of us are far down the scale from that, and we must learn to live with that, accept it, and be content with where and who we are.

The irony is, I think if Charles Haddon Spurgeon lived today, most churches would never even consider extending a call to him. They couldn't get over his style. And if they knew in-depth the whole story behind the Tabernacle, most pastors today would not want to serve in that place. (It's amazing what a hundred years' history will do to enhance our vision of a church or a man.)

The importance of two-way tolerance is extremely significant. A pastor needs to be very tolerant of the people he is serving. And the people who are being served by the minister need to be very tolerant of him. We need to give each other a lot of wobble room. Congregations need to give each other—and their pastors—room to be themselves. Religion, by the way, resists such freedom.

Please understand, I'm not saying anyone should live a lie; nor am

I promoting an unaccountable, sinful lifestyle. I'm simply encouraging grace here . . . giving room for others to be who they really are. All of us have quirks. All of us are unique in our own way. It's important that we adapt to a broad spectrum of personality types.

I smiled when I read this little sign recently:

Welcome to the Psychiatric Hotline!

IF YOU ARE OBSESSIVE-COMPULSIVE: Please press 1 repeatedly.

IF YOU ARE CO-DEPENDENT: Please ask someone to press 2.

IF YOU HAVE MULTIPLE PERSONALITIES: Please press 3, 4, 5, and 6.

IF YOU ARE PARANOID-DELUSIONAL: We know who you are and what you want. Just stay on the line so we can trace the call.

IF YOU ARE SCHIZOPHRENIC: Listen carefully—a little voice will tell you which number to press.

IF YOU ARE MANIC-DEPRESSIVE: It doesn't matter which number you press. No one will answer.[3]

If we're going to live together comfortably over a long period of time, we have to accept one another's idiosyncrasies and styles. This is an appropriate time for me to repeat something I wrote earlier: A good sense of humor is essential, especially if you hope to survive many years in church and/or the ministry.

Two Biblical Principles Regarding Ministry

I've expressed my concern about all this because we have come to a section in Peter's letter that sort of stands on its own as it deals with the pastor and the flock among whom he ministers. It's helpful because Peter's counsel doesn't have a religious ring to it. It's refreshingly insightful. The opening lines of the chapter offer a couple of effective and important principles worth mentioning.

> Therefore, I exhort the elders among you, as your fellow elder and witness of the sufferings of Christ, and a partaker also of the glory that is to be revealed, shepherd the flock of God among you . . . . (1 Pet. 5:1–2a)

The first principle is this: *The pride of position must be absent.* Remember who wrote these words: Peter the apostle, the spokesman for the early church, the one who saw Jesus with his own eyes, who literally walked with the Messiah for more than three years. What honor had been his . . . what privileges, and yet he never hints at his own position of authority. Any sense of pride of position is absent from Peter's opening remarks. He simply calls himself, "a fellow elder, a witness of the sufferings of Christ, and a partaker of the glory that is to be revealed."

I consider these very humble words. He says nothing about his authoritative apostleship. Nothing about the importance of the recipients of his letter being obedient to his advice. He simply identifies with the elders as a "fellow elder." And if you want to make the word "partaker" a little bit more understandable, think of the word *partner.* "I'm a partner with you in the same glory that's going to be revealed hereafter." He saw himself on the same level as the other elders.

A religious ministry is an easy place to secretly construct a proud life. Unfortunately, pride can consume a person in ministry. It not only can, it *has* for some.

Stop and think about why. We speak for God. We stand before large groups of people regularly. Most ministers address more people more often (without being interrupted) than most executives of large corporations do in their work. Those in ministry can live virtually unaccountable. We are respected and trusted by most. And throughout our careers, only rarely are we questioned. When we are, our answers are seldom challenged. We do our preparation away from the public eye as we work alone in our studies. All of that is fine . . . but it's like a mine field of perils and dangers. Because before you know it, we can begin to fall into the trap of believing only what we say and seeing only what we discover. This is especially true if your ministry grows and your fame spreads. When that happens, your head can swell and your ears can become dull of hearing.

If Peter, one of the original Twelve, the earliest spokesman for the church, an anointed servant of God, would not mention his role of importance, I think we can learn a lesson about humility. Mark it down. Don't forget it. The pride of position must be absent.

There is a second principle, equally significant: *The heart of a shepherd must be present.* Remember his opening imperative? "Shepherd the flock of God which is among you." The original root word means "to act as a shepherd, to tend a flock." And don't miss the flip side of the coin: He calls the people "the flock of God."

That is why I have never cultivated the habit of referring to any congregation I serve as "my people." The flock isn't owned or controlled by the under-shepherd; they are God's people! They must ultimately answer to Him. They live their lives before Him. They are to obey *Him.* It is His Word that guides us all, shepherd and flock alike.

I like this description: "By definition, the true elder is the shepherd of the flock in which God has placed him . . . who bears them on his heart, seeks them when they stray, defends them from harm, comforts them in their pain, and feeds them with the truth."

This is a good time to add that unless you have the heart of a shepherd, you really ought not to be in a pastorate. You might wish to teach. You might choose to be involved in some other realm of ministry, and there are dozens of possibilities. But if you lack the heart of a shepherd, my advice is simple: don't go into the pastorate. It soon becomes a mismatch, frustrating both pastor and flock.

This saying used to hang in the office of my good friend and former minister of worship, Dr. Howie Stevenson. "Never try to teach a pig to sing. It wastes your time, and it annoys the pig!"

I've heard some people say, "Well, I'll just learn how to be a shepherd." Sorry. There is more to it than that. Shepherding has to be in your heart. There isn't a textbook, there isn't a course, there isn't some relationship that will turn you into a shepherd. It is a calling.

It's a matter of gifting by God, as we saw in the previous chapter. You are not educated into becoming a shepherd. Seminary may help, for during their years in seminary, most students discover whether or not they have a shepherd's heart. If they do not, I repeat, they should not pursue the pastorate.

I've seen evangelists filling pulpits, and the church is evangelized. But it isn't shepherded. I've seen teachers, bright and capable teachers, filling the pulpit, and the church is carefully instructed and biblically educated. But it isn't shepherded. A shepherd's heart certainly includes evangelism, teaching and exhortation, but it must also include love and tolerance, servant-hearted patience and understanding, and a lot of room for those lambs and sheep who don't quite measure up. Pastoring a church isn't a religious profession, not really. It isn't a business decision but rather a call of God that links certain shepherds with certain flocks.

Religion speaks in terms of hiring qualified professionals to fulfill certain responsibilities. The result is "hirelings," as Jesus called them (John 10:11–15). But in God's flock, shepherds are gifted; they are called to serve and to give themselves, to love and to encourage, to model the Savior's style. When this occurs churches are blessed and they enjoy hope beyond religion.

Three Essential Attitudes for Non-Religious Shepherds

Shepherd the flock of God among you, exercising oversight not under compulsion, but voluntarily, according to the will of God; and not for sordid gain, but with eagerness; nor yet as lording it over those allotted to your charge, but proving to be examples to the flock. (1 Pet. 5:2–3)

I find at least three vital attitudes set forth in the verses you just read. Each attitude begins with a negative, followed by the positive side.

1. Not under compulsion . . .
   but voluntarily, according to the will of God

2. Not for gain . . .
    but with eagerness
3. Nor yet as lording it over those allotted to your charge . . .
    but proving to be examples to the flock.

Attitude number one is *an attitude of willingness.* "Not under compulsion, but voluntarily." *Compulsion* means "to be compelled by force." Like getting your teenager out of bed early in the morning to go to school. That is compulsion. Peter, however, isn't referring to a teenager at school but a shepherd with his flock.

This reminds me of a story I heard several years ago. A young man was sleeping soundly one Sunday morning when his mother came in, shook him, and said, "Wake up, son. You've got to get up . . . you've got to get out of bed." He groaned and complained. "Give me three good reasons why I have to get up this morning." Without hesitation his mother said, "Well, first of all, it's Sunday morning, and it's only right that we be in church. Second, because it's only forty minutes until church starts, so we don't have much time. And third, *you're the pastor!*"

Paul writes in his swan song that God's messengers are to "be ready in season and out of season" (2 Tim. 4:2). Faithful shepherds are to be willing "in season and out of season." . . . when we feel like it, when we don't . . . when the church is growing as well as when it's not.

One of the things that intensifies burnout in ministry is a lack of willingness. And willingness depends on resting when we should so we can give it our all when we must. That's why, each time I speak to them, I encourage ministers to take a day off every week—when possible, a day and a half or two days. Why? To replenish the soul, to refresh the spirit. Furthermore, it is also imperative to take sufficient vacation time, to get away. I encourage "mini-vacations" as well—to get away with your mate, to spend time in refreshment and romance and simply the enjoyment of one another. By doing so, we are better able to do our work willingly and "not under compulsion."

I see many a frowning face and weary body when I go to pastors' conferences. Candidly, of all the groups that I minister to, few are more depressed and exhausted than a group of pastors. They are overworked, usually underpaid, and almost without exception underappreciated, though most of them are doing a remarkable piece of work.

Mild depressions can come upon us unexpectedly that erode our willingness. Often we can't explain such depressions at the time. Later, perhaps, but not when they occur.

I was reading to Cynthia the other day from the book I mentioned earlier in the chapter, Spurgeon's *Lectures to My Students*. She was in the kitchen working, and I walked over and said, "You've got to hear this." Then I read her about three pages! (Talk about a willing spirit!) Though writing more than one hundred years ago, Spurgeon described exactly some of the reasons we suffer from "burn out" in ministry today. He even admitted to depression in his own life, often before a great success, sometimes after a great success, and usually because of something he couldn't explain. He called this chapter "The Minister's Fainting Fits" (great title!). Listen to his candid remarks.

> Fits of depression come over most of us. Usually cheerful as we may be, we must at intervals be cast down. The strong are not always vigorous, the wise not always ready, the brave not always courageous, and the joyous not always happy. There may be here and there men of iron . . . but surely the rust frets even these.[4]

Let me add one final comment here . . . for the flock of God. Be tolerant with your pastor. A better word is *patient*. Try your best not to be too demanding or set your expectations too high. Multiply your own requests by however many there are in your church, and you'll have some idea of what the shepherd of the flock must live with. Be very understanding. Remember, if you write a letter that will bring his spirit down, it could wound him for weeks. Sometimes a confrontation is necessary. But even then, be kind. Be tactful. Pray for him! Encourage him! When you do, you'll find him all the more willing to serve his Lord among you.

Now, look at the second attitude: *an attitude of eagerness*. This next phrase describes not just willingness but an attitude of enthusiastic eagerness. Look how Peter expresses this: "Not for sordid gain, but with eagerness." The old King James Bible called sordid gain (money) "filthy lucre." Make certain your ministry is not motivated by the monetary, external perks. Religious circles emphasize, think about, and make a big thing of money. Guard against that.

I challenge preachers—and I have done it myself through the years—not to do a wedding just because they may get fifty dollars (or whatever) to do that wedding. Be eager to serve, not greedy! And if you're invited to participate in a week-long conference, do it because you really want to, not because you'll get an honorarium. Money is not a healthy motivation, so watch your motives.

When I was in seminary, my sister made me a small black-and-white sign that I hung on the wall in front of my desk where I studied. It read simply, *"What's your motive?"* What a searching question. I looked at it, off and on, for four years. It's a question every shepherd needs to ask on a weekly basis. Motives must forever be examined.

There is nothing quite as exciting or delightful as a shepherd who emits enthusiasm. Such zeal is *contagious*! His love for the Scriptures becomes the flock's love for the Scriptures. His zest for life becomes the congregation's zest for life. His commitment to leisure and enjoyment of life becomes their commitment to leisure and enjoyment of life. His joyful commitment to obeying God becomes theirs. No wonder Peter emphasizes eagerness. His passion for the unsaved becomes their passion. How refreshing it is to be around shepherds who are getting up in years but still eager and enthusiastic!

There's a third attitude Peter highlights: *an attitude of meekness*. I think it was with an extra boost of passion that he wrote:

> . . . nor yet as lording it over those allotted to your charge, but proving to be examples to the flock. (1 Pet. 5:3)

I like the way Eugene Peterson paraphrases this:

Not bossily telling others what to do, but tenderly showing them the way. (MSG)

What concerns the old apostle here is a shepherd's exercising undue authority over others. We as shepherds must learn to hold our congregations loosely. We must watch our tendency to try and gain dominion over them, thinking of them as underlings. To avoid this, we must think of ourselves as servants, not sovereigns. Give the flock room to disagree. Assure them that they are to think on their own. But make no mistake. A shepherd who is "meek" is not weak. It takes great inner strength and security to demonstrate grace. He's willing to serve rather than demand. How beautiful, how marvelous it is, to witness one who is gifted and strong of heart, yet secure enough to let God's people grow and learn without having to fall in line with him at every point and march in lockstep to his drumbeat. The best shepherds are those who do their work unto the Lord, expecting no one to bow down before them.

While reading a recent issue of *Sports Illustrated*, I came across an article about Al Davis, owner of the Oakland Raiders football team. If you're a sports fan, you know that Davis is considered by many as one of the most greedy and proud of all owners in the business. He goes through more coaches in a decade than some owners do in a lifetime. This article reports that . . .

> Davis's abuses of power have become increasingly visible. For example, after practice it is customary for him to enter the equipment room, drop a towel on the floor and wait for an employee to clean his shoes. "I saw him make someone wipe his shoes in front of 75 people," says Denver Broncos coach Mike Shanahan, who coached the Raiders in 1988.[5]

When I read that, I thought—here's the *opposite* of servant-hearted leadership. Yet I've witnessed leaders in ministry positions who have abused their positions almost as blatantly.

I've just finished listening to a cassette tape. It's the voice of a man who has been in ministry for years, and it was as if I were listening to another Jim Jones as he preached. My heart ached for that flock who sat and endured his self-serving style. Here was a man who had gained the mastery; verbal abuse was commonly practiced. He snapped his fingers . . . they jumped. He cracked his whip . . . they bowed down. Friend, that is not "proving to be an example to the flock." That is religious abuse . . . the manipulation of a congregation . . . legalistic religion at its worst.

The pastorate brings an enormous amount of authority. Not even a board of elders or deacons, as powerful as they may be, can take the shepherd's place in the pulpit on Sunday. It is a place where he can wield incredible authority and, if he chooses to do so, pull rank. All the more reason not to abuse it. The shepherd is not a stand-in for the Lord!

What God's people need most in their minister is a model of the life of Jesus Christ. There is something convincing about a model. That's Peter's point here. The very best thing for the minister to do is live a life of authenticity, accountability, and humility. Few things win the hearts of sheep like a tender shepherd!

You may remember that Moses, toward the end of his life, was said to have been "very humble, more than any man who was on the face of the earth" (Num. 12:3). Here was a man who "pastored" millions of people, but he refused to pander to his fame. He cared nothing for the applause of the public. He would not manipulate the people. In fact, brokenhearted before God, he even said, "Just take me out of the way." This wonderful section of Scripture is a good reminder that as important as it is to be a decisive leader with strong convictions, accepting the responsibilities of the position, it is never appropriate for the shepherd to "lord it over" those in his care.

No extra charge for this little comment, but I want to underscore an earlier observation that taking control of others is a mark of insecurity. Those who must have absolute agreement from everyone are terribly insecure people. Isn't it interesting that Christ Jesus never demanded that His disciples write anything down, never once exhorted them to memorize things He said? What He told them most of all was, "Do not be afraid." That was His most frequent command. "Do not be afraid." And the other was given by implication, "Watch Me and follow My model." No one has ever had the authority over a flock like Christ, but only on the rarest of occasions did He even raise His voice . . . or rebuke His followers. Sheep do best when they are led, not driven . . . when they are released, not controlled . . . when they know they are loved, not shamed.

An Eternal Reward to Be Claimed

And when the Chief Shepherd appears, you will receive the unfading crown of glory. (1 Pet. 5:4)

I've mentioned crowns before in this book, but I've not mentioned *this* crown. Unlike the others, this is an exclusive crown. It is reserved for those who faithfully shepherd God's flock God's way. Only those who serve in this capacity will be able to receive the "unfading crown of glory." Notice, as a result of fulfilling these two principles and these three attitudes, the "crown of glory" will be awarded by "the Chief Shepherd" Himself.

Count on it, fellow shepherds. We have this to anticipate when we meet our Lord face to face.

Personal Suggestions for Both Sides of Ministry

To summarize, let me first address you who lead by saying, *keep a healthy balance.* If you teach, also be teachable. Read. Listen. Learn. Observe. Be ready to change. Then change! Admit wrong where you were wrong. Stand firm where you know you are right. You cannot win them all. And keep in mind, you're a servant of God, not a slave of the flock.

Since you are called to be a leader, when it's necessary, be a good follower—which takes us back to servanthood. When you lead, put yourself in the followers' shoes; think about what it would be like if you were sitting there listening to those things you are saying.

Neither underestimate your importance nor exaggerate your role. You are, admittedly, called of God. You represent Him, His message, His vision. You can become whipped by a congregation. (It happened to me once. It will never, by the grace of God, happen to me again.) Something tragic happens to a leader who has lost his drive and his determination. But you cannot do it all, so delegate. It's a big job to do, so invite others to help you do it. And when they do it well, give them credit.

Stay balanced. You are engaged in serious work, but (I repeat) keep a good sense of humor. Laugh often and loudly! And don't be afraid to laugh at yourself. My fellow laborers at Insight for Living make sure I do! On several occasions they have presented me with a tape containing all the "outtakes"—things they cut out of my taped messages during the year. Sort of my own private "bloopers." Some have even had the audacity to play this tape at a Christmas party for hundreds to hear and enjoy! As I listen, I cannot believe the dumb things I have said in any given year. It's enough to reduce even a strong-hearted shepherd to the size of a nit-pickin' termite!

Take God seriously, but don't take yourself too seriously.

Now, finally, to those of you being led, may I suggest that you *be a reason for rejoicing*. What a wonderful assignment!

Read the following slowly . . .

> Obey your leaders, and submit to them; for they keep watch over your souls, as those who will give an account. Let them do this with joy and not with grief, for this would be unprofitable for you. (Heb. 13:17)

Think of ways to encourage your minister or leader. Pray often for him. Model gratitude and love. Demonstrate your affection with acts of generosity. Defend the shepherd whenever possible. And when you can't, tell him face to face, and tell no one else. Do it briefly, graciously, then forgive quickly. Try to imagine being in the shoes of the one who lives with the burden of the whole flock and is never free of that. And one more thought . . . think of how it would be if everyone else in the flock were *just like you*. C'mon, have a heart! The guy's not Spurgeon . . . and even if he were, you wouldn't agree with him either.

If you will do these things for your shepherd-leader, not only will you be rewarded, you will give him and yourself new hope . . . hope to press on, hope for the second mile, and everyone in the flock will enjoy hope beyond religion.

A Prayer for Hope Beyond Religion

Father, we consider it a priceless privilege to serve You, the living God. You've made all of us with different personalities, given us different gifts and responsibilities, and yet chosen to mingle us together in the same body, over which Christ is head. There are great temptations we face as shepherds and as sheep . . . to be in charge, to force others to get in line, to make things more uniform and rigid, to get narrow and demanding, to set our expectations too high . . . to handle ministry as if it were a secular enterprise. God, we need You to keep things fresh and unpredictable and especially to keep us authentic, servant-hearted people, and easy to live with.

So give us new hope . . . hope beyond religion, hope that motivates us to press on, serving You with pure motives and eager hearts. Thank You for Your grace, our only hope, dear Savior . . . in Your name.

AMEN

15

Hope Beyond Dissatisfaction

A Formula That Brings Relief

OUR SOCIETY HAS gorged itself on the sweet taste of success. We've filled our plates from a buffet of books that range from dressing for success to investing for success. We've passed the newsstands and piled our plates higher with everything from *Gentleman's Quarterly* and *Vogue*, to the *Wall Street Journal* and *Time*. When we've devoured these, we have turned our ravenous appetites toward expensive, success-oriented seminars. We've gobbled down stacks of notebooks, cassette albums, and video tapes in our hunger for greater success.

The irony of all this is that "there is never enough success in anybody's life to make one feel completely satisfied."[1] Instead of fulfillment, we experience the bloated sensation of being full of ourselves—*our* dreams, *our* goals, *our* plans, *our* projects, *our* accomplishments. The result of this all-you-can-eat appetite is not contentment. It's nausea. How terribly dissatisfying!

"The trouble with success is that the formula is the same as the one for a nervous breakdown," says *The Executive's Digest*. If you find yourself a little queasy after just such a steady diet, you don't need a second helping of success. You need a healthy dose of relief.

Interestingly, very few address that which most folks want but seldom find in their pursuit of success, and that is contentment, fulfillment, satisfaction. Rarely, if ever, are we offered boundaries and encouraged to say, "Enough is enough." And so we work harder and harder, make more and more, yet enjoy all of it less and less.

If we're hung up on any one subject in America today, we are hung up on the pursuit of success. Yet I don't know of another pursuit that is more deceptive—filled with fantasy dreams, phantoms, mirages, empty promises, and depressing disappointments.

Johnny Cash wasn't far off when he groaned, "If you don't have any time for yourself, any time to hunt or fish—that's success."

Today's Major Messages, Promising "Success"

The ad campaigns that come out of Madison Avenue promise much more than they can deliver. Their titillating messages fall into four categories: fortune and fame, power and pleasure.

Fortune says that to be successful you need to make the big bucks. Why else would the Fortune 500 list make such headlines every year? Anyone who is held up as successful must have more money than the average person.

Understand, there is nothing wrong with money earned honestly. Certainly there is nothing wrong in investing or giving or even spending money if the motive is right, if the heart is pure. But I have yet to discover anyone who has found true happiness simply in the gathering of more money. Although money is not sinful or suspect in itself, it is not what brings lasting contentment, fulfillment, or satisfaction.

Fame says that to be successful you need to be known in the public arena. You need to be a celebrity, a social somebody. Fame equates popularity with significance.

Power says that to be successful you need to wield a lot of authority, flex your muscles, take charge, be in control, carry a lot of weight. Push yourself to the front. Expect and demand respect.

Pleasure implies that to be successful you need to be able to do whatever feels good. This philosophy operates on the principle: "If it feels good, do it." It's just a modern version of the ancient epicurean philosophy, "Eat, drink, and be merry, for tomorrow you may die."

Fortune. Fame. Power. Pleasure. The messages bombard us from every direction. But what's missing in all this? Stop and ask yourself that question. Isn't something very significant absent here?

You bet. A *vertical* dimension. There's not even a hint of God's will or what pleases Him in the hard-core pursuit of success. Note also that nothing in that horizontal list guarantees satisfaction or brings relief deep within the heart. And in the final analysis, what most people really want in life is contentment, fulfillment, and satisfaction.

My sister, Luci, told me about the time she visited with a famous opera singer in Italy. This woman owned a substantial amount of Italian real estate, a lovely home, and a yacht floating on the beautiful Mediterranean in a harbor below her villa. At one point, Luci asked the singer if she considered all this the epitome of success.

"Why, no!" said the woman, sounding a bit shocked.

"What is success then?" asked Luci.

"When I stand to perform, to sing my music, and I look out upon a public that draws a sense of fulfillment, satisfaction, and pleasure from my expression of this art, at that moment I know I have contributed to someone else's need. That to me describes success."

Not a gathering of expensive possessions but a deliberate investment in the lives of others seems to be a crucial factor in finding fulfillment and contentment. Service. Help. Assistance. Compassion for others. Therein lies so much of what brings a sense of peace and true success.

In light of that, it seems, success is not a pursuit as much as it is a surprising discovery in an individual's life. All this brings us back to Peter's letter—old, but as we're discovering, ever relevant.

God's Ancient Plan: The Three A's

You younger men, likewise, be subject to your elders; and all of you, clothe yourselves with humility toward one another, for God is opposed to the proud, but gives grace to the humble.

Humble yourselves, therefore, under the mighty hand of God, that He may exalt you at the proper time, casting all your anxiety upon Him, because He cares for you. (1 Pet. 5:5–7)

The world's strategy to climb the ladder of success is simple: Work hard, get ahead, then climb higher—even if you have to claw and step on and climb over the next guy; don't let anything get in your way as you promote yourself. The goal is to make it to the top. It doesn't matter how many or who you push aside along the way, and it doesn't matter who you leave behind, even if it's your family or your friends or your conscience. It's a dog-eat-dog world, friends and neighbors, and the weak puppies don't make it. To survive, you have to hold on to the ladder for dear life. To succeed, you have to fight your way to the top . . . and never stop climbing.

I shook my head in disappointment when I read of Jimmy Johnson's decision to walk away from his wife and family several years ago when he became head coach of the Dallas Cowboys. He didn't deny it or hide it or apologize for his decision. He saw this major career promotion from the University of Miami to the Cowboys organization as his opportunity to make it to the top, big time. There was no way he would let anyone or anything get in his way; this was his moment to succeed, to move into big money. And things like home and family and kids (and grandkids!) were not going to stop him. He dropped all those responsibilities like a bad habit and split for Dallas like a hungry leopard searching for food.

In the world's eyes, he's now reached the pinnacle. A winning record, two Super Bowl rings, enormous amounts of money, fame, a yacht, several private enterprises, and now the Miami Dolphins with even greater hopes for more and more and more. As the public watches and reads of Johnson's accomplishments, most salivate. "The man's got it made!" would be the general opinion of athletes and sports fans and entrepreneurs and executives around the country. That, to them, represents success at its best.

God's plan, His ancient plan, is much different. We see it spelled out for us here in Peter's strategy for the right kind of success. In the three verses above, we see a series of contrasts to the kind of thinking I just illustrated. To keep everything simple, I call them the three A's: authority, attitude, and anxiety.

Authority

Peter's first piece of counsel advises us to submit ourselves to those who are wise and to "clothe" ourselves with humility.

> You younger men, likewise, be subject to your elders; and all of you, clothe yourselves with humility toward one another, for God is opposed to the proud, but gives grace to the humble. (1 Pet. 5:5)

The "clothe yourself" metaphor comes from a rare word that pictures a servant putting on an apron before serving those in the house. Perhaps Peter was recalling that meal in the upper room when Jesus wrapped Himself with a towel and washed the disciples' dirty feet (see John 13). Reclining at the table for their last meal with the Master, Peter and the other disciples had come to the table with dirty feet. The Savior, humbling Himself to the role of a servant, "clothed Himself" with a towel and, carrying a basin of water, washed their feet. I really believe the old fisherman was remembering that act of humility as he wrote these words in verse 5.

"Be subject to," he says—it's in the present tense here, "Keep on being subject to . . ." In other words, submission is to be an ongoing way of life, a lifestyle. We are to listen to the counsel of our elders in the faith, to be open to their reproofs, watch their lives, follow the examples they set, respect their decisions, and honor their years of seasoned wisdom. We must always remember that we need others. Their advice and model, their warnings and wisdom, are of inestimable value, no matter how far along in life we are.

I remember Dr. Howard Hendricks telling me years ago, "Experience is not the best teacher. *Guided* experience is the best teacher." The secret lies in the "guide"!

Bricklaying is a good illustration of this. As a novice, you can lay brick from morning to night, day in and day out, gaining several weeks of experience on your own, and you'll probably have a miserable-looking wall when you're finished. But if you work from the start with a journeyman bricklayer who knows how to lay a course of brick, one after the other, your guided experience can create a wall that is an object of beauty.

Proud independence results in a backlash of consequences, the main one being the opposition of God (see James 4:6). The original idea of God's opposing the proud is found in Proverbs 3.

> Do not envy a man of violence,
> And do not choose any of his ways.
> For the crooked man is an abomination to the LORD;
> But He is intimate with the upright.
> The curse of the LORD is on the house of the wicked,
> But He blesses the dwelling of the righteous.
> Though He scoffs at the scoffers,
> Yet He gives grace to the afflicted.
> The wise will inherit honor,
> But fools display dishonor. (Prov. 3:31–35)

In contrast to the humble, those who are proud in their hearts *scoff* at the Lord. This term expresses scorn and contempt. But God, not the proud, has the last scoff! As Solomon put it, "He scoffs at the scoffers."

When you submit yourself to those who are wise, instead of flaunting your own authority, you will have a greater measure of grace.

> But He gives a greater grace. Therefore it says, "God is opposed to the proud, but gives grace to the humble." (James 4:6)

And that is certainly what today's models of success could use a lot more of—a greater measure of grace. Isn't it noteworthy how rarely those who are on an aggressive, self-promoting fast track to the top even use the word *grace*. Grace, says Peter, is given by God to the humble, not to the proud.

Attitude

Peter's second strategy for success has to do with attitude. We must, he says, humble ourselves under God's mighty hand.

> Humble yourselves, therefore, under the mighty hand of God, that He may exalt you at the proper time. (1 Pet. 5:6)

In the Old Testament, God's hand symbolizes two things. The first is discipline (see Exod. 3:20, Job 30:21, and Ps. 32:4). The second is deliverance (see Deut. 9:26 and Ezek. 20:34). When we humble ourselves under the mighty hand of God, we willingly accept His discipline as being for our good and for His glory. Then we gratefully acknowledge His deliverance, which always comes in His time and in His way.

In other words, as we saw in the previous chapter, we don't manipulate people or events. We refuse to hurry His timing. We let Him set the pace. And we humbly place ourselves under His firm, steadying hand. As a result of this attitude—don't miss it!—"He may exalt you at the proper time."

I must confess there are times when God's timing seems awfully slow. I find myself impatiently praying, "Lord, hurry up!" Is that true for you too?

In today's dog-eat-dog society, if something isn't happening as quickly as we want it to, there are ways to get the ball rolling, and I mean *fast*. There are people to call, strings to pull, and strong-arm strategies that make things happen. They are usually effective and always impressive . . . but in the long run, when we adopt these methods, we regret it. We find ourselves feeling dissatisfied and guilty. God didn't do it—we did!

When I was led by God to step away from almost twenty-three marvelous years at the First Evangelical Free Church in Fullerton, California, and step into the presidency of Dallas Theological Seminary, Cynthia and I immediately faced a challenge . . . in many ways, the greatest challenge of our lives and ministry. What about our radio ministry, Insight for Living?

The seminary is in Dallas, Texas; IFL is in Anaheim, California. In order for Cynthia to remain in leadership at IFL and provide the vision that ministry needs, she has to be in touch with and available to our radio ministry, and she and I, both, need to be engaged in some of the day-to-day operations of IFL. Meanwhile my work at the seminary requires my presence and availability on many occasions. If I hope to be more than a figurehead, and I certainly do, then my presence on and around that campus is vital. But it's hard to be two places at once. I tried that several years ago, and it hurt!

Obviously, then, it makes sense for IFL to move to Dallas. But moving an organization that size (with around 140 employees) is a costly and complicated process. We have a continuing lease on our building in Anaheim, no property or building as of yet in Dallas . . . but she and I cannot continue to commute indefinitely. We have been doing that for well over two years—long enough to know we don't want to do that much longer! On top of all that, there's no money to move us.

So . . . we have two options, humanly speaking. We can run ahead, make things happen, manipulate the money needs, and get the move behind us . . . or we can "humble ourselves under the mighty hand of God" and pray and wait and watch Him work, counting on Him to "exalt us at the proper time" (answer our prayers, provide the funds, help us find a place in Dallas for relocating IFL, and end our commuting). And so we wait. We make the need known . . . and we wait.

We're still waiting. We're still praying. We *refuse* to rush ahead and "make things happen." Admittedly, we get a little impatient and anxious at times, but we're convinced He is able to meet our needs and He will make it happen! Meanwhile we must be content to humble ourselves under God's mighty hand.

What does it mean to humble *yourself* under the mighty hand of God in *your* job, vocation, or profession? What if you're not getting the raise or the promotion you deserve? What if you are in a situation where you could make things happen . . . but you really want God to do that?

Think of David, the young musician, tending his father's sheep back on the hills of Judea many centuries ago. He was a self-taught, gifted musician. He didn't go on tour, trying to make a name for himself. Instead, he sang to the sheep. He had no idea that someday his lyrics would find their way into the psalter or would be the very songs that have inspired and comforted millions of people through long and dark nights.

David didn't seek success; he simply humbled himself under the mighty hand of God, staying close to the Lord and submitting himself to Him. And God exalted David to the highest position in the land. He became the shepherd of the entire nation!

You don't have to promote yourself if you've got the stuff. If you're good, if you are to be used of Him, they'll find you. God will promote you. I don't care what the world system says. I urge you to let *God* do the promoting! Let *God* do the exalting! In the meantime, sit quietly under His hand. That's not popular counsel, I realize, but it sure works. Furthermore, you will never have to wonder in the future if it was you or the Lord who made things happen. And if He chooses to use you in a mighty way, really "exalt" you, you won't have any reason to get conceited. He did it all!

How refreshing it is to come across a few extremely gifted and talented individuals who do not promote themselves . . . who genuinely let God lead . . . who refuse to get slick and make a name for themselves! May their tribe increase.

Anxiety

Peter's third strategy for success tells us to cast all our anxiety upon God.

Humble yourselves . . . casting all your anxiety upon Him, because He cares for you. (1 Pet. 5:6–7)

The original meaning of the term *cast* literally is "to throw upon." We throw ourselves fully and completely on the mercy and care of God. This requires a decisive action on our part. There is nothing passive or partial about it.

When those anxieties that accompany growth and true success emerge and begin to weigh you down (and they will), throw yourself on the mercy and care of God. Sometimes the anxiety comes in the form of people, sometimes it comes in the form of the media, sometimes it comes in the form of money and possessions, or a dozen other sources I could mention. The worries multiply, the anxieties intensify. Just heave those things upon the Lord. Throw them back on the One who gave them.

I love David's advice:

> Cast your burden upon the LORD, and He will sustain you;
> He will never allow the righteous to be shaken. (Ps. 55:22)

I have a feeling David wrote that one after he'd "made it," don't you?

If you've ever carried a heavily loaded pack while hiking, mountain climbing, or marching in the military, you know there is nothing quite like the wonderful words from the leader, "Let's stop here for a while." Everybody lets out a sign of relief and *thump, thump, thump, thump*, all those packs start hitting the ground. That's the word picture here. Release your burden. Just drop it. Let it fall off your back. Reminds me of John Bunyan's pilgrim when he came to the place of the sepulcher and the cross; the burden of sin fell off his back.

So here's the simple formula that will enable you to handle whatever success God may bring your way and will provide you with the relief you need while waiting:

SUBMISSION + HUMILITY − WORRY = RELIEF

Submission to others plus humility before God minus the worries of the world equals genuine relief. It will also provide hope and contentment without the pain of dissatisfaction.

Our Great Need: Effecting Change

Now I wish all this were as simple as just reading it and saying, "That's it. I'm changed. It's gonna happen." Believe me, it doesn't work that way. So let me suggest some things we need in our lives to effect these changes.

To grasp what true success really is and how to obtain it, we need to tune out the seductive messages from the world and tune in to the instructive messages from the Word. How? It occurs to me we need at least three things to make this happen.

First, we need direction so we can know to whom we should submit.

Let's understand . . . start trying to please everybody, and you're assured of instant failure and long-term frustration. We need God to direct us to those to whom we should submit.

Who are the people I should follow? Who are the folks I should watch? Whose writings should I read? Whose songs should I sing? Whose ministry should I support financially? Whose model should I emulate?

We need direction from God. So begin to pray, "Lord, direct me to the right ones to whom I should submit." Count on Him for direction.

Second, we need discipline to restrain our hellish pride.

Pride will keep rearing its ugly head. The more successful we get, the stronger the temptation to rely on the flesh. We've thought about that already in previous chapters. I use the words "hellish pride" because it is just that. Pride will whisper ways to promote ourselves (but look very humble and pious). Pride will tell us how and when to manipulate or intimidate others. We need discipline to keep ourselves from being our own deliverers. We need discipline to stay *under* the hand of God. Remember that—*under* His mighty hand. But pride hates being *under* anything or anyone. So ask God for discipline here.

Third, we need discernment so we can detect the beginning of anxiety.

Ever have something begin to kind of nag you? You can't put your finger on it. It's fuzzy. Sort of a slimy ooze. It's just growing in the corners, nagging you, getting you down. That is the beginning of a heavy anxiety. We need discernment to detect it, identify it, and get to its root so we can deal with it. When we see the beginning of anxiety for what it is, that's the precise moment to cast it on God, to roll that pack on Him. At that moment we say, "I can't handle it, Lord. You take over."

And how are these needs met? Through the Word of God. The principles and precepts of Scripture give us direction, discipline, and discernment.

Do you find yourself caught up in the success syndrome? Are you still convinced that the world's formula is best? Do you find yourself manipulating people and pulling strings to get ahead? Are you, at this moment, in the midst of a success syndrome you started, not God? No wonder you feel dissatisfied! That type of success *never* satisfies. Only God-directed success offers the formula that brings contentment, fulfillment, satisfaction, and relief.

God's success is never contrived. It is never forced. It is never the working of human flesh. It is usually unexpected—and its benefits are always surprising.

The hand of God holds you firmly in His control. The hand of God casts a shadow of the cross across your life. Sit down at the foot of that cross and deliberately submit your soul to His mighty hand. Accept His discipline. Acknowledge His deliverance. Ask for His discernment.

Then be quiet. Be still. Wait. And move over so I can sit beside you. I'm waiting too.

A Prayer for Hope Beyond Dissatisfaction

We are so grateful, Father, for the truth of Your Word—for the Old and New Testaments alike . . . the teachings of Jesus, the

writings of Peter, the profound songs of David, the law of Moses. All of it blends together in a harmony, a symphony of theological and practical significance. You have us under Your hand, and in our more lucid moments we really want to be there. In times of impatience and wildness we want to squirm free and run ahead. Thank You for holding us, for forgiving us, for cleaning us up, for accepting us, for reshaping us, for not giving up on us. And at this moment, we give You the full right to discipline, to direct, to deliver in Your way and in Your time. Give us great patience as we wait. Humbly, I pray and submit to You in Jesus' name.

AMEN

16

Hope Beyond the Battle

Standing
Nose-to-Nose
with the Adversary

"AS YOU LOOK back over your life, at what places did you grow the most?"

Whenever I ask this question, almost without exception the person will mention a time of pain, a time of loss, a time of deep and unexplained suffering in his or her life. Yet when suffering rains down upon us, our tendency is to think that God has withdrawn His umbrella of protection and abandoned us in the storm. Our confusion during those inclement times stems from our lack of understanding about the role of pain in our lives. Philip Yancey is correct in his analysis.

> Christians don't really know how to interpret pain. If you pinned them against the wall, in a dark, secret moment, many Christians would probably admit that pain was God's one mistake. He really should have worked a little harder and invented a better way of coping with the world's dangers.[1]

Nevertheless, the pain rages on. With relentless regularity, we encounter hardship and heartache. We give ourselves to a friendship, only to lose that person in death. We grieve the loss and determine not to give ourselves so completely again . . . so loneliness comes to haunt us. Is there no hope beyond this? We find the answer to that age-old question, according to Peter, is a resounding YES!

Interestingly, the apostle never once laments the fact that the people he was writing to were suffering pain and persecution, nor does he offer advice on how to escape it. Instead, he faces suffering squarely, tells them (and us) not to be surprised by it, and promises that God provides benefits for enduring life's hurts. Even when life is dreary and overcast, rays of hope pierce through the clouds to stimulate our growth. In fact, without pain there would be little growth at all, for we would remain sheltered, delicate, naive, irresponsible, and immature.

Let's get something straight. Our real enemy is not our suffering itself. The real culprit is our adversary the Devil, the one responsible for much of the world's pain and danger. Although God is at work in the trials of life, so is Satan. While God uses our trials to draw us closer to Him, Satan tries to use them as levers to pry us away from Him. That tug-o'-war only intensifies the battle! Not surprisingly, Peter gives us some crucial advice on how to do battle with the Devil and how to keep him from gaining victory over our lives.

Battle Tactics

In his book *Your Adversary the Devil*, Dwight Pentecost compares the tactics of a physical battle to those of the spiritual one.

> No military commander could expect to be victorious in battle unless he understood his enemy. Should he prepare for an attack by land and ignore the possibility that the enemy might approach by air or by sea, he would open the way to defeat. Or should he prepare for a land and sea attack and ignore the possibility of an attack through the air, he would certainly jeopardize the campaign.
>
> No individual can be victorious against the adversary of our souls unless he understands that adversary; unless he understands

his philosophy, his methods of operation, his methods of temptation.[2]

This being the case, it should not surprise us that Peter begins by identifying the enemy and his general modus operandi. Whoever denies the fact that there is a literal enemy of our souls chooses to live in a dream world, revealing not only a lack of understanding but also a lack of reality. Throughout the Old Testament and the New we find ample evidence of a literal Devil, an actual Satan—a very real "adversary," to use Peter's word.

His Identity, Style, and Purpose

Be of sober spirit, be on the alert. Your adversary, the devil, prowls about like a roaring lion, seeking someone to devour. But resist him, firm in your faith, knowing that the same experiences of suffering are being accompanied by your brethren who are in the world. (1 Pet. 5:8–9)

The original term translated *adversary* refers to an opponent in a lawsuit. This individual is a person on the other side. An adversary is neither a friend nor a playmate. An adversary is no one to mess around with—and no one to joke about.

Satan's constant relationship with the child of God is an adversarial relationship. Make no mistake about it; he despises us. He hates what we represent. He is our unconscionable and relentless adversary, our opponent in the battle between good and evil, between truth and falsehood, between the light of God and the darkness of sin.

"Your adversary, the devil," puts it well. That's the way Peter identifies the Enemy—boldly, without equivocation. "The devil" comes from the word *diabolos*, which means "slanderer" or "accuser." Revelation 12:10 states that the enemy of our souls is "the accuser of our brethren." He accuses us "day and night," according to that verse. Not only does he accuse us to God, he also accuses us to ourselves. Many of our self-defeating thoughts come from the demonic realm. He is constantly accusing, constantly building guilt, constantly prompting shame, constantly coming against us with hopes of destroying us.

Did you notice his style? "He prowls about." The Devil is a prowler. Think about that. He comes by stealth, and he works in secret. His plans are shadowy. He never calls attention to his approach or to his attack. Furthermore, he is "like a roaring lion." He is a beast, howling and growling with hunger, "seeking someone to devour"! To personalize this, substitute your name for "someone." When you do, it makes that verse all the more powerful. "Your adversary, the devil, prowls about like a roaring lion, seeking to devour _____ ." I find that has a chilling effect on my nervous system.

He isn't simply out to tantalize or to tease us. He's not playing around. He has a devouring, voracious appetite. And he dances with glee when he destroys lives, especially the lives of Christians.

A. T. Robertson wrote, "The devil's purpose is the ruin of mankind. Satan wants all of us." It's wise for us to remember that when we travel. It's wise for us to remember that when we don't gather for worship on a Sunday and we're really out on our own. It's wise to remember that when we find ourselves alone for extended periods of time, especially during our more vulnerable moments. He prowls about, stalking our every step, waiting for a strategic moment to catch us off guard. His goal? To devour us . . . to consume us . . . to eat us alive.

I hope you've gotten a true picture of your enemy. He's no sly-looking imp with horns, a red epidermis, and a pitchfork. He is the godless, relentless, brutal, yet brilliant adversary of our souls who lives to bring us down . . . to watch us fall.

Our Response

Peter's opening command alerts us to our necessary response: "Be of sober spirit, be on the alert."

Satan doesn't like chapters like this. He hates exposure. He hates being talked about. He certainly hates it when truth replaces fantasy and people are correctly informed. He especially hates having all of his ugly and filthy plans and destructive ways identified.

> *Be Alert.* As his possible prey, however, our primary response should be to keep on the lookout for the predator.

Satan is a dangerous enemy. He is a serpent who can bite us when we least expect it. He is a destroyer . . . and an accuser . . . . He has great power and intelligence, and a host of demons who assist him in his attacks against God's people . . . . He is a formidable enemy; we must never joke about him, ignore him, or underestimate his ability. We must "be sober" and have our minds under control when it comes to our conflict with Satan.[3]

The Devil's great hope is that he will be ignored, written off as a childhood fairy tale, or dismissed from the mind of the educated adult. Like a prowler breaking into a home, Satan doesn't want to call attention to himself. He wants to work incognito, undetected, in the shadows. The thing he fears most is the searchlight of the Scriptures turned in his direction, revealing precisely who he really is and what comprises his battle plan.

> *Respect Him.* To defeat the Devil we must first be alert to his presence . . . respect him—not fear or revere him, but respect him, like an electrician respects the killing power of electricity.

One caution here, however.

A part of this soberness includes not blaming everything on the devil. Some people see a demon behind every bush and blame Satan for their headaches, flat tires, and high rent. While it is true that Satan can inflict physical sickness and pain (see Luke 13:16 and the Book of Job), we have no biblical authority for casting out demons of headache or demons of backache. One lady phoned me long-distance to inform me that Satan had caused her to shrink seven and a half inches. While I have great respect for the wiles and powers of the devil, I still feel we must get our information about him from the Bible and not from our own interpretation of experiences.[4]

Please be careful that you don't identify every ache and pain or every significant problem you encounter as being satanic in origin. My brother mentioned to me that he once counseled a woman who said she had "the demon of nail-biting." I've met a few who said they fought against "the demon of gluttony." (From their appearance, they were losing the war.) That is not a sign of maturity. I get real concerned about folks who blame the Devil every time something happens that makes life a little bit difficult for them. In fact, it can even become an excuse for not taking responsibility for your own life and your own decisions and choices.

So be alert and be sober. Be calm and watchful. Or, as Moffatt renders it, "Keep cool. Keep awake." We use that word *cool* very lightly today, but here it means a calm coolness. Like professionals in an athletic contest. The best in the game stay cool, calm, collected, and clear-headed, even in the last two minutes as they drive hard for the win, the ultimate prize. So be calm, but be on the alert. Satan's prowling around. This is no time for a snooze in the backyard hammock. He's silently maneuvering a brilliant strategy with plans to destroy us. This is serious stuff!

By the way, I've never seen a prowler who wore a beeper. I've never heard of a prowler who came honking his way down the street with a loudspeaker, saying, "I'm gonna slip in through the sliding door of that home at 7147 Elm at two o'clock in the morning." No, you know a prowler doesn't do that. He comes with stealth. He silently slides his way in. And you never even know he's in your house until he's robbed you blind.

Last fall Cynthia and I had the scare of our lives—literally. I was ministering at a hotel in Cancun—a nice, safe, well-equipped hotel. We turned in for the night around 11:30 or so and were soon in Dreamland. Shortly before 1:00 A.M. Cynthia's loud, shrill scream startled me awake. "There's a man in our room!!"

I looked toward the sliding-glass door that opened onto the patio . . . and there he stood, silent and staring into our room. A chill raced down my spine. The door had been slid open, and the curtains were blowing like sails into the room from the wind off the gulf waters. In fact, it was the surge of the surf that had awakened Cynthia, not the intruder. He had not made a sound . . . nor was he easily visible, since he was dressed in dark clothing.

I jumped out of bed and stood nose-to-nose with him . . . and yelled at the top of my lungs, hoping to frighten him away. For all I knew he had a gun or a knife, but this was no time to close my eyes and pray and lie there like a wimp. Slowly, he backed out of the room, jumped off the seawall, and quickly escaped. Hotel security never found a trace of him, except for a few footprints in the sand. He was a prowler who came, most likely, to steal from our room. Talk about a lasting memory!

Our adversary is a prowler. He comes without announcement, and to make matters worse, he comes in counterfeit garb. He is brilliant, and you and I had better *respect* that brilliance.

I've heard young Christians say things like, "This Christian life is thrilling. I'm ready to take on the Devil." When I can, I pull them aside and say, "Don't say that. It's a stupid comment! You're dealing with the invisible realm. You're dealing with a power you cannot withstand in yourself and a presence you have no knowledge of when you say something like that. Get serious. Be on the alert." Usually that's enough to wake 'em up. Every once in a while it's helpful to be knocked down a notch or two, especially when we're starting to feel a little big for our britches.

I heard a funny but true story recently about Muhammad Ali. It took place in the heyday of his reign as heavyweight champion of the world. He had taken his seat on a plane and the giant 747 was starting to taxi toward the runway when the flight attendant walked by and noticed Ali had not fastened his seat belt.

"Please fasten your seat belt, sir," she requested.

He looked up proudly and snapped, "Superman don't need no seat belt, lady!"

Without hesitation she stared at him and said, "Superman don't need no plane . . . so buckle up."

Don't be fooled by your own pride or softened by some medieval caricature of an "impish" little devil. Our adversary is a murderer, and except for the Lord Himself, he's never met his match. We may hate him . . . but, like any deadly enemy, we had better respect him and keep our distance. There's a war on!

Resist Him. After we are alert to him and respect him, we must resist him. Don't run scared of the enemy. Don't invite him in; don't play with him. But don't be afraid of him either. Resist him. Through the power of the Lord Jesus Christ, firmly resist him.

"But resist him, firm in your faith," writes Peter. Kenneth Wuest has a wise word of counsel on this.

> The Greek word translated "resist" means "to withstand, to be firm against someone else's onset" rather than "to strive against that one." The Christian would do well to remember that he cannot fight the devil. The latter was originally the most powerful and wise angel God created. He still retains much of that power and wisdom as a glance down the pages of history and a look about one today will easily show. While the Christian cannot take the offensive against Satan, yet he can stand his ground in the face of his attacks. Cowardice never wins against Satan, only courage.[5]

I like that closing line.

Once we have enough respect for Satan's insidious ways to stay alert and ready for his attacks, the best method for handling him is strong resistance. That resistance is not done in our own strength, however, but comes from being "firm in faith." An example of this can be seen in the wilderness temptations of Christ when He resisted Satan with the Word of God (see Matt. 4:1–11).

You know what helps me when I sense I'm in the presence of the enemy? Nothing works better for me in resisting the Devil than the actual quoting of Scripture. I usually quote God's Word in such situations. One of the most important reasons for maintaining the discipline of Scripture memory is to have it ready on our lips when the enemy comes near and attacks. And you'll know it when he does. I don't know how to describe it, but the longer you walk with God, the more you will be able to sense the enemy's presence.

And when you do, you need those verses of victory ready to come to the rescue. The Word of God is marvelously strong. It is alive and active and "sharper than a two-edged sword." And its truths can slice their way into the invisible, insidious ranks of the demonic hosts.

Although our own strength is insufficient to fend him off, when we draw on the limitless resources of faith, we can stand against him nose-to-nose, much like I did with that intruder at Cancun. And such faith is nurtured and strengthened by a steady intake of the Scriptures.

Furthermore, the strength that comes from faith is supplemented by the knowledge of that company of saints stretching down through history, as well as present-day believers joining hands in prayer across the globe. There is something wonderfully comforting about knowing that we are not alone in the battle against the adversary.

In spite of faith and in spite of friends, however, the battle is *exhausting*. I don't know of anything that leaves you more wrung out, more weary. Nothing is more demanding, nothing more emotionally draining, nothing more personally painful than encountering and resisting our archenemy.

The devil always has a strategy, and he is an excellent strategist. He's been at it since he deceived Eve in the Garden. He knows our every weakness. He knows our hardest times in life. He knows our besetting sins. He knows the areas where we tend to give in the quickest. He also knows the moment to attack. He is a master of timing . . . and he knows the ideal place.

But I have good news for you. Better still, Scripture has good news for you. When you resist through the power and in the name of the Lord Jesus Christ, the Devil will ultimately retreat. He will back down. He won't stay away; he'll back away. He will retreat as you resist him, firm in your faith.

Remember Ephesians 6:10–11: "Be strong in the Lord, and in the strength of His might. Put on the full armor of God, that you may be able to stand firm against the schemes of the devil."

This is where the Christian has the jump on every unbeliever who tries to do battle against the enemy. Those without the Lord Jesus have no power to combat or withstand those supernatural forces. No chance! They are facing the enemy without weapons to defend themselves. But when the Christian is fully armed with the armor God provides, he or she is invincible. Isn't that a great word? Invincible! That gives us hope beyond the battle.

It's a mockery to say to those who are not Christians, "Just stand strong against the enemy." They can't. They have no equipment. They have no weapons. A person must have the Lord Jesus reigning within to be able to stand strong in His might.

Our Rewards

Will there be suffering in resisting Satan? Yes. Will it be painful? Without a doubt. I have found that there are times we emerge from the battle a little shell-shocked. But after the dust settles, our Commander-in-Chief will pin medals of honor on our lapels. And what are they? Peter tells us.

> And after you have suffered for a little while, the God of all grace, who called you to His eternal glory in Christ, will Himself perfect, confirm, strengthen and establish you. (1 Pet. 5:10)

He will "perfect, confirm, strengthen and establish" us. Talk about hope beyond the battle! Here is the biblical portrait of a decorated war hero, a seasoned veteran from the ranks of the righteous whose muscles of faith have been hardened by battle. It is the portrait of a well-grounded, stable, mature Christian. Christ will make sure the portrait of our lives looks like that, for He himself will hold the brush. And His hand is vastly more powerful than our enemy's.

I remember one night when I was taking care of a couple of our grandchildren. It was late in the evening, but since grandfathers usually let their grandchildren stay up longer than they should, they were still awake. We were laughing, messing around, and having a great time together when we suddenly heard a knock at the door. Not the doorbell, but a mysterious knocking. Immediately one of my grandsons grabbed hold of my arm. "It's OK," I said. The knock came again, and I started to the door. My grandson followed me, but he hung onto my left leg and hid behind me as I opened the door. It was one of my son's friends who had dropped by unexpectedly. After the person had left and I'd closed the door, my grandson, still holding on to my leg, said in a strong voice. "Bubba, we don't have anything to worry about, do we?" And I said, "No, we don't have anything to worry about. Everything's fine." You know why he was strong? Because he was hanging on to protection. As long as he was clinging to his grandfather's leg, he didn't have to worry about a thing.

That happens to us when we face the enemy. When he knocks at the door or when he prowls around back or when he looks for the chink in your armor, you hang on to Christ. You stand firm in faith. You put on the "armor of God" (Eph. 6:11–20—please read it!). You have nothing to worry about. *Nothing.* For, as Peter reminds us, our Lord has "dominion forever and ever. Amen" (1 Pet. 5:11). He is the one *ultimately* in control, and that is something in which every believer can find strength to hope again.

Necessary Reminders

Now, I want to tie a couple of strings around your finger as reminders as we bring these thoughts to a close. This advice has helped me throughout my Christian life, and I think you may find it useful.

First, never confuse confidence in Christ with cockiness in the flesh.
Confidence and cockiness are two different things. When you're facing the enemy, there's no place for cockiness. There is a place for confidence, however, and it's all confidence in Christ. You tell Him your weakness. You tell Him your fears. You ask Him to assist you as you equip yourself with His armor. You ask Him to think through you and to act beyond your own strength and to give you assurance. He'll do it. I repeat, it's all confidence in Christ. It's not some sense

of cockiness in the flesh. You're a Christian, remember, not Superman or Wonder Woman.

Second, always remember that suffering is temporal but its rewards are eternal. Paul's wonderful words come to mind:

> Therefore we do not lose heart, but though our outer man is decaying, yet our inner man is being renewed day by day. For momentary, light affliction is producing for us an eternal weight of glory far beyond all comparison, while we look not at the things which are seen, but at the things which are not seen; for the things which are seen are temporal, but the things which are not seen are eternal. (2 Cor. 4:16–18)

Our Lord set the example for us, "who for the joy set before Him endured the cross" (Heb. 12:2). We have all read the Gospel accounts that chronicle Christ's suffering on the cross. We have all heard the Good Friday sermons that recount the horrors of crucifixion. As we look up at Him there on the cross, we can sense His shame and feel the anguish of His heart as we stand at arm's length from His torn and feverish flesh. What we can't see is the joy that awaited Him when He surrendered His spirit to His Father. But He saw it. He knew.

Imagine for a minute how horrible that nightmare of the cross really was. Then imagine, if you can, how wonderful the joy awaiting Jesus must have been for Him to have willingly endured that degree of suffering and injustice. That same joy awaits us. But we have to stoop through the low archway of suffering to enter into it. And part of that suffering includes doing battle with the adversary.

There is probably no book, other than the Bible, that is as insightful or creatively written concerning the strategies of Satan than C. S. Lewis's *The Screwtape Letters*. Here is a sampling of Satan's strategy as articulated by the imaginary Screwtape, a senior devil, who corresponds with his eager nephew to educate the fledgling devil for warfare against the forces of "the Enemy"—that is, God.

> Like all young tempters, you are anxious to be able to report spectacular wickedness. But do remember, the only thing that matters is

the extent to which you separate the man from the Enemy. It does not matter how small the sins are, provided that their cumulative effect is to edge the man away from the Light and out into the Nothing. Murder is no better than cards if cards can do the trick. Indeed, the safest road to Hell is the gradual one—the gentle slope, soft underfoot, without sudden turnings, without milestones, without signposts.[6]

A Prayer for Hope Beyond the Battle

Almighty God, You are our all-powerful and invincible Lord. How we need You, especially when the battle rages! Thank You for standing by our side, for being our strong shield and defender. We have no strength in ourselves. We are facing an adversary far more powerful, more brilliant, and more experienced than we. And so, with confidence, we want to put on and wear the whole armor of God . . . and, in Your strength alone, resist the wicked forces that are designed to bring us down.

Give new hope, Lord—hope beyond the battle. Encourage us with the thought that, in Christ, we triumph! In His great name I pray.

AMEN

Hope Beyond Misery

Lasting
Lessons

I HAVE BEEN encouraged by the fact that in his writings Peter gets us beyond the misery part of suffering.

You have noticed, haven't you, how we all throw pity parties for ourselves when suffering comes? It's almost as though we capitalize on the downside rather than focus on the benefits that come from the hard times. How easily we forget that growth occurs when life is hard, not when it's easy. However, it is not until we move beyond the misery stage that we're able to find the magnificent lessons to be learned. The problem is, we almost delight in our own misery.

In keeping with that, Dan Greenburg has written a very funny book, *How to Make Yourself Miserable*, in which he says:

> Too long have you . . . gone about the important task of punishing yourself . . . by devious or ineffective means. Too long have you had to settle for poorly formulated anxieties . . . simply because this vital field has always been shrouded in ignorance—a folk art rather than a science. Here at last is the frank report you have been waiting for. . . . It is our humble but earnest desire that through these pages you will be

able to find for yourself the inspiration and the tools for a truly painful, meaningless, miserable life.[1]

The truth is, of course, that we don't need any help in this area. We have perfected the art of misery all by ourselves. We know very well how to capitalize on misery, how to multiply our troubles rather than learn—through the sometimes torturous and yes, humiliating experiences of life—the vital lessons that bring about true joy, true meaning, and true significance in life.

I think it was Charlie "Tremendous" Jones who said, "There is something wrong with everything." Have you found that true? No matter where you go or what you do, is there something wrong with it? Murphy's Law says, "If something can go wrong, it will." Another of Murphy's Laws says, "That's not a light at the end of the tunnel. That's an oncoming train." And then one wag adds, "Murphy was an optimist."

The problem is, when we're all alone, when we are feeling the brunt of the experience, when we are in the midst of the swirl, when we can't see any light at the end of any tunnel, it isn't funny.

As the apostle Peter so masterfully presents in his letter, however, suffering is not the end; it's a means to the end. Best of all, God's end for us is maturity. It is growth. It is a reason for living and going on.

Five Observations and a Set of Bookends

As we look back at the things we've seen in this book, a few broad-stroked observations stand out in sharp relief. Perhaps by reviewing where we've been, we'll be able to sharpen our perspective to an even keener edge.

First, Peter wrote the letter. Though it may seem simplistically obvious, this fact offers us a unique encouragement. Along with James and John, Peter was one of the inner circle of three confidants to whom Jesus revealed himself most fully. Of the twelve disciples, Peter was regarded as the spokesman. Never one to teeter on the fence of indecision, Peter was impulsive, impetuous, and outspoken. He often put his foot in his mouth. He knew the heights of ecstasy on the Mount of Transfiguration and the depths of misery and shame on the night of his denials. And yet, in spite of his flaws and his failures, he is called an apostle of Jesus Christ. What grace!

This is tremendous encouragement for all who fear that their flaws are too numerous or their failures too enormous to be given another chance.

I'm sure Peter looked back on many occasions and thought, *I wish I hadn't said that.* (Haven't we all?) But I'll tell you something else about Peter; he wasn't afraid to step forward—to put it all on the line.

Are you one of those people who never goes anywhere without a thermometer, a raincoat, an aspirin, or a parachute? Not Peter. He went full-bore into whatever he believed in. No lack of passion in Peter! What he lacked in forethought he made up for in zeal and enthusiasm.

Admittedly, that kind of lifestyle is a bit risky and unpredictable.

Do you ever envy some of the experiences of Peter kind of people—folks who are willing to say what they think or admit how they feel, even though they may be wrong? How much more fun it is to be around people like that than around those who are so careful and so closed-in and so protected you never know what they really feel or where they really stand. They're very, very cautious, ultra-conservative thinkers who wouldn't even consider taking a risk. And they get very little done for the kingdom because they are so busy guarding everything they do and say.

Not Peter. Peter says, in effect, "I wrote this. Yes, I'm the Disciple who blew it. I failed Him when He was under arrest. I spoke when I shouldn't have. But I write now as one who has learned many things the hard way, things about pain and suffering. I don't write out of theory; I write from experience."

Second, hurting people received the letter. They are not named, but their locations are stated in the first verse of the letter. Peter wrote "to those who reside as aliens, scattered throughout Pontus, Galatia, Cappadocia, Asia, and Bithynia."

These hurting people, scattered outside their homeland, were lonely and frightened aliens, unsure of their future. But though they were homeless, they were not abandoned; though they were frightened, they were not forgotten. Peter reminds them of that. They were chosen by God and sanctified by His Spirit, and His grace and peace would be with them "in fullest measure."

Whenever you find yourself away from home, whenever you find yourself feeling abandoned and frightened, overlooked and forgotten, Peter's first letter is magnificent therapy. I suggest you read it in several versions. The Living Bible, the New International Version, J. B. Phillips's paraphrase, and Eugene Peterson's paraphrase, *The Message*, will give you a good start. Read through without a break, if possible. Read it through sitting there in that hotel room or alone in your cell or apartment or home. It is excellent counsel for those who are hurting. It will assure you of your calling and reassure you that grace and peace are yours to claim in fullest measure.

Third, this letter came through Silas. The person to whom Peter dictated his words was Silas, one of the leaders in the early church (referred to in 1 Peter 5:12 as Silvanus).

Silas was a cultured Roman citizen, well educated and well traveled. Peter was a rugged fisherman, a blue-collar Galilean with little or no schooling, but apparently (beginning with 5:12) he took the pen in his own hand and wrote the final lines of the letter. We know that, not only because of the substance of verses 12–14, but because of the style. The grammar, syntax, and vocabulary become simpler in the Greek text.

The rest of the letter, however, came *through* Silas. If you're like most people, you don't know enough about Silas to fill a three-by-five card. Some people know him only as the guy who carried Paul's bags on long trips. Paul gets all the attention, yet it was Paul *and* Silas who carried the gospel. Silas was Barnabas's replacement on Paul's missionary journeys. Paul *and* Silas were the ones who sang in the jail there in Philippi at midnight. And Silas was the one alongside Paul when the man was stoned. Silas was one who really understood the hearts of Paul and Peter.

Look at Acts 15:22 in case your respect for Silas needs a little bolstering.

> Then it seemed good to the apostles and the elders, with the whole church, to choose men from among them to send to Antioch with Paul and Barnabas—Judas called Barsabbas, and Silas, leading men among the brethren.

Here is a man who was one of the "leading men" of the church in the first century, and at the writing of this letter, he remained alongside Peter. In fact, Peter calls him "our faithful brother (for so I regard him)" (1 Pet. 5:12).

God gives Peter the message, Silas writes it down, and the Spirit of God ignites it. There may have been times when Silas was the wind beneath Peter's wings. We all need a Silas . . . someone willing to stand alongside us.

Fourth, the letter concludes with a greeting from a woman.

> She who is in Babylon, chosen together with you, sends you greetings, and so does my son, Mark. (1 Pet. 5:13)

Now, obviously, everybody wonders who "she" is; who is the woman "who is in Babylon"? Most interpretations fall into two categories: Peter could either be referring to "woman" in the figurative sense, as the bride of Christ, or he could be using the word literally. If the latter is correct, the woman referred to may possibly be Peter's wife. We know Peter had a wife because Jesus healed Peter's mother-in-law. Then, in 1 Corinthians 9:5, Paul makes note of the other apostles' wives, which likely included Peter's wife. Clement of Alexandria states that she died as a martyr for the faith, so she may have been well-known among the early Christians. No doubt those who first received this letter knew who the woman was whether or not we do.

Fifth, the letter's final command is one of intimate affection. This old fisherman still has a lot of love left in him. He has not become jaded. Look how he expresses himself.

Greet one another with a kiss of love.
Peace [*Shalom*] be to you all who are in Christ. (1 Pet. 5:14)

The kiss of the Christian was called "the shalom," or "the peace." With the passing of time, the practice of the kiss of peace has disappeared from the church. It is fascinating to trace through church history how the kiss shared between people of the faith became less and less intimate. In fact, if you are a romantic-type person given to warm affection, it's enough to completely deplete all wind from your sails! In the first century, a kiss was placed on the cheek of believers as they arrived and as they left the fellowship of the saints. As time passed, people began kissing the precious documents rather than each other. And before long, a wooden board was passed among the people and everyone kissed that plank of wood. (That sounds exciting, doesn't it? "Let's go to church tonight. We'll get to kiss the board.") Anyway, through it all, the church lost the sense of affection and intimacy along with the embrace of peace.

Originally, as they kissed each other's cheeks, they would say to one another, "Peace be with you," or simply *Shalom*. And that's exactly what Peter does here. "Greet one another with the kiss of peace."

Augustine said that when Christians were about to communicate, "they demonstrated their inward peace by the outward kiss."

The formal kiss was the sign of peace among early Christians, demonstrating their love and unity. This outward sign reflected an inward peace between believers, a sign that all injuries and wrongdoing were forgiven and forgotten. Some traditions should be reinstated!

Personal Applications

Well, so much for the bookends that open and close Peter's letter. Now let's take a last look at the contents and how they can speak to us in our personal situations.

Three times in the letter Peter refers to the reader, which gives us a clue to the letter's structure. In fact, the letter falls neatly into three distinct sections, each one detailing the "how" of an important truth: a living hope and how to claim it (1:1–2:10), a pilgrim life and how to live it (2:11–4:11), and a fiery trial and how to endure it (4:12–5:11). An application of these three major messages should give us hope beyond our misery.

A Living Hope and How to Claim It

> Blessed be the God and Father of our Lord Jesus Christ, who according to His great mercy has caused us to be born again to a living hope through the resurrection of Jesus Christ from the dead. (1 Pet. 1:3)

The idea of "living hope" occupies Peter's mind throughout this section of the letter. And how do we claim that living hope? By focusing on the Lord Jesus Christ and by trusting in "the living and abiding word of God." Living hope requires faith in the living Lord and His Word.

The grass withers and dies, flowers bloom and die, but the Word of God "abides forever."

That's a great image, isn't it? Especially in a culture like ours where people are so grass conscious. Just look at the commercials that start appearing on television in late winter, and the countless "garden centers" devoted to our yards and gardens that you can find across the country. We know what happens when we neglect our grass or our gardens—but the truth is, they will eventually wither and die anyway.

There is nothing tangible on this earth that is inspired but the Word of God, this book that holds God's counsel. It doesn't tell us about the truth; it *is* truth. It doesn't merely contain words about God; it *is* the Word of God. We don't have to try real hard to make it relevant; it *is* relevant. Don't neglect it. You can neglect your grass. You can neglect your garden. But you dare not neglect the Word of God! It is the foundation of a stable life. It feeds faith. It's like fuel in the tank. Don't wait till Sunday to see what the Scripture teaches.

We have a living hope, and Peter's words in this section tell us how to claim it—by faith in our Lord Himself and by faith in what He has written, His Word.

The Pilgrim Life and How to Live It

As Christians we live in a world that is not our home. We looked at this, in depth, in chapter 11. We live as pilgrims on a journey in another land. If you want to know how to live the life of an alien, a stranger, a pilgrim, Peter's letter will help.

We claim our living hope through faith, and we live the pilgrim life by submission. In fact, if there is one theme that stretches through this central section of Peter's letter, it is submission. We need to be reminded of it again and again and again because we are an independent lot. Especially here in America, we are so ornery and stubborn. It's come to be known as "the American way." It's the reason many sailed the Atlantic and later came west. It's built into our independent spirit to make it on our own, to decide for ourselves, to prove, if only to ourselves, we can do it! That may be the explorer's life or the pioneer's life . . . but it's not the pilgrim life. The pilgrim life is a life of submission, which works directly against our nature.

But where? When? To whom do we submit? As we saw earlier, Peter spells it out.

In government and civilian affairs. "Submit yourselves for the Lord's sake to every human institution, whether to a king . . . or to governors . . ." (1 Pet. 2:13–14). If you have a president, submit to the president. In Peter's case, they had an emperor. And what a monster he was. Nero. Yet Peter said, "Don't fight the system. Submit."

At work. "Servants, be submissive to your masters" (1 Pet. 2:18). My, that cuts cross-grain in our day of unions and strikes and lawsuits and stubborn determination to have it our own way. Peter says, in effect, "Submit to your boss or quit!"

Submit! Make the thing work or get out. Submit.

At home. "In the same way, you wives, be submissive to your own husbands." And in order for that to work, "You husbands likewise, live with your wives in an understanding way" (1 Pet. 3:1, 7). "Likewise" is a rope-like word that wraps itself around this chapter and part of the previous one, sustaining the thought of submission.

I remember talking with a young couple a few years ago when I observed a sterling example of this. He was a dentist in his mid- to late thirties, and he and his wife had come to a meeting where they found themselves rethinking their life plans for the future. Afterward, he said to me, "I'm thinking seriously about going into the ministry."

I said, "Really? Have you had any training at all?"

He said, "No, not formally. I'd have to go back to school. I'd like to have your suggestion about seminary and what you think would be best for me."

So we talked for a few minutes, and I concluded with this counsel. "If you are happy doing what you're doing, don't just jump into ministry because it seems fascinating or appealing to you."

The next day he came to me and said, "Your words really made me think throughout the night. To tell you the truth, I am very fulfilled in dentistry, and I find a lot of satisfaction in it."

His wife was standing beside him, and I turned to her and said, "And how do you feel about this?" She had a terrific answer. She said, "You know, Chuck, when I married this man I really gave myself to this marriage. And I determined that this man who is walking with God was worth working alongside of, no matter what and no matter where. However God leads him, I'm a part of that plan."

"How do you feel about going into ministry?" I asked.

"If he's convinced, I'm convinced," she said.

Now I know this woman. She's no dummy. She's no vanilla shadow, standing there sighing, "Whatever he wants is fine with me." She's not a beaten-down, doormat kind of wife. That's not the kind of woman she is, and that's not the kind of woman Peter is talking about here. There's vitality and zeal and strength of soul in her life. And she can say, "I am confident God is working in my husband. I wouldn't think of going some other direction." A harmonious blend of give and take is what Peter has in mind here.

In the church. "To sum up, let all be harmonious, sympathetic, brotherly, kindhearted, and humble in spirit; not returning evil for evil, or insult for insult, but giving a blessing instead; for you were called for the very purpose that you might inherit a blessing" (1 Pet. 3:8–9). Now isn't there a lot of submission at work there?

And a few verses later (3:22) we see that even the angels, the authorities, and the powers are subjected to Him. Just picture those magnificent angelic creatures bowing in submission to the risen Christ.

My suggestion on the heels of all this? Work on a submissive spirit. Don't wait for the media to encourage you to do this . . . it'll never happen. Ask God, if necessary, to break the sinews of your will so that you become a person who is cooperative, submissive, harmonious, sympathetic, brotherly or sisterly, kindhearted in every area of this pilgrim life.

Remember, ultimately we are not submitting to human authority but to divine authority. God will never mistreat us. Bowing before Him is the best position to take when we want to communicate obedience.

The Fiery Trial and How to Endure It

No matter how fiery the trial, the main thing is that you and I remember the temperature is ultimately regulated by God's sovereignty (see 1 Pet. 4:12–19). It's also important to understand that we don't suffer our trials in isolation; we are part of a flock that is lovingly tended by faithful shepherds (see 1 Pet. 5:1–5). Finally, we need to know that no matter how formidable our adversary, the power of God is available to help us endure (see 5:6–11).

And how do we endure the fiery trials that engulf us? By cooperation. We need to cooperate with God by trusting Him—with the leaders of the church by submitting to them, and with faith by standing firm and resisting the assault of the devil.

As you struggle with fiery trials, call to mind the sovereignty of God. Nothing touches you that hasn't come through the sovereign hand and the wise plan of God. It must all pass through His fingers before it reaches you. Ultimately He is in control.

As you endure the fiery trial, be in touch with and faithful to the flock of God.

And through it all, rely on the power of God. As we learned in the previous chapter, we must rely on that.

Four Lasting Lessons/Secrets of Life

We have finished his letter . . . but the ink from Peter's pen leaves an indelible impression on our lives. Along with everything else he tells and teaches us, I want to mention four lasting lessons, four secrets of life, that stand out in bold relief. All of these give us hope beyond our misery.

First, when our faith is weak, joy strengthens us.

> In this you greatly rejoice, even though now for a little while, if necessary, you have been distressed by various trials, that the proof of your faith, being more precious than gold which is perishable, even though tested by fire, may be found to result in praise and glory and honor at the revelation of Jesus Christ; and though you have not seen Him, you love Him, and though you do not see Him now, but believe in Him, you greatly rejoice with joy inexpressible and full of glory. (1 Pet. 1:6–8)

> Beloved, do not be surprised at the fiery ordeal among you, which comes upon you for your testing, as though some strange thing were happening to you; but to the degree that you share the sufferings of Christ, keep on rejoicing; so that also at the revelation of His glory, you may rejoice with exultation. (1 Pet. 4:12–13)

No matter how dark the clouds, the sun will eventually pierce the darkness and dispel it; no matter how heavy the rain, the sun will ultimately prevail to hang a rainbow in the sky. Joy will chase away the clouds hovering over our faith and prevail over the disheartening trials that drench our lives. In this regard I am often reminded of the promise from the Psalms.

> Weeping may last for the night,
> But a shout of joy comes in the morning. (Ps. 30:5)

Second, when our good is mistreated, endurance stabilizes us.

For this finds favor, if for the sake of conscience toward God a man bears up under sorrows when suffering unjustly. For what credit is there if, when you sin and are harshly treated, you endure it with patience? But if when you do what is right and suffer for it you patiently endure it, this finds favor with God. (1 Pet. 2:19–20)

The word *endure* in verse 20 means "to bear up under a load," as a donkey bears up under the load its owner has stacked high on its back. This patient bearing of life's cumbersome loads is made possible by love, made steadfast by hope, and made easier by example.

When we suffer, even though we have done what is right, there is something about endurance that stabilizes us. When our good is mistreated, endurance stabilizes us.

My hope for every one who reads these pages is that you will learn how to endure. Picture yourself as that little burro, abiding under the heavy load piled upon its back. Such quiet and confident endurance stabilizes us.

Third, when our confidence is shaken, love supports us.

Above all, keep fervent in your love for one another, because love covers a multitude of sins. (1 Pet. 4:8)

Love is the pillar of support when our world comes crumbling down around us. That's why, when warning about the end times, Peter puts love on the top of the survival checklist.

Fourth, when our adversary attacks, resistance shields us.

Be of sober spirit, be on the alert. Your adversary, the devil, prowls about like a roaring lion, seeking someone to devour. But resist him, firm in your faith, knowing that the same experiences of suffering are being accomplished by your brethren who are in the world. (1 Pet. 5:8–9)

When Satan stalks us like a roaring lion, we're not instructed to freeze, to hide, or to tuck tail and run. We're told to resist. And that resistance forms a shield to protect us from our adversary's predatory claws.

What Really Counts

And so we reach the end of Peter's letter that has endured the centuries . . . and the end of my book that may not endure to the end of this century, less than five years from now. But that is as it should be. God's Word will never fade away, though human works are quickly erased by the sands of time.

My concern is not about how long these pages remain in print but how soon you will put these principles to use in your life. That's what really counts in the long run. That's the important issue. Frankly, that's why the old fisherman wrote his letter in the first place. To help us hope again.

Hope to go on, even though we're scattered aliens.

Hope to grow up, even though we, like Peter, have failed and fallen.

Hope to endure, even though life hurts.

Hope to believe, even though dreams fade.

A Prayer for Hope Beyond Misery

Our Father, we thank You for sustaining us in Your grace through times that absolutely defy explanation, times of suffering and misery, times of mistreatment and disappointment.

Thank You for being a Friend who is closer than a brother, for meaning more to us than a mother or a father. Thank You for Your mercy that takes us from week to week through a life that isn't easy, dealing with people who aren't always loving and encountering battles that leave us exhausted. Thank You for strength that has come from a little letter written by an old fisherman who understood life in all its dimensions: failure and disappointment and victory and joy and intimacy. We commit to You, our Father, the truth of what we have read. Help us to find hope again as a result of putting these truths into practice. In the lovely and gracious name of Jesus Christ I pray.

AMEN

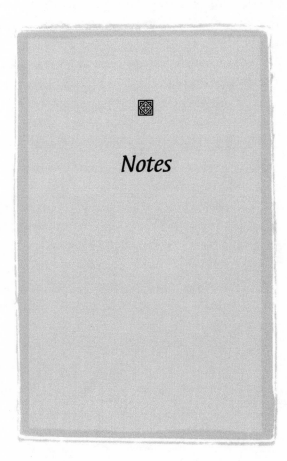

Notes

CHAPTER 1   HOPE BEYOND FAILURE

1   Eugene H. Peterson, *The Message: The New Testament in Contempo-
rary English* (Colorado Springs, Colo.: Navpress, 1993), 486.

CHAPTER 2   HOPE BEYOND SUFFERING

1   Warren W. Wiersbe, *Be Hopeful* (Wheaton, Ill.: SP Publications,
Victor Books, 1982), 11.
2   Julie Ackerman Link, "Fully Involved in the Flame," *Seasons: A
Journal for the Women of Calvary Church*, Spring 1996, 1. Copyright
Calvary Church, Grand Rapids, Michigan. Used by permission.

CHAPTER 3   HOPE BEYOND TEMPTATION

1   Kenneth S. Wuest, *In These Last Days*, vol. 4 in *Wuest's Word Studies
from the Greek New Testament* (Grand Rapids, Mich.: Eerdmans,
1966), 125–26.
2   Randy Alcorn, "Consequences of a Moral Tumble," *Leadership*
magazine, Winter 1988, 46.
3   Stuart Briscoe, *Spiritual Stamina* (Portland, Oreg.: Multnomah
Press, 1988), 133.

CHAPTER 4   HOPE BEYOND DIVISION

1   Kenneth S. Wuest, *First Peter: In the Greek New Testament* (Grand
Rapids, Mich.: Eerdmans, 1956), 48.
2   Edward Gordon Selwyn, *The First Epistle of St. Peter*, 2d ed.
(London, England: Macmillan Press, 1974), 153.

CHAPTER 5   HOPE BEYOND GUILT

1   Quoted in *Dear Lord*, comp. Bill Adler (Nashville: Thomas Nelson, 1982).

2   Quoted in *More Children's Letters to God*, comp. Eric Marshall and Stuart Hample (New York: Simon and Schuster, 1967).

3   Quoted in William Barclay, *The Letters of James and Peter*, rev. ed., The Daily Study Bible Series (Philadelphia, Pa.: Westminster Press, 1976), 203.

4   Wiersbe, *Be Hopeful*, 57.

CHAPTER 6   HOPE BEYOND UNFAIRNESS

1   Barclay, *The Letters of James and Peter*, 210–11.

2   J. H. Jowett, *The Epistles of St. Peter*, 2d ed. (London: Hodder and Stoughton, n.d.), 92.

CHAPTER 7   HOPE BEYOND "I DO"

1   Joseph C. Aldrich, *Secrets to Inner Beauty* (Santa Ana, Calif.: Vision House, 1977), 87–88.

2   Philip Yancey, *I Was Just Wondering* (Grand Rapids, Mich.: Eerdmans, 1989), 174–75.

3   Barclay, *The Letters of James and Peter*, 218.

4   Edwin A. Blum, "1 Peter" in *The Expositor's Bible Commentary*, vol. 12, ed. Frank E. Gaebelein (Grand Rapids, Mich.: Zondervan, 1981), 237.

5   *Los Angeles Times*, 23 June 1988.

6   Gary Smalley and John Trent, *The Gift of Honor* (Nashville: Thomas Nelson, 1987), 23, 25–26.

CHAPTER 8   HOPE BEYOND IMMATURITY

1   Robert A. Wilson, ed., *Character Above All* (New York: Simon and Schuster, 1995), 219–21.

2   Oswald Chambers, *My Utmost for His Highest*, special updated

edition, ed. James Reimann (Grand Rapids, Mich.: Discovery House, 1995), November 16, n.p.

3   Alvin Goeser quoted in *Quote-Unquote*, comp. Lloyd Cory (Wheaton, Ill.: SP Publications, Victor Books, 1977), 200.

4   Cited in Jon Johnston, "Growing Me-ism and Materialism," *Christianity Today*, 17 January 1986, 16-I.

CHAPTER 9   HOPE BEYOND BITTERNESS

1   Retold from "Toads and Diamonds," *The Riverside Anthology of Children's Literature*, 6th ed. Boston: Houghton Miffiin, 1985), 291–93.]

2   Malcolm Muggeridge, *Twentieth-Century Testimony*, (Nashville: Thomas Nelson, 1988), 18–19.

3   Barclay, *The Letters of James and Peter*, 230–31.

CHAPTER 11   HOPE BEYOND THE CULTURE

1   J.R. Baxter, Jr., "This World Is Not My Home," © copyright 1946. Stamps-Baxter Music. All rights reserved. Used by permission of Benson Music Group, Inc..

2   Quotes from Georgia Harbison, "Lower East Side Story," *Time*, 4 March 1996, 71.

3   Wuest, *First Peter: In the Greek New Testament*, 110.

4   D. Martyn Lloyd-Jones, *The Christian Warfare* (Grand Rapids, Mich.: Baker, 1976), 41.

5   John Hus, quoted in John Moffatt, *The General Epistles: James, Peter, and Judas* (London: Hodder and Stoughton, 1928), 147.

CHAPTER 12   HOPE BEYOND EXTREMISM

1   Wiersbe, *Be Hopeful*, 107.

2   Mahatma Gandhi quoted in Brennan Manning, *Lion and Lamb* (Old Tappan, N.J.: Revell, Chosen Books, 1986), 49.

3   Jowett, *The Epistles of St. Peter*, 166–67.

4   Ibid., 167.

5   Anne Ross Cousin, "The Sands of Time Are Sinking."

CHAPTER 13   HOPE BEYOND OUR TRIALS

1   C. S. Lewis, *The Problem of Pain* (New York: Macmillan, 1962), 106.
2   R. C. H. Lenski, *The Interpretation of the Epistles of St. Peter, St. John and St. Jude* (Columbus, Ohio: Wartburg Press, 1945), 213.
3   Andre Crouch, "Through It All," © 1971, by Manna Music Inc., 35255 Brooten Road, Pacific OR. 97135. International copyright secured. All rights reserved. Used by permission.
4   Lewis, *The Problem of Pain*, 107.
5   M. Craig Barnes, *When God Interrupts* (Downers Grove, Ill.: InterVarsity, 1996), 54.
6   Wiersbe, *Be Hopeful*, 115–16.

CHAPTER 14   HOPE BEYOND RELIGION

1   J. G. G. Norman, "Charles Haddon Spurgeon," in *The New International Dictionary of the Christian Church*, rev. ed., ed. J. D. Douglas (Grand Rapids, Mich.: Zondervan, 1978), 928.
2   C. H. Spurgeon, *Lectures to My Students* (Grand Rapids, Mich.: Zondervan, 1962), 7–8.
3   Source unknown.
4   Spurgeon, *Lectures*, 154.
5   Michael Silver, "White Tornado," *Sports Illustrated*, 3 June 1996, 71.

CHAPTER 15   HOPE BEYOND DISSATISFACTION

1   Jean Rosenbaum, quoted in *Quote-Unquote*, 315.

CHAPTER 16   HOPE BEYOND THE BATTLE

1   Philip Yancey, *Where Is God When It Hurts?* (Grand Rapids, Mich.: Zondervan, 1977), 22–23.
2   J. Dwight Pentecost, *Your Adversary the Devil* (Grand Rapids, Mich.: Zondervan, 1969), Introduction.
3   Wiersbe, *Be Hopeful*, 138.
4   Ibid.
5   Wuest, *First Peter: In the Greek New Testament*, 130.
6   C. S. Lewis, *The Screwtape Letters* (New York, N.Y.: Macmillan, 1961), 3.

CHAPTER 17   HOPE BEYOND MISERY

1   Dan Greenburg, *How to Make Yourself Miserable*, (New York: Random House, 1966), 1–2.

ABOUT THE AUTHOR

CHARLES R. SWINDOLL serves as president of Dallas Theological Seminary. He is also president of Insight for Living, a radio broadcast ministry aired daily worldwide. He was senior pastor at the First Evangelical Free Church in Fullerton, California for almost twenty-three years and has authored numerous books on Christian living, including the best-selling *Grace Awakening*, *Laugh Again*, and *Flying Closer to the Flame*.